Access to History
FOR THE **IB DIPLOMA**

Causes and effects of 20th-century wars

Study and Revision Guide

PAPER 2

Kate Harker
Nicholas Verrill

Access to History
FOR THE **IB DIPLOMA**

Causes and effects of 20th-century wars

Study and Revision Guide

PAPER 2

Kate Harker
Nicholas Verrill

HODDER
EDUCATION
AN HACHETTE UK COMPANY

Dedications

Nicholas Verrill: For my wife Emily and son Sebastian. Without your sympathy, encouragement and support this book would have been finished in half the time. And for my students always remember the following: war is bad, peace is good.

Kate Harker: Thank you to my parents and husband, for always encouraging me to take on the next venture.

The Publishers would like to thank the following for permission to reproduce copyright material.

Photo credits: p61 Chronicle/Alamy Stock Photo; **p65** Punch Ltd; **p79** ITAR-TASS News Agency/Alamy Stock Photo; **p85** World History Archive/Alamy Stock Photo; **p89** Photo 12/Alamy Stock Photo.

Acknowledgements: Allen Lane, *China's War with Japan* by Rana Mitter, 2013. Basic Books, *Empires on the Pacific: World War II and the Struggle for the Mastery of Asia* by Robert Smith Thompson, 2001. Bloomsbury, *Mao's Great Famine* by Frank Dikötter, 2010. Cambridge University Press, *A History of East Asia from the Origin of Civilization to the Twenty-first Century* by Charles Holcombe, 2011. HarperCollins, *Modern China: The Fall and Rise of a Great Power, 1850 to the Present* by Jonathan Fenby, 2008. MacDonald, *War by Time-Table: How the First World War Began* by A.J.P. Taylor, 1969. Macmillan, *The Economic Consequences of the Peace* by John Maynard Keynes, 1919. Martinus Nijhoff, 'History's long shadow: the Lausanne Treaty and contemporary Greco-Turkish relations' by Renée Hirsch in *In the Long Shadow of Europe: Greeks and Turks in the Era of Postnationalism* edited by O. Anastasakis, K.A. Nicolaidis and K. Öktem, 2009. Oxford University Press, *A Modern History of Japan: From Tokugawa Times to the Present* by Andrew Gordon, 2003. Penguin Books, *Embracing Defeat: Japan in the Aftermath of World War II* by John Dower, 1999. Praeger, *The Pacific War: Japan Versus the Allies* by Alan J. Levine, 1995. Routledge, *Mao* by Michael Lynch, 2004; *The Rise of Modern China* by Immanuel Hsu, 1990. Salamander Books, *War in the Pacific: Pearl Harbour to Tokyo Bay* edited by Bernard C. Nalty, 1991. University of West Florida Press, *Nicaragua Divided: La Prensa and the Chamorro Legacy* by Patricia Taylor Edmisten, 1990. Vintage, *What is History?* by E.H. Carr, 1961. W.T. Press, *The Great War: Myth and Reality* by D.E. Marshall, 1988. W.W. Norton, *Origins of the First World War* by L.C.F. Turner, 1970; *The Search for Modern China* by Jonathan D. Spence, 2013.

Every effort has been made to trace all copyright holders, but if any have been inadvertently overlooked, the Publishers will be pleased to make the necessary arrangements at the first opportunity.

Although every effort has been made to ensure that website addresses are correct at time of going to press, Hodder Education cannot be held responsible for the content of any website mentioned in this book. It is sometimes possible to find a relocated web page by typing in the address of the home page for a website in the URL window of your browser.

Hachette UK's policy is to use papers that are natural, renewable and recyclable products and made from wood grown in well-managed forests and other controlled sources. The logging and manufacturing processes are expected to conform to the environmental regulations of the country of origin.

Orders: please contact Hachette UK Distribution, Hely Hutchinson Centre, Milton Road, Didcot, Oxfordshire, OX11 7HH. Telephone: +44 (0)1235 827827. Email education@hachette.co.uk Lines are open from 9 a.m. to 5 p.m., Monday to Friday. You can also order through our website: www.hoddereducation.com

ISBN: 978 1 510432 37 6

First published 2019 by
Hodder Education
An Hachette UK Company
Carmelite House
50 Victoria Embankment
London EC4Y 0DZ

www.hoddereducation.com

Impression number 10 9 8 7 6 5 4 3

Year 2024

Cover photo: © Aloysius Patrimonio/ImageZoo/Corbis
Produced and typeset in Goudy and Frutiger by Gray Publishing, Tunbridge Wells
Printed and bound by CPI Group (UK) Ltd, Croydon, CR0 4YY

A catalogue record for this title is available from the British Library.

FSC www.fsc.org MIX Paper | Supporting responsible forestry FSC™ C104740

Contents

How to use this book

- Welcome to the *Access to History for the IB Diploma: Causes and effects of 20th-century wars: Study and Revision Guide*. This book has been written and designed to help you develop the knowledge and skills necessary to succeed in the Paper 2 examination. The book is organized into double-page spreads.
- On the left-hand page you will find a summary of the key content you will need to learn. Words in bold in the key content are defined in the glossary and key figures list (see pages 168–72).
- On the right-hand page you will find exam-focused activities related to and testing the content on the left-hand side. These contain questions so that you can develop essay-writing skills. Answers for some of the activities can be found at the back of the book.
- At the end of each chapter, you will find an exam focus section. Here, you will find examples of student responses, with examiner comments and annotations, to help you understand how to improve your grades. There are also exam-style questions that you can answer yourself.

Together, these two strands of the book will provide you with the knowledge and skills essential for examination success.

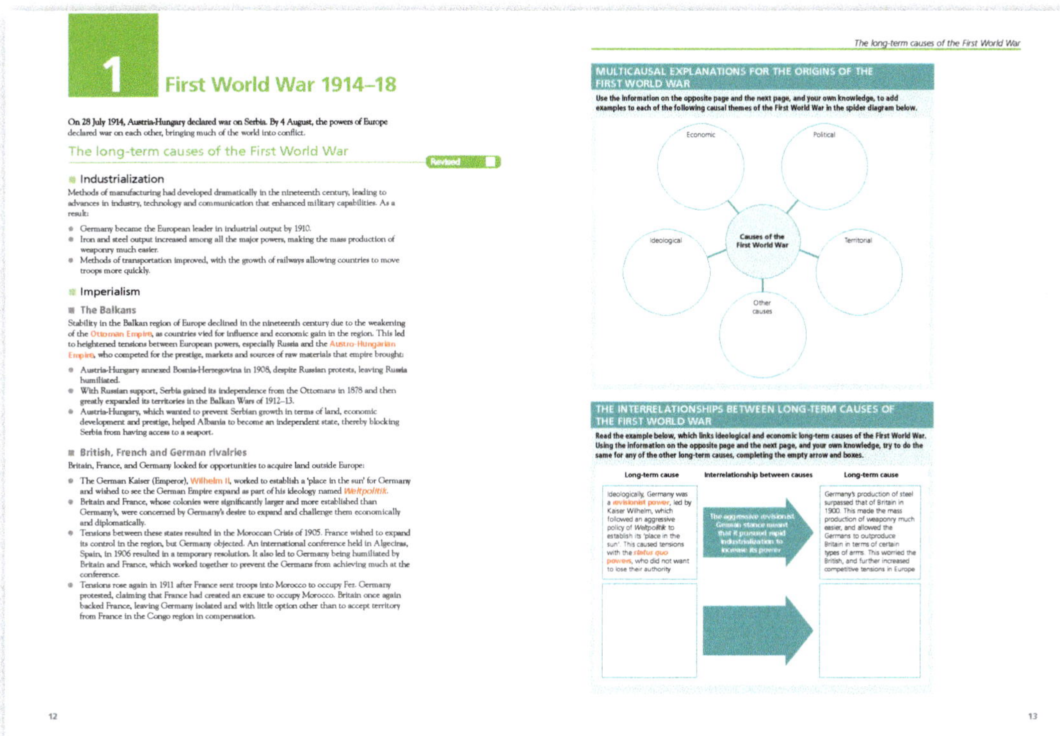

Key historical content | Exam-focused activities

At the end of the book, you will find:

- Glossary and Key figures – key terms in the book are defined and key figures are highlighted.
- Answers for some of the exam-focused activities.

Understanding the prescribed content

Paper 2 requires you to write two essays, each from a different topic; there will be a choice of two questions for each topic. You should answer only one of these questions for Topic 11: Causes and effects of 20th-century wars and a second question for the other topic that you have studied. Questions for Topic 11 may address:

- the causes of 20th-century wars
- the practices of 20th-century wars and their impact on the outcomes
- the effects of 20th-century wars.

Below, you will find guidance and information on the skills and knowledge that you will need to successfully answer questions on each of these areas of the prescribed content.

Causes of war

Topic	Prescribed content
Causes of war	• Economic, ideological, political, territorial and other causes • Short- and long-term causes

Here, the focus is on causation, more specifically, why a war broke out. In order to effectively explain this, you need to have a good understanding of causal analysis.

SOURCE 1

Extract from E.H. Carr, *What is History?*, Vintage, London, 1961, page 113.

If milk is set to boil in a saucepan, it boils over. I do not know, and have never wanted to know, why this happens; if pressed, I should probably attribute it to a propensity in milk to boil over, which is true enough but explains nothing. But then I am not a natural scientist. In the same way, one can read, or even write, about the events of the past without wanting to know why they happened, or be content to say that the Second World War occurred because Hitler wanted war, which is true enough but explains nothing. But one should not then commit the solecism of calling oneself a student of history or a historian. The study of history is a study of causes. The historian, as I said at the end of my last lecture, continuously asks the question, 'Why?'; and, so long as he hopes for an answer, he cannot rest. The great historian – or perhaps I should say more broadly, the great thinker – is the man who asks the question, 'Why?', about new things or in new contexts.

In *What is History?*, E.H. Carr states that, 'the study of history is a study of causes'. One of the fundamental endeavours of a historian is to explain why events occur. This is no simple matter: establishing causation is a tricky business. This is especially true in the case of explaining the genesis of an event as complex as the First World War, for example. So, how do we do this? The first step is to identify the causes of an event and categorize them into larger historical themes, which will then form the basis of the paragraphs in an IB essay. Secondly, very little happens in history for one reason, so an essay should examine the interrelationship between causes to explain why an event occurred, and how causes combined to produce that outcome. Thirdly, by showing this interrelationship, the historian tries to prioritize causes, and argue that certain factors were more important than others in causing events. This prioritization should be justified persuasively with reference to evidence. These three elements are essential in a strong IB Paper 2 essay in this area of the prescribed content, as the focus here is on causation.

It is therefore worth noting what weak and strong causal analysis looks like in a history essay.

Weak causal analysis may be characterized by the following three elements:

1. **A reductionist view:** focused on an insufficient number of causes. Perhaps even a monocausal argument where only one cause is presented.
2. **Compartmentalization:** treats causes as distinct entities, and fails to show how they combined to cause an event.

3 **A lack of prioritization:** does not offer a line of argument, but treats all causes as equal in terms of importance.

Strong causal analysis may be characterized by the following three elements:

1 **A consideration of multiple events:** deals with a range of causes – three or four would be sufficient in an IB Paper 2 essay – across a variety of historical themes, or categories. Examples of categories include economic, political, ideological and territorial.

2 **An examination of the interrelationship between causes:** analyses how different causes interrelate with each other to cause an event to occur. Unpacks and explains these links between factors.

3 **Prioritization:** offers an argument, and tries to argue that certain factors, or combinations of factors, are more important than others when explaining why an event occurs. This is an attempt to establish some type of hierarchy of causes based on how they interrelate.

Practices of war and their impact on the outcome

Topic	Prescribed content
Practices of war and their impact on the outcome	• Types of war: civil wars; wars between states; guerrilla wars • Technological developments; theatres of war – air, land and sea • The extent of the mobilization of human and economic resources • The influence and/or involvement of foreign powers

Here, the focus is still on causation, but now it is on how and why the various practices of war affected the outcome of a conflict. To effectively explain this, you need to understand the technical terminology in the prescribed content, as defined in the table below.

Prescribed content	Definition
Civil war	Also referred to as an intrastate war. This is a war between organized groups within the same state, or country. Aims may vary. They include: trying to control the country or region; attempting to achieve independence; aiming to change some governmental policy
War between states	This is when different countries go to war with each other. Aims may vary, but common causes are economic, political, territorial and religious
Guerrilla war	A form of unconventional warfare in which small groups of mobile irregular forces carry out surprise attacks against regular forces. Tactics of such a force include ambushes, sabotage, hit-and-run attacks, booby traps and raids
Technological developments	Advances in technology that affect how a war is fought. For them to be effective in aiding victory they need to fit the theatre of war. It is not always the side with the most modern technology that wins, but more often than not throughout history it has helped
Theatre of war	The area, or environment, in which a war takes place. This will affect the tactics and weaponry that armies use and can have a huge impact on their effectiveness. Air, land and sea are examples of this. Jungle warfare, urban warfare and trench warfare are further types
Human resources	The human beings available to the sides in a war. The number, motivation and military skills of these people are vital to the success of a war effort
Economic resources	The finances available to the sides in a war. The ability of an army to be victorious can rest to a large degree on how much money is available to support the war effort with weapons, logistics and training. However, in some irregular types of warfare there have been historic examples where finance has not been decisive
Foreign powers	This refers to foreign powers intervening in a domestic conflict, such as a civil war, that is already being fought. Sometimes the intervention of these foreign powers can prove decisive in helping the side that they are supporting to win. However, in other cases, such intervention can prove detrimental to the side it is intended to help and have unintended consequences

Effects of war

Topic	Prescribed content
Effects of war	• The successes and failures of peacemaking • Territorial changes • Political repercussions • Economic, social and demographic impact; changes in the role and status of women

Here, the focus is on the consequences of warfare, and the effects that it has across a variety of areas listed in the prescribed content. This section requires students to consider the effects of war in a range of different ways, and decide whether they have been positive, negative, or somewhere in between. Students need to understand the effects of warfare for the different countries involved, and to assess which ones emerged in better, or worse, shape. To do well, it is once again integral that you understand the meaning of the prescribed content, as defined in the table below.

Prescribed content	Definition
Peacemaking	The attempts to uphold peace after a war. Major aims include trying to prevent further loss of life and conflict, trying to rebuild a nation by ensuring civilians are protected and rebuilding infrastructure. However, peace terms are often decided by the victors, who have other motives, such as revenge and gain for their nation. These motives may result in unsustainable peace terms
Territorial changes	Changes to who governs areas of land. This can involve the creation of new countries and empires, and the end of others. The implications for the populations of these areas are often significant
Political repercussions	Repercussions of war for political systems. War can often lead to significant upheavals to the governing classes of countries, and result in regime changes and new ideologies taking precedence. Sometimes these include greater rights for people, other times the complete opposite occurs
Economic impact	Warfare can impact on the economy in areas such as gross domestic product and employment levels. It can also leave countries facing huge war debts in the form of reparations. The reconstruction of an economy after a war can be a tricky, protracted process
Social impact	Warfare can impact on society in areas such as culture, religion, familial relations, relations between different groups in society, lifestyle changes, wealth and living conditions
Demographic impact	Demographic studies attempt to measure quantifiable characteristics of a given population. War may impact the number of people left alive, the average age in a country, the ethnic makeup of a country and the gender balance, to name a few of the most common indicators
Changes in the role and status of women	War may have a big impact on the role and status of women as the demands of war may require greater numbers of women to enter the workforce or join the army. This can lead to the enfranchisement and empowerment of women

Getting to know the exam

Command terms

A key to success is to understand the demands of the question. Questions use key terms and phrases known as command terms.

Command term	Description
Compare and contrast	• **Discuss** the **similarities** and **differences** of wars, referring to both throughout your answer and not treating each separately • You should not give an overview of each war and should focus on the most **important similarities and differences** in relation to the question
Discuss	• **Review various arguments** regarding a war, or wars, and conclude with an argument **supported by evidence**
Evaluate	• **Make a judgement** based on how strong or weak the evidence may be
Examine	• **Analyse** the **strengths and weaknesses** of various arguments, with a **concluding opinion**
To what extent	• **Determine the extent to which something is true or false**, with answers usually being 'to a limited extent', 'to some extent' or 'to a great extent'

Answering questions

- You will have five minutes of reading time at the start of the examination. It is during this time that you should review the questions in the two or more topics that you have studied.
- Once you have identified which ones you are able to address, choose the Topic 11 question for which you have the most knowledge and whose demands you fully understand.
- Many students may have great knowledge regarding one or more 20th-century wars, but they may not understand fully what the question wants them to do. If you find the wording of a question confusing, consider addressing another question if you feel more comfortable doing so.
- Once you have chosen your question for Topic 11, you should look at your other topic of study and repeat this exercise.
- Once you have made a decision on your second question for Paper 2, return to your Topic 11 question and begin to think about how you will address it, waiting for the end of the reading time.

Marks

All questions on Paper 2 are worth 15 marks each for a total of 30 possible marks for this paper. In order to attain the highest mark band (13–15), your essays should include:

- answers that clearly address the demands of the question and are well structured and clear
- correct, relevant historical knowledge used appropriately to support your argument
- evidence that is critically analysed
- historical events that are placed in their context
- evidence that you understand that there are different historical interpretations.

Timing your writing

- You will have 1 hour 30 minutes to complete both Paper 2 essays. This breaks down to 45 minutes per essay on average. You will also have five minutes' reading time.
- Part of your writing time, however, should be spent preparing a basic outline which will help you keep your answer structured and focused.

Making an argument

- Your essays should make an argument, not just repeat details about a war, its causes, practices or effects.
- Your argument should be stated explicitly in your essay's introduction and conclusion, with the supportive evidence discussed in the body of the essay.
- To strengthen your argument, use a range of supporting evidence. This evidence should be explained and connected to the question.

- Try to bring in conceptual understanding and historical comparison points within your writing to increase the sophistication of your analysis and evaluation.
- Higher-level responses will also discuss different perspectives. These could include the views of historians, opinions from the time period in question and your own interpretations. An evaluation of perspectives is required to reach the 13–15-mark band.

Planning your essay

- A good plan will contain an argument and set out the structure of your essay, which will be designed to facilitate your argument.
- You should spend perhaps five minutes preparing this.

Writing an introduction

- The introduction is of vital importance for the rest of your essay, as it is the first thing an examiner will read, and needs to create the right impression about you as a student and young historian.
- The most important three elements of a history introduction are that the reader leaves it knowing that you: (a) understand the question, (b) have a complex argument and (c) are able to structure your essay logically and unambiguously, accounting for each body paragraph you are going to write.
- There should be no surprises for the reader as they make their way through the main body of your essay. In other words, you need to make clear in your introduction what you will be arguing, and how you will be arguing it.
- Follow the four steps in the table below to enable you to do this effectively.

Step 1: Contextualizing statement	Using an explanation (and maybe a flowery anecdote), show that you understand the demands of the question
Step 2: Rhetorical question(s)	To show mastery over the question, pose a couple of rhetorical questions that expose the heart of the topic in the question. Perhaps explore the fact that the history will change depending on the lens through which you look at it
Step 3: State your argument	This is your answer to the question, so use the words of the question. It should show the interrelationship between factors and the ability to prioritize factors. It should be multilayered and nuanced
Step 4: Explain the structure of your essay (the agenda for the essay)	You should explicitly account for every paragraph. Try to use historical themes or factors. These may include: (1) economic, social, political, military factors; (2) long- and short-term factors; (3) historiographical arguments, for example 'intentionalism' and 'functionalism'

It is also important that you define the terms you use in the introduction of your essay.

If the question asks you:	Be sure to …
• about guerrilla warfare	• explain what guerrilla warfare means
• to discuss two wars, each from a different region	• state clearly the regions in which the wars were fought, and the wars you will be discussing, with dates of the conflict
• to discuss post-war peacemaking	• explain what peacemaking is and what formats you will address as part of your structure, such as treaties, economic reconstruction or international observers

Writing body paragraphs

- In a Paper 2 essay you should aim for three or four body paragraphs.
- Each paragraph should develop your argument and stay focused on the question.
- You should use historical themes, or factors, for each body paragraph. An example of this would be basing paragraphs around economic, social, political or military factors.
- Follow the four steps on page 11 to enable you to effectively write body paragraphs. You may need to repeat steps 2 and 3 within each paragraph as you will probably be discussing more than one piece of evidence in each paragraph. Aim for three pieces of evidence to support your point, as a general rule.

Step 1: Your point, or mini-argument	Start with an argument that answers the question and makes your historical theme clear. Use the words of the question to make sure you are doing this
Step 2: Evidence	Support your argument with evidence. This evidence should be detailed and precise and should be both qualitative and quantitative. You may include expert opinion, for example historians' arguments
Step 3: Analyse	Explain the meaning and significance of the evidence in relation to the question. Analyse how it supports your argument, and consider the implications of the evidence for the question
Step 4: Link	At the end of the paragraph make a link back to the question, reasserting your main point in the paragraph. Make sure you use the words of the question to ensure you stay relevant to it

Writing a conclusion

- In your conclusion make the final, powerful case for your argument.
- Restate your main arguments and unpack them.
- Try to ensure that all of your body paragraphs are accounted for to show how they all contributed to your argument. In this way, your essay will not lose its nuance, or its layers of analysis.
- Do not contradict arguments that you have made earlier in your essay.
- Make sure that you refer back to the question throughout your conclusion, and unpack the complexities in the question.
- If you have time, for the grand finish, try to reposition your essay in a wider historical context. The final sentence could perhaps refer back to the first contextualizing statement in your introduction to try to give your essay a profound finish.

Essays which focus on two case studies

Essays that focus on two case studies are common on Paper 2. There are some key points that are worth keeping in mind for this type of essay:

- There should be a 50–50 split between usage of the two case studies. In other words, they need to be discussed equally.
- Try to find big historical themes and refer to both case studies in relation to each theme. This thematic approach will encourage you to be analytical. Although this approach is preferable, there is no strict guidance on this, so you could write two paragraphs on one case study, and then two paragraphs on the other, discussing each separately. It will largely depend on the question set, so you will need to be flexible.
- For example, if the question asks you to 'compare and contrast' two case studies, then you will get your marks by analysing similarities and differences between them. Here you will need to use a thematic structure in which you discuss both case studies in each paragraph, comparing and contrasting them.
- If the question presents you with one of the other four command terms – examine, evaluate, to what extent or discuss – then you could either sequence the case studies or adopt a thematic approach. The latter is preferable though.

Good luck with your studies and the exam!

1 First World War 1914–18

On 28 July 1914, Austria-Hungary declared war on Serbia. By 4 August, the powers of Europe declared war on each other, bringing much of the world into conflict.

The long-term causes of the First World War

Revised

Industrialization

Methods of manufacturing had developed dramatically in the nineteenth century, leading to advances in industry, technology and communication that enhanced military capabilities. As a result:

- Germany became the European leader in industrial output by 1910.
- Iron and steel output increased among all the major powers, making the mass production of weaponry much easier.
- Methods of transportation improved, with the growth of railways allowing countries to move troops more quickly.

Imperialism

The Balkans

Stability in the Balkan region of Europe declined in the nineteenth century due to the weakening of the **Ottoman Empire**, as countries vied for influence and economic gain in the region. This led to heightened tensions between European powers, especially Russia and the **Austro-Hungarian Empire**, who competed for the prestige, markets and sources of raw materials that empire brought:

- Austria-Hungary annexed Bosnia-Herzegovina in 1908, despite Russian protests, leaving Russia humiliated.
- With Russian support, Serbia gained its independence from the Ottomans in 1878 and then greatly expanded its territories in the Balkan Wars of 1912–13.
- Austria-Hungary, which wanted to prevent Serbian growth in terms of land, economic development and prestige, helped Albania to become an independent state, thereby blocking Serbia from having access to a seaport.

British, French and German rivalries

Britain, France, and Germany looked for opportunities to acquire land outside Europe:

- The German Kaiser (Emperor), **Wilhelm II**, worked to establish a 'place in the sun' for Germany and wished to see the German Empire expand as part of his ideology named ***Weltpolitik***.
- Britain and France, whose colonies were significantly larger and more established than Germany's, were concerned by Germany's desire to expand and challenge them economically and diplomatically.
- Tensions between these states resulted in the Moroccan Crisis of 1905. France wished to expand its control in the region, but Germany objected. An international conference held in Algeciras, Spain, in 1906 resulted in a temporary resolution. It also led to Germany being humiliated by Britain and France, which worked together to prevent the Germans from achieving much at the conference.
- Tensions rose again in 1911 after France sent troops into Morocco to occupy Fez. Germany protested, claiming that France had created an excuse to occupy Morocco. Britain once again backed France, leaving Germany isolated and with little option other than to accept territory from France in the Congo region in compensation.

MULTICAUSAL EXPLANATIONS FOR THE ORIGINS OF THE FIRST WORLD WAR

Use the information on the opposite page and the next page, and your own knowledge, to add examples to each of the following causal themes of the First World War in the spider diagram below.

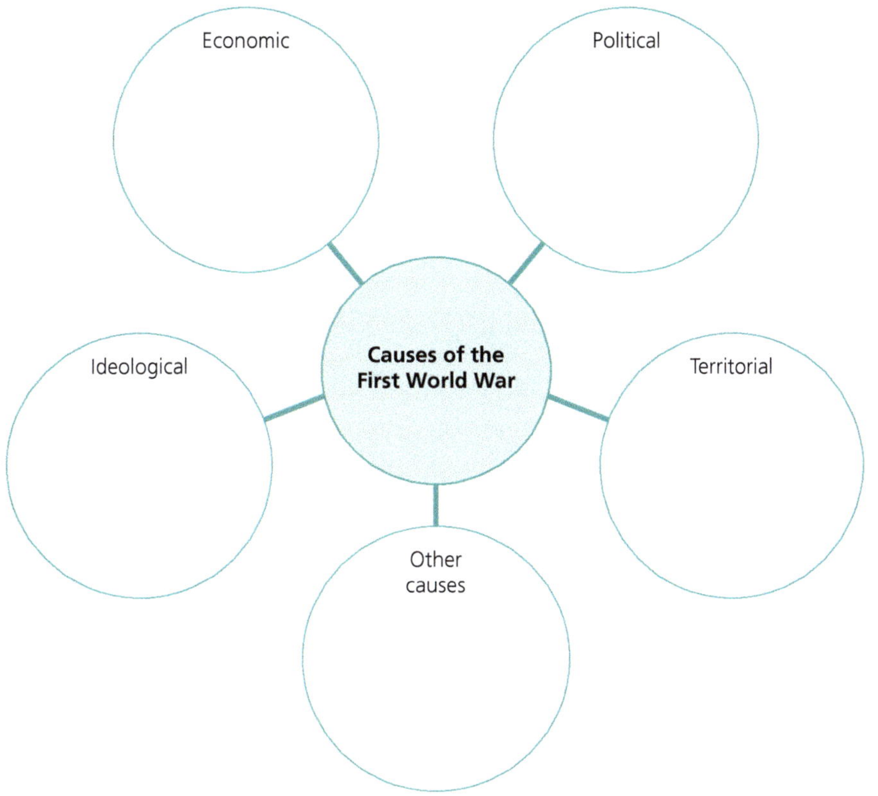

THE INTERRELATIONSHIPS BETWEEN LONG-TERM CAUSES OF THE FIRST WORLD WAR

Read the example below, which links ideological and economic long-term causes of the First World War. Using the information on the opposite page and the next page, and your own knowledge, try to do the same for any of the other long-term causes, completing the empty arrow and boxes.

Long-term cause	Interrelationship between causes	Long-term cause
Ideologically, Germany was a **revisionist power**, led by Kaiser Wilhelm, which followed an aggressive policy of *Weltpolitik* to establish its 'place in the sun'. This caused tensions with the ***status quo* powers**, who did not want to lose their authority	The aggressive revisionist German stance meant that it pursued rapid industrialization to increase its power	Germany's production of steel surpassed that of Britain in 1900. This made the mass production of weaponry much easier, and allowed the Germans to outproduce Britain in terms of certain types of arms. This worried the British, and further increased competitive tensions in Europe

Alliance systems

European powers were all members of rival alliances, increasing the likelihood of a small dispute escalating into a much larger one.

- Germany and Austria-Hungary formed the Dual Alliance in 1878 as a way of bolstering strength in central Europe after Russian–German relations deteriorated.
- The Dual Alliance turned into the **Triple Alliance** in 1882 with Italy joining. Members agreed to provide military support to one another in the case of a military attack by another European power (Germany and Italy's agreement concerned a French attack only).
- Russia, fearing isolation against a now hostile Germany and Austria-Hungary along most of its western border, formed an alliance with France in 1894, known as the Franco-Russian military alliance. Both countries agreed to support each other in the event of an attack from a country in the Triple Alliance.
- In 1904, Britain and France signed the Entente Cordiale, a series of agreements that resolved long-term colonial disputes and tensions between the two countries. While this was not technically an alliance and they did not promise military support to one another, it established a working relationship between the two countries.
- In 1907, Britain signed a similar agreement with Russia, ending colonial tensions. Thus, the so-called **Triple Entente** was born.

Militarism

The increased capacity to produce weaponry due to industrialization, combined with a desire for influence and territory abroad among the European powers, led to an **arms race** at the start of the twentieth century.

- Russia had the largest army in 1914, totalling 1.3 million troops from a population of 167 million.
- All countries had substantially increased the size of their armies. For example, Austria-Hungary's army more than doubled to 810,000 by 1910.
- Britain continued to focus its efforts on maintaining naval superiority and developed the *Dreadnought* battleship in 1906. The battleship far surpassed any previous vessels in terms of machinery and capacity to attack from a great distance.
- Germany responded by launching its own Dreadnought in 1908.
- By 1914, Britain had 29 dreadnoughts compared to Germany's 14.

Military plans

Rapid advances in machinery and weaponry meant new military strategies.

- Germany developed the **Schlieffen Plan**, which aimed to prevent war breaking out simultaneously on its eastern border with Russia and its western border with France. Germany would launch a rapid attack against France, defeating it within six weeks, and then the vast majority of its army could be used against Russia before the Russians were fully ready for war. Russia was seen as the greater threat over the long term.
- Russian plans were developed to rapidly move against Germany in order to counter its logistical and organizational problems, which would be an issue in a long-term war.
- Plan XVII was drawn up in France, emphasizing the importance of launching an attack against Germany on their shared border.
- Britain planned to send its army to France in the event of war and concentrate its efforts on destroying Germany's navy, which would lead to supply problems, of both food and raw materials, that would hinder Germany militarily and economically.

Nationalism

Nationalism gained in popularity throughout the nineteenth century.

- Germany's unification was achieved through a series of wars orchestrated by Chancellor Otto von Bismarck of Prussia, the largest German-speaking state other than Austria. This led to a swell in nationalism, leading to calls for empire, as well as a large army and navy.
- The desire for autonomous rule led to several ethnic groups declaring independence from the declining Ottoman Empire, such as Bulgaria, Greece and Serbia; all achieved independence by the early twentieth century.
- Charles Darwin's theory of evolution and natural selection was misappropriated and gave rise to the idea that some races and nations were superior to others and therefore were meant to dominate weaker groups or states.

USING HISTORIANS' ARGUMENTS TO HELP WITH THE PRIORITIZATION OF CAUSES

It is a good idea to quote from expert opinion – that of historians – a couple of times in your essays. You can then evaluate these quotations with evidence, arguing whether you agree or disagree with them. This will help with prioritizing arguments, as you can see which causes the experts place emphasis on and engage with their line of thinking.

For each historian's argument below, explain which cause or causes of the First World War you think it supports.

SOURCE 1

Extract from A.J.P. Taylor, *War by Time-Table: How the First World War Began*, MacDonald, London, 1969, page 45.

It is the fashion nowadays to seek profound causes for great events. But perhaps the war which broke out in 1914 had no profound causes. For thirty years past, international diplomacy, the balance of power, the alliances and the accumulation of armed might, produced peace. Suddenly the situation was turned round, and the very forces which had produced the long peace now produced a great war. In much the same way, a motorist who for thirty years has been doing the right thing to avoid accidents makes a mistake one day and has a crash. In July 1914 things went wrong.

SOURCE 2

Extract from D.E. Marshall, *The Great War: Myth and Reality*, W.T. Press, Wellington, 1988, page 36.

The Schlieffen Plan must rank as one of the supreme idiocies of modern times … It restricted the actions of the German government disastrously. In July 1914 they had just two choices; either to abandon the only plan they had to win the next war, or to go to war immediately.

SOURCE 3

Extract from L.C.F. Turner, *Origins of the First World War*, W.W. Norton, London, 1970, page 112.

None of the rulers of the Great Powers really knew what they were fighting about in August 1914 … the crisis gathered pace and the calculations of statesmen were overwhelmed by the rapid succession of events, the tide of emotion in the various capitals, and the demands of military planning.

PRIORITIZATION OF CAUSES

Create your own argument by organizing the causes of the First World War (listed in the boxes on the right) into the pyramid below to show their relative importance. You can put more than one cause in the different sections if you feel that helps your argument. Explain your reasoning around the pyramid. Use your own knowledge and the opposite pages to help with your reasoning.

- Ideological
- Economic
- Political
- Territorial
- Other causes

The short-term causes of the First World War

Revised

The assassination of Archduke Franz Ferdinand and the July Crisis

On 28 June 1914, a Bosnian Serb, Gavrilo Princip, from the secret **Black Hand** organization (also known as the Unification or Death movement) assassinated the heir to the Austro-Hungarian Empire in Sarajevo, the capital of Bosnia-Herzegovina, which Austria-Hungary had annexed in 1908. This incident, often regarded as the catalyst cause of the First World War, was followed by a month of deliberations and negotiations known as the **July Crisis**, which led to the outbreak of the First World War:

- Austria-Hungary, now in a stronger military position due to its alliance with Germany and Italy, felt confident enough to act against Serbia, even though Serbia had Russian support. Serbia supported Slav nationalism and as Austria-Hungary had many Slavs, this was a threat to the unity of the empire.
- As it was a political assassination, it led to Austro-Hungarian hopes that the international community would be sympathetic and refuse to side with Serbia.
- On 5 July, Germany offered Austria-Hungary its full support in the event of war (a 'blank cheque') and encouraged it to take whatever action necessary to resolve the crisis.
- Austria-Hungary sent an ultimatum to the Serbian government on 23 July, including a demand that Austria-Hungary lead the investigation into the assassination. This would involve Serbia allowing Habsburg officials onto Serbian territory to investigate the assassination. Serbia was given 48 hours to accept all terms of the ultimatum.
- Russia condemned the ultimatum but refused to support Serbia militarily at this point.
- Serbia refused to have Austria-Hungary involved in the investigation but accepted all other ultimatum terms. Since Serbia did not unconditionally accept all terms, Austria broke off diplomatic relations with Serbia and mobilized its army. At this point Russia officially offered support to Serbia, as a fellow Slav state was being threatened. Russian prestige in the Balkans was at stake.
- Realizing the seriousness of the situation, on 27 July, Britain sent a series of appeals to Germany to attend an international conference to attempt to resolve the crisis. France, Italy and Russia all agreed to attend. Germany and Austria-Hungary rejected these diplomatic appeals.
- Britain, France, Italy and Russia agreed to attend a conference for resolution; Germany refused.
- Once war was certain, the German government urged Austria-Hungary to only occupy the Serbian capital, which was just across the border from Austria-Hungary, to limit the war and keep other states from joining the conflict. Austria-Hungary ignored this request.

Timeline of the outbreak of war

Date	Event
28 July	Austria-Hungary formally declared war on Serbia
29 July	Tsar Nicholas II sent a telegram to the Kaiser still hoping to avert a war with Germany. Germany was not responsive, and maintained its aggressive stance
30 July	Russia mobilized, or prepared, its army for war, causing Germany to issue an ultimatum that Russia demobilize and that France declare it would not become involved in the war
1 August	Both Germany and France mobilized their troops Germany and Russia declared war against each other
2 August	Germany delivered an ultimatum to Belgium requiring that it remain neutral while German troops occupied the country
3 August	Britain indicated that it would defend Belgian neutrality, as Belgium rejected Germany's ultimatum Germany declared war on France
4 August	Germany invaded Belgium as a step towards invading northern France; Britain declared war on Germany
6 August	Austria-Hungary declared war on Russia
12 August	Britain and France declared war on Austria-Hungary

PLANNING AN IB ESSAY

Below is an example plan for the following essay question.

'Territorial ambition was the most significant cause of war.' With reference to one 20th-century war, to what extent do you agree with this statement?

Argument

Territorial ambition was the most significant cause of the First World War, as the imperial ambitions of Germany, and territorial conflicts in the Balkans, were the primary causes of this war. This can be seen by the July Crisis, which was sparked by a territorially motivated assassination, and escalated into war due to German intransigence based on their imperial designs. That being noted, other significant causes, such as the military preparations for war and the arms race, were also contributing factors that increased tensions in Europe and made war more likely. However, ultimately they were caused by territorial disputes and without such disputes war would not have occurred in Europe in 1914.

Structure

Paragraph 1 theme: Territorial ambitions of the countries in and surrounding the Balkan region (Austria-Hungary, Serbia, Germany, Russia) and the assassination of Archduke Franz Ferdinand were the most significant factors as they triggered the July Crisis. Before that, war was not imminent.

Paragraph 2 theme: German ideology and Weltpolitik meant that tensions during the July Crisis could not de-escalate. This was based on the territorial ambitions of Kaiser Wilhelm II, who wanted 'a place in the sun'.

Paragraph 3 theme: Territorial ambitions were not the sole cause, of course. The arms race and war plans created an environment of competitive tension that made war more likely. Territorial ambitions, however, were the underlying cause of conflict and created the July Crisis.

Read the question below and then plan out your answer in the box provided. You should spend approximately five to ten minutes on a plan for an IB essay in the exam.

Evaluate the importance of long-term and short-term causes of one 20th-century war.

Argument:

Paragraph 1 theme:

Paragraph 2 theme:

Paragraph 3 theme:

Paragraph 4 theme:

The course of the First World War

Revised

The First World War lasted for four years and mobilized entire communities. New weapons were introduced throughout the war, changing the nature of warfare.

The land war

War on the Western Front

Germany declared war on 1 August and began the initial phase of the Schlieffen Plan. Germany invaded Belgium, a neutral country. The German advance was slowed by Belgian, French and British resistance in both Belgium and northern France. By the end of August, German troops and supplies were exhausted and fell behind the schedule of the Schlieffen Plan. In September, the German advance was halted in France and German soldiers dug trenches to secure their positions. British and French attempts to go around the Germans failed, with Germany extending its trenches in the 'race to the sea'. The Schlieffen Plan failed and both sides developed **trench systems** to secure their positions.

Trench warfare posed new problems for both sides due to the dangers for soldiers crossing 'no man's land', the area between opposing trenches. Trenches were fortified with barbed wire and attacking soldiers lacked protection from artillery bombardment, machine guns and sniper fire.

The war on the Western Front became a **war of attrition** as both sides attempted to break the **stalemate**. Devastating cross-fire contributed to this; machine guns could fire 450–500 bullets in one minute.

Germany introduced poison gas in 1915 during the **Second Battle of Ypres**. Although this had great psychological effect and led to many deaths, it failed to end the stalemate. Germany, Britain, France, the USA and Austria-Hungary would all use poison gas during the war.

In February 1916, Germany launched a series of attacks against France at Verdun. It was hoped that France would prioritize saving Verdun and weaken its other positions across the Western Front. The **Battle of Verdun** raged for ten months, with around 1 million troops killed or wounded. Germany eventually called off the battle having gained only eight kilometres (five miles) of territory.

The British launched an offensive in July 1916 near the Somme River in the hope of drawing German forces away from Verdun. The **Battle of the Somme** was a clear example of the deadly nature of trench warfare, with 20,000 British soldiers being killed on the first day. The territorial gain made was minimal.

Several attempts were made by the Allies in 1917 to break through the German lines, such as the **Battle of Passchendaele** in which the Allies gained eight kilometres (five miles). These attempts were not decisive and failed to make significant gains. The USA joined the war on the side of the Allies in April 1917 and by 1918 over a quarter of a million US troops were arriving on the Western Front each month.

Use of tanks

Tanks were first used against trenches by Britain in September 1916. While clunky and unreliable to begin with, they proved successful in the latter parts of the war, such as at the **Battle of Cambrai** in 1917, when 476 British tanks took 9.5 km (six miles) of land in a few hours.

Numbers of tanks produced by country in the First World War are listed below:

Year	Britain	France	Germany	Italy	USA
1916	150	0	0	0	0
1917	1277	800	0	0	0
1918	1391	4000	20	6	84

In an attempt to counter strengthening Allied forces, the Germans launched the **Ludendorff Offensive** in March 1918 to try to achieve a decisive victory, as they lacked the manpower and resources to fight on much longer. Germany changed its tactics by employing a shorter artillery bombardment, known as a hurricane barrage, followed by smaller, staggered infantry detachments. The new tactics appeared successful, but Germany was not able to sustain the offensive and began to retreat after the Allies attacked at Marne in July. Germany was forced into an armistice, an agreement to stop fighting, on 11 November 1918.

WESTERN FRONT BATTLE MATCH-UP

Below are the names of various battles that took place on the Western Front, along with definitions of each battle.

Match the battle with the definition.

Battle	Definition
Second Battle of Ypres	Took place in 1916. Lasted for ten months, killing 1 million. The Germans gained 8 km of territory
Battle of Verdun	Took place in 1917. Was an attack launched by the Allies in which they gained 8 km of territory
Battle of the Somme	Took place in 1917. An example of a battle where the Allies used tanks effectively, gaining 9.5 km of land in a few hours
Battle of Passchendaele	Took place in 1915. Was the battle where Germany introduced poison gas. Finished in a stalemate
Battle of Cambrai	Took place in 1916. Was an attack launched by the British; 20,000 British soldiers died on the first day

REASONS FOR THE RESULTS OF KEY BATTLES

Using the information on the page opposite and your own knowledge, complete the following table to analyse which side, if any, won the key battles and campaigns on the Western Front and why the fighting turned out the way that it did.

Battle or campaign	Which side, if any, won? What was achieved?	Why did it turn out this way? Explain your thinking
Schlieffen Plan		
Second Battle of Ypres		
Battle of Verdun		
Battle of the Somme		
Battle of Passchendaele		
Battle of Cambrai		
Ludendorff Offensive		

War on the Italian Front

Italy joined the war in 1915 having signed the Treaty of London, an agreement which would see Italy fight on the side of the Allies in return for Italy gaining Austro-Hungarian territory after the war. Italian and Austro-Hungarian soldiers engaged in trench warfare, with neither side making any meaningful territorial gains. German and Austro-Hungarian troops launched a major offensive against Italy in 1917, killing 300,000 Italians in the Battle of Caporetto.

War on the Eastern Front

Russian forces mobilized more quickly than the Germans anticipated and invaded eastern Germany on 7 August 1914. This meant that Germany's Schlieffen Plan was immediately ruined. Germany defeated the Russians at the **Battle of Tannenberg** in late August 1914, destroying the Russian Second Army. Germany's use of railways to manoeuvre its troops to take on Russian armies one at a time, and the failure of Russia to encode radio messages, were key reasons for the defeat of the Russians.

In June 1916, Russia launched what became known as the **Brusilov Offensive** against Austria-Hungary. While the offensive had initial success, the Russians suffered from a lack of supplies and were overwhelmed by German reinforcements arriving from Verdun. Russia succeeded in crippling the Austro-Hungarian army, but the cost was high, depleting its resources.

The Russian ruler, the tsar, was overthrown in February 1917. The Provisional Government, supported by the army, was established, but was itself overthrown in October 1917 in the **Bolshevik Revolution**. The **Bolshevik Party**, later known as the Communist Party, quickly brought an end to Russia's role in the First World War by agreeing to the terms of the **Treaty of Brest-Litovsk**, leaving German troops on the Eastern Front free to deploy to the Western Front for the Ludendorff Offensive.

War on the Ottoman Front

The Allies launched an attack against Ottoman forces on the **Gallipoli Peninsula** in 1915 in an attempt to:

- remove the Ottoman Empire from the war by capturing Istanbul, the Ottoman capital
- improve Allied supply routes between Britain/France and Russia
- weaken Germany and Austria-Hungary by forcing them to fight on a third front.

The Gallipoli campaign failed to make gains against entrenched Ottoman soldiers and the Allies conceded defeat early in 1916 after over 100,000 lives had been lost on both sides.

War in the Middle East

The **Caucasus Campaign** was fought between Russia and the Ottomans, starting in 1914. The Ottomans aimed to recover territory which had been lost to Russia in the nineteenth century. Although the Ottomans had some initial success, by 1917 Russia had captured large areas of what is today eastern Turkey. The Russian army, however, fell apart in 1917 with the revolutions in Russia.

The **Mesopotamian Campaign** began in 1914 and was initially successful for Britain against the Ottomans. The Ottomans began better resistance in 1915 and by 1916 British troops surrendered. In March 1917, the important city of Baghdad was captured by Britain. Little else was accomplished.

In January 1915, Ottoman forces attacked the British-controlled Suez Canal in Egypt, causing the British government to encourage an Arab revolt against the Ottomans while promising Arab independence after the war. The Arab Revolt lasted from June 1916 to October 1918 and led to the Ottomans leaving the Arabian Peninsula, Palestine, and much of Syria and Lebanon. The campaign ended when the Ottomans surrendered at the end of the war.

COMPLETE THE TABLE

Using the information on the page opposite and your own knowledge, complete the following table to identify how each front proved a victory or failure for the Allied and Central Powers. Explain your decision using factual details from the text.

Campaign	Allied powers	Central Powers
The Italian Front		
The Eastern Front		
The Ottoman Front		
War in the Middle East		

STATEMENTS ON THE FIGHTING ON THE EASTERN FRONT, ON THE OTTOMAN FRONT AND IN THE MIDDLE EAST

For each statement below, explain whether you agree or disagree with it, and why.

Statement	Agree or disagree?
Russia was defeated on the Eastern Front in 1917 primarily because of the superior military strength of the Germans	
The Schlieffen Plan was unrealistic and never really stood a chance of being successful	
The Gallipoli Campaign was a complete disaster for the Triple Entente	
The fighting in the Middle East mainly resulted in victories for the Triple Entente	

War in the air

At first, aircraft were only used for **reconnaissance**, but fighter planes were developed to shoot down observation aircraft. By 1915, forward-firing machine guns were placed on most aircraft. By 1917, planes had the capability of flying at over 200 km/h (124 mph) and were able to carry two machine guns, while dropping shells, some with poison gas.

Aircraft were used by both sides for **strategic bombing** campaigns. The British launched bombing attacks on Germany from 1916, and the Germans on Britain in 1917; these had no real effect on the outcome of the war.

Aircraft were also used to support infantry campaigns. Bombs and grenades were dropped from planes flying at a low altitude and machine guns were fired at infantry soldiers. However, this had no effect on the outcome of any battle.

In 1915, Germany launched air-raid attacks against Britain and France using Zeppelin airships. The large size and slow speed of the airships made them easy targets for anti-aircraft fire. By the end of the war, 60 of the 84 Zeppelin airships built had been destroyed.

Countries used seaplanes for reconnaissance and attacks on navies in the war. These had no effect on the outcome of any battle. During the war, planes were launched from ships for the first time.

Aircraft production saw the building of 50,000 aircraft each for Britain and France, indicating their perceived importance by the military.

War at sea

Britain established a naval blockade against Germany from August 1914 until 1919. Mines were placed and naval patrols guarded the English Channel and North Sea exits to the Atlantic Ocean to stop German ships being able to leave ports and trade with the rest of the world.

The only major naval battle of the war was the **Battle of Jutland**, which occurred in May 1916. Germany hoped to cause enough damage to break the naval blockade, and while the battle was costlier for Britain in terms of battleships lost (Britain lost fourteen compared to Germany's eleven), Germany failed to break this blockade. The stopping of imports, such as food, getting into Germany was a key factor in Germany's eventual surrender in 1918.

Britain was vulnerable to starvation as it imported much of its food. As a result, Germany targeted merchant, as well as military, ships in unrestricted submarine warfare intermittently from 1915 until 1918.

Britain attempted to combat the threat of U-boats by developing Q-ships (battleships that looked like merchant ships) and using a **convoy system**. German U-boats inflicted significant damage on British ships (with almost 5000 ships sunk over the course of the war), but failed to force Britain into a surrender through starvation.

TO WHAT EXTENT DID TECHNOLOGY USED ON LAND, AIR AND SEA AFFECT THE OUTCOME OF THE FIRST WORLD WAR?

For each of the different military technologies used across air, land and sea, use the preceding pages and your own knowledge to decide how important they were in deciding the outcome of the First World War. Then arrange the nine types into the diamond nine to show their importance. Place the most important at the top. Around the diamond nine, add in explanations and examples to explain your thinking.

Submarines

Battleships

Fighter planes

Zeppelin airships

Poison gas

Machine guns

Tanks

Artillery

Radio

The practices of the First World War and their impact on its outcome

Revised

Military manpower

Almost all the war strategies developed by the major powers before the outbreak of the First World War involved the rapid mobilization of troops. Germany succeeded in mobilizing the 1.5 million troops needed for the Schlieffen Plan, but Russia mobilized its troops more rapidly than Germany had anticipated.

All major powers introduced **conscription**, mobilizing civilian populations into the military on a scale unlike anything before. As a result, population size became increasingly important as the war went on, with the Allies benefiting from Russia's huge population and the colonies of the British and French Empires. German campaigns in the latter stages of the war did not have enough troops to resist the advances of the Allies, especially after the entry of the USA. By 1918 over a quarter of a million US troops were arriving on the Western Front each month.

War production

Few anticipated that the war would go on for as long as it did, thus nations were faced with significant shortages of ammunition and weapons in the early stages of the war. Production of war supplies rose rapidly in all countries as the war progressed. The Allies were able to make the most significant gains as they benefited from US supplies (from 1917 onwards) and Germany struggled to access the raw materials that it needed because of the naval blockade. Entire populations were mobilized, including women. In Austria-Hungary, women made up 42.5% of industrial workers by 1916 (compared to 17.5% in 1913), with all other countries seeing similar increases.

The graph below compares British and German explosives production during the war.

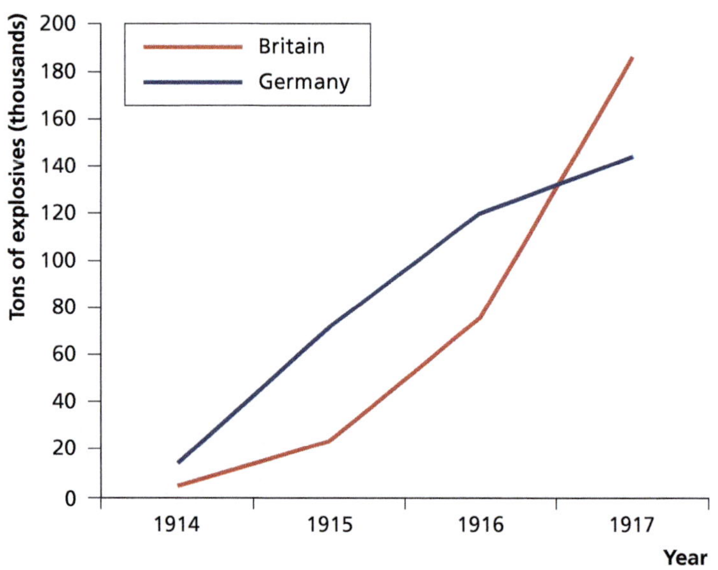

Food shortages

Keeping the military and civilian population fed was a difficult challenge for all countries, particularly Britain, which imported 60% of its food before 1914. Propaganda campaigns helped to raise awareness of the need to save food and reduce the number of merchant ships that risked journeying to Britain past German submarines. Britain was forced to adopt a rationing programme and at times was weeks away from starvation.

Germany introduced big changes to the way its population ate as a result of the blockade. Imports were halved and substitutes were introduced to keep the population fed. A decision to slaughter millions of pigs led to a shortage of fertilizer, limiting Germany's ability to grow its own produce, leading to further hunger.

In Russia, food shortages led to massive price increases. The price of meat rose by 232% in the first two years of war, affecting those in urban areas most as agricultural labourers in rural areas kept hold of their produce as money lost its value. There was little the agricultural labourers could buy with money in any case, as all production was for the war effort.

THE RELATIVE SIGNIFICANCE OF DIFFERENT VARIABLES IN EXPLAINING THE OUTCOME OF THE FIRST WORLD WAR

For each of the following variables, use the previous pages and your own knowledge to explain the impact that they had on the outcome of the First World War. Then decide on the significance of the variable. Complete the blank sections.

Variable	Explain the impact that this variable had on the outcome of the First World War	How significant was the impact of this variable on the outcome of the First World War?
Technological developments	• The use of machine guns (cross-fire) and artillery bombardment meant that trench warfare ensued • Germany introduced poison gas in 1915 during the Second Battle of Ypres. The shock caused by the gas allowed the Germans to advance, but they were unable to take Ypres	• Technology led to huge casualties on both sides for very limited gains • Modern technological developments resulted in a long four-year war, as neither side could strike decisively. They actually made it harder for one side to win • Gas had a terrible impact on the troops involved, but did not prove significant in altering the outcome of the war
Land war		
War in the air		
War at sea		
Human resources	• The USA joined the war on the side of the Allies in April 1917, and by 1918 over a quarter of a million US troops were arriving on the Western Front each month	• Hugely significant. With the entry of the USA into the war, alongside the forces of Britain and France, the Germans could not sustain the fight against this increased manpower and were overpowered in 1918
Economic resources		

The effects of the First World War

Revised

The First World War led to significant political, economic and social changes for the countries involved. Political systems were affected, empires collapsed, territories changed hands and governments had to work out how to meet the needs of their citizens, who had endured four years of total war.

The peace treaties

Various peace treaties were created at the end of the war, aiming to create a lasting peace.

Treaty	Country concerned	Key terms
Treaty of Versailles	Germany	• **Reparation payments** of 132 billion gold marks (never fully paid) • Rhineland, bordering France, to be demilitarized • Lost ten per cent of its land and all colonies • Military severely reduced, with no tanks, air force or artillery, and maximum army of 100,000 men • Unification with Austria, ***Anschluss***, forbidden
Treaty of St Germain	Austria	• Much land lost to neighbouring countries • Military reduced to 30,000 men and no air force or navy • Reparations required (not paid as the result of national bankruptcy)
Treaty of Trianon	Hungary	• Two-thirds of territory lost • Massive reparations (never fully paid) • Military reduced to 35,000 men and no air force or navy
Treaty of Sèvres	Turkey	• Empire dismantled, with Middle Eastern lands put under French and British control • Military reduced to 50,000 men and no air force or navy • No reparations • Bosporus Straits and Dardanelles to be international zone with no restrictions on shipping
Treaty of Neuilly	Bulgaria	• Land given to Greece and Serbia • Military severely reduced to 20,000 men and no air force • Reparations set at £100 million

Both the Ottoman and Austro-Hungarian Empires were dismantled at the end of the war, leading to the formation of new nation-states such as Yugoslavia and Czechoslovakia.

US President **Woodrow Wilson**'s principle of self-determination was carefully considered as the territorial boundaries of Europe were redrawn, with new nations being formed with homogeneous peoples. However, this process was not smooth and led to thousands of civilians being moved and thousands more becoming a minority population in a new nation.

The political impact of the First World War

Western Europe

There were many great political changes in Western Europe as a result of the war:

- Germany became democratic at the end of 1918 with the abdication of the Kaiser, the German emperor, just before the end of the war, and the founding of a republic.
- The Treaty of Versailles was met with great protest in Germany and was referred to as the diktat ('dictated peace'). It resulted in anti-democratic, violent, **right-wing** support and actions.
- The new **Weimar Republic**, named after the city where the new constitution was signed, faced difficult political challenges immediately, with revolutions attempted by various extreme political groups over several years.
- Italy was politically divided after the war, leading to violence and the emergence of **fascism** and its leader, soon to be dictator of Italy, **Benito Mussolini**.

Central and eastern Europe

There were also great changes in central and eastern Europe:

- Russia had two revolutions in 1917 and pulled out of the war in early 1918. The Russian Civil War, between various political groups, was mostly over by 1921, leaving the Bolsheviks, or Communists, in power. They established the Soviet Union as the world's first communist state.
- With the break-up of the Austro-Hungarian and Ottoman Empires, new nation-states, such as Poland, Czechoslovakia and Yugoslavia, were created.
- Austria and Czechoslovakia became republics, while Poland developed into a military dictatorship. Czechoslovakia and Poland were stable, but Austria was much less so.
- Hungary, Romania, Bulgaria and Yugoslavia (an expanded Serbia that included parts of the former Austro-Hungarian Empire) all became versions of constitutional monarchies.

THE SUCCESSES AND FAILURES OF THE PEACE TREATIES

Read the two sources below and use them, along with the information on the previous page, to answer the questions below.

SOURCE 4

Extract from John Maynard Keynes, *The Economic Consequences of the Peace*, Macmillan, London, 1919, page 211.

The Treaty includes no provisions for the economic rehabilitation of Europe, – nothing to make the defeated Central Empires into good neighbours, nothing to stabilise the new States of Europe, nothing to reclaim Russia; nor does it promote in any way a compact of economic solidarity amongst the Allies themselves; no arrangement was reached at Paris for restoring the disordered finances of France and Italy, or to adjust the systems of the Old World and the New.

The Council of Four paid no attention to these issues, being preoccupied with others, – Clemenceau [France's prime minister] to crush the economic life of his enemy, Lloyd George [Britain's prime minister] to do a deal and bring home something which would pass muster for a week, the President to do nothing that was not just and right.

SOURCE 5

Extract from Renée Hirsch on, 'History's long shadow: the Lausanne Treaty and contemporary Greco-Turkish relations' in O. Anastasakis, K.A. Nicolaidis and K. Öktem (editors), *In the Long Shadow of Europe: Greeks and Turks in the Era of Postnationalism*, Martinus Nijhoff, Leiden, 2009, page 75.

The Lausanne Convention (LC or Convention), and the Treaty to which it was a protocol, ratified a unique compulsory exchange. It was one of many international treaties signed in the aftermath of the First World War and was deliberated in the climate of nation-state formation after the break-up of the great empires. The Convention was applied as a solution to conflict of the most brutal kind. In order to stop the bloodshed, two states agreed to eliminate the 'Other' from their midst through the compulsory expulsion of its minorities, in order to create homogeneous societies. It was, strikingly, the first internationally ratified programme for 'ethnic cleansing', a term which did not exist at the time but which neatly describes what happened.

1. What evidence is there that the peacemaking process was a success?
2. What evidence is there that the peacemaking process was a failure?
3. Overall, to what extent do you consider the peacemaking process to be a success?

THE POLITICAL REPERCUSSIONS OF THE FIRST WORLD WAR

Using the opposite page and your own knowledge, complete the table below, noting down the major political repercussions for the countries listed, and why these repercussions were significant.

Country	Describe the main political repercussions of the First World War	Why were these political repercussions significant?
Germany		
Italy		
Russia		
Turkey		

The social impact of the First World War

The First World War had a great social impact on the countries involved:

- The war inflicted more casualties than had any previous European conflict, with around 10 million men killed.
- Germany suffered the most in terms of men lost, with over 2 million dead and a further 5.6 million wounded.
- Civilian casualties were also high, with 500,000 Russians dying as a result of the war, excluding the **Russian Civil War** period.
- Although women joined the workforce in unprecedented numbers during the war, most left industry at the war's conclusion. In France, women's employment returned to 1911 levels by 1921.
- The war gave women a sense of freedom and independence that continued to develop in the 1920s. Fashions began to change and accepted social norms regarding employment status, marital status and more began to shift.
- One of the biggest consequences of the war for women in many countries involved, such as Britain and Germany, but not France, was gaining the vote.

The economic effects of the First World War

Germany

Germany's economy was affected greatly by the war:

- The naval blockade devastated Germany's economy.
- Germany lost key industrial territory under the terms of the Treaty of Versailles, such as the Saar coalfields, which were placed under the supervision of the **League of Nations**. The North Sea port of Danzig was also controlled by the League of Nations after the war, and placed in a customs union with Poland, which needed the port for international trade.
- The Reparations Commissions, created by the Treaty of Versailles, placed reparations at £6.6 billion; Germany managed the first instalment in 1921, but not the second in 1922.
- France and Belgium occupied the industrialized Ruhr area of Germany in 1923 to take its profits as reparations. Germany responded by asking its workers to go on strike in the Ruhr and continued paying their wages. The government was able to pay their wages by printing more money, leading to **hyperinflation**, destroying the currency's value.
- As Germany's land was not invaded during the war, damage was minimal, and German industry recovered by 1928 to 1914 levels.

France

France, too, was affected economically by the war:

- Most of the Western Front war had been fought in France, which led to the destruction of both civilian and industrial areas. Huge areas were designated as '*zone rouge*', meaning they were too physically and environmentally damaged for human occupation.
- France lent money to Russia during the war, but the Bolshevik government in Russia refused to pay the old government's debts, leading to France needing German reparations to rebuild the country.
- France's economy slowly began to recover through the 1920s.

WRITING INTRODUCTIONS TO IB ESSAYS

Highlight the four elements of a good introduction in the example introduction below. These four steps are outlined in the 'Getting to know the exam' section of this book (pages 9–10).

Compare and contrast the economic and social effects of one 20th-century war on two countries.

The economic and social effects of the First World War varied greatly from country to country. This essay will focus on France, one of the countries on the winning side in the First World War, and on Germany, one of the countries on the losing side. Despite their contrasting fortunes at the end of the war, how did the economic and social effects compare and contrast between these two countries? Did one country lose more from the First World War than the other? It will be argued that the economic and social effects of the First World War were paradoxically more detrimental to France than Germany, despite the fact that France was on the winning side. First, this essay will discuss the economic impact of the war, and it will be argued that both countries' industries suffered in the short term as a result of the First World War, but Germany recovered quicker than France as there was hardly any fighting on their soil. Second, the social effects of the war will be considered, and it will be argued that immense human suffering affected both countries in similar ways, although it was on a larger scale in Germany. Finally, we will turn to consider opportunities for women as a result of the war, and it will be argued that women benefited more in Germany, as their socioeconomic status was raised as they gained political rights and entered the workforce in greater numbers, which did not happen in France.

PLANNING ESSAYS IN TIMED CONDITIONS

Read the IB Paper 2-style question below, and then write out your introduction using the boxes provided to help guide you. You should give yourself five to ten minutes to plan the essay before you write the introduction to replicate exam conditions.

Evaluate the effects of one 20th-century war on two countries.

Step 1: Contextualizing statement	
Step 2: Rhetorical question(s)	
Step 3: State your argument	
Step 4: Explain the structure of your essay (the agenda for the essay)	

Britain

Britain's economy was also affected by the war:

- In order to survive the conflict, Britain was forced to borrow money from the USA, leaving the country in debt.
- As Britain shifted its manufacturing focus towards the war effort, the USA took over many of Britain's markets, leaving Britain without outlets for its goods after the war.
- Britain needed Europe to recover quickly economically so that it could resume trading with other countries, especially Germany, and boost its own economy in turn.

United States

Unlike most countries, the USA prospered as a result of the war:

- The US economy expanded greatly during the war. Before the USA entered the war in 1917, it lent money and sold food and supplies to the Allies.
- War created an industrial boom as the demand for factories, homes and infrastructure increased.
- Many people from the agricultural South travelled North to find work and benefited from the industrial boom.
- The USA's economic growth continued post-war, and the 1920s were known as the 'Roaring Twenties', as the nation's wealth more than doubled from 1920 to 1929.
- Yet, by the late 1920s, the economic situation was precarious because of excessive borrowing, and in 1929 the Wall Street Crash occurred, causing the **Great Depression**.

Central and eastern Europe

Significant economic effects were felt across central and eastern Europe:

- The newly created states in central and eastern Europe struggled to sustain their own economies now that they were no longer part of much larger imperial economies and trade networks.
- Austria had been the administrative district of the Austro-Hungarian Empire, meaning that the new country had very little in terms of agricultural infrastructure, but still had a large government with few people left to govern. Agriculturally, it had been supported by Hungary and industrially by what was now Czechoslovakia. In short, Austria's economy was not sustainable.
- The League of Nations, established under the terms of the Treaty of Versailles, provided loans to Austria and Hungary, which helped the countries to achieve some economic stability while their economies were slowly transformed.

Russia/Soviet Union

Economic changes in Russia were perhaps greater than for any other state participating in the war:

- After Russia descended into civil war in 1918, the Bolshevik government established War Communism, an economic policy that abolished the use of currency, nationalized all property and forced agricultural labourers to give food to the Bolsheviks.
- War Communism led to the starvation of millions but it allowed the Bolsheviks to supply their troops and win the war.
- The Bolsheviks introduced the New Economic Policy (NEP) in 1921 to try to tackle the problems caused by War Communism. The NEP allowed for small private industries and for agricultural labourers to pay taxes in food, keeping excesses to sell for profit.
- The NEP built trade links with other countries, exporting grain to purchase machinery.
- By 1928, the Soviet Union matched Russia's pre-war production levels.

THE VARYING EFFECTS OF THE FIRST WORLD WAR ON THE DIFFERENT COUNTRIES INVOLVED

Using the preceding pages and your own knowledge, complete the table below, noting the positive and negative effects of the First World War on each of the countries involved. Then give each country an overall rating of 1–9, 1 being the country that suffered the most negative effects from the First World War, and 9 being the country that experienced the most positive effects.

Country/empire	Positive effects of the First World War	Negative effects of the First World War	Overall rating 1–9
France			
Germany			
Britain			
USA			
Russia			
Austria			
Hungary			
Turkey			
Italy			

CHAPTER 1 Exam focus

Sample question and answer

Have a look at the answer to the essay question below. Consider the strengths and limitations of the response.

'Territorial ambition was the most significant cause of war.' With reference to one 20th-century war, to what extent do you agree with this statement?

The First World War took place in the years 1914–18. The war was caused by a multitude of factors including nationalism, militarism and imperialism. Territorial ambition, as evidenced by the rivalries of various European powers in Europe and north Africa, was a significant cause of the war. Territorial ambition, however, stemmed from strong nationalist sentiment and therefore nationalism was the most significant cause of war.

> This is a focused introduction that states a clear thesis which is relevant to the question. The introduction could be clearer about how the essay will be structured.

Territorial ambition proved itself to be a highly significant cause of the First World War when considering the newly unified country of Germany. Germany's 'Weltpolitik' ideology meant that it tried to upset the status quo powers of Britain and France and establish its 'place in the sun', meaning empire. France and Britain were established imperialist powers with colonies across the world, and Germany wanted to shift the power balance in Europe by building an empire of its own for the reasons of prestige, markets and sources of raw materials. Germany, led by ambitious nationalist Kaiser Wilhelm II, saw an opportunity to expand German power and influence in northern Africa. The Moroccan crises of 1905 and 1911 were instances where Germany tried, and failed, to increase its territory in the region. On both occasions, Germany's desires were blocked by Britain and France, which were not prepared to give power or significant territory to Germany. Germany clearly had territorial ambitions in Europe. These were outlined in the September Programme, a document released just after the start of the war in 1914. This document indicated that Germany would expand into Russia, but also make vassal states of Belgium and France. As Germany clearly desired to expand, Austria was supported in its dispute with Serbia, with Germany offering its ally a 'blank cheque' to go to war. A war would give Germany the excuse needed to make war on France and Russia and realize the goals of the September Programme.

> This paragraph is well developed with a range of detailed examples, relating to the territorial causes of the First World War.

What the argument above doesn't fully consider, however, is why Germany was intent on territorial expansion. Germany experienced a wave of nationalism in the nineteenth century and many in the country believed that Germans were superior to others and therefore deserved to have their own impressive empire like that of Britain's. Kaiser Wilhelm's Weltpolitik was born from a nationalist desire to see Germany as the great European power. I would argue that this strong sense of nationalism also propelled Germany's rapid military expansion and industrialization. Therefore, while German territorial ambition did contribute significantly to the outbreak of war, nationalism was the driving force.

> This is a clear counterargument which is relevant to the question and the student's thesis. Points on militarism and industrialization are left undeveloped.

Territorial ambition can also be regarded as a significant cause of the First World War when considering the Balkan region. The Ottoman Empire was declining and the surrounding countries, particularly Russia, Serbia and Austria-Hungary, saw the opportunity to gain territory in the region. For example, the Austro-Hungarians annexed Bosnia-Herzegovina in 1908 and Serbia expanded its territories after winning the Balkan Wars of 1912–13. Desire for territory increased tensions rapidly between these

> This paragraph begins with a clear point sentence, which is well focused.

nations in the years leading up to war and was further heightened after the archduke's assassination at the hands of a Serb. The ultimatum Austria-Hungary sent to Serbia after the assassination was never likely to be accepted and could arguably have been created to encourage Serbia into war with Austria-Hungary in the hope that Austria-Hungary could acquire Serbian land in the Balkan region. Thus, the argument that territorial ambition was the most significant cause of war holds merit.

This paragraph is concise and contains relevant and precise examples.

It is necessary, again, however, to consider what drove territorial ambition in the Balkans. Serbia and Russia wished to see the growth of pan-Slavism (political and cultural union of Slavic peoples) and this was a huge motivation for the Balkan Wars and the archduke's assassination. Austria-Hungary felt threatened because its empire contained many Slavic people and this fear of the strength of nationalist sentiment from the Serbs and Russians would definitely have encouraged Austria-Hungary to seek an alliance with and assistance from Germany. Therefore, once again, territorial ambition did contribute to the outbreak of war, but the desire for increased territories came from a sense of nationalism.

This paragraph once again counters the paragraph above and contains a clear line of argument.

To conclude, territorial ambitions motivated the key countries in Europe which were responsible for the outbreak of the First World War, but this motivation stemmed from a strong nationalistic belief. A highly nationalistic Serbian group assassinated the archduke, Russia – a monarchy – sided with its fellow Slavic nation Serbia rather than sympathize with a country that had had a member of its royal family assassinated. Germany offered Austria-Hungary a blank cheque as it saw the opportunity to expand its own territory and therefore see the power and identity of the German peoples elevated.

The conclusion is fairly short; however, it argues consistently with the rest of the essay and is well focused on the question.

This is a fairly well-argued response which follows a clear structure. The stated factor of territorial ambition is considered in depth, with a good amount of appropriate evidence, and the argument taken is consistent. The student could have developed ideas on other causes of the war to strengthen the overall argument.

Exam practice

Try one of the following questions or develop a different answer to the question above.

1 Compare and contrast the economic causes of two 20th-century wars, each from a different region.

2 Naval warfare is rarely critical in determining the outcome of war. Discuss with reference to two 20th-century wars.

3 Evaluate the peacemaking efforts of one 20th-century war.

2 Spanish Civil War 1936–9

The long-term causes of the Spanish Civil War

Revised

Economic and social problems

There were deep-seated socioeconomic divisions in both rural and urban Spain.

Rural poverty

Profound socioeconomic divisions between the small, wealthy landowning elite and vast masses of poor, landless labourers created great tensions in rural Spain.

- These problems were especially acute in the south of Spain where huge estates, called ***latifundia***, dominated rural life. Labourers suffered from low pay, underemployment due to seasonal work and little financial security, as they were hired by the day.
- Unions organized strikes and demonstrations against landlords, and, by 1918, 700,000 people had joined the union Confederación Nacional del Trabajo.
- By 1930, 45.5 per cent of all workers were rural labourers, making rural issues very important politically.
- A deeply divided central government was unable to solve rural problems.

Urban poverty

There was a huge divide in urban areas too, with wealthy factory owners exploiting poor industrial workers.

- By 1930, 42 per cent of Spain's population lived in towns of at least 10,000 people.
- These industrial workers faced terrible living and working conditions. They resided in overcrowded, insanitary slums and enjoyed few rights at work, with no minimum wage, no limits to working hours and no protection from hazardous working conditions.
- Trade unions increased in popularity, as did the idea of a social revolution similar to the October 1917 Bolshevik Revolution in Russia. The Catholic Church, factory owners and landlords grew fearful of workers and farm labourers.

Political instability

The Spanish political scene was highly unstable, with divisions existing between the **left-wing** and **right-wing**. Broadly speaking, these divisions are summarized in the table below:

Left-wing	Right-wing
Reformist	Conservative
Republican	Monarchist
Poorer farmers and urban working class	Wealthy landowners and industrialists
Anti-Catholic, separation of Church and State	Catholic

Separatism in Spain

Even though Spain was politically unified, strong **separatist** movements existed in Catalonia and the Basque country, both of which have their own distinctive culture, language and history.

- Both regions grew economically, leading to more demands for independence.
- Catalan separatists argued that only five per cent of taxes paid to the central government were returned to Catalonia.
- Left-wing groups indicated that they were willing to reduce the central government's control over these regions and grant more autonomy. This was opposed by right-wing groups.

The dictatorship of Primo de Rivera (1923–30) and the collapse of the monarchy (1931)

During the rule of Prime Minister **Primo de Rivera**, the deep divisions in Spanish society and politics developed into crisis, leading to his resignation in 1930. The monarchy ended in 1931, leaving an unstable democratic republic as the political system as Spain entered the Second Republic.

- Primo de Rivera established a dictatorship through a military coup in 1923, supported by the army and king.
- He attempted to introduce a number of reforms to heal the divisions in Spanish society. However, these reforms were too radical for the right, but not radical enough for the left, and led to further polarization. They were costly reforms and these financial demands further made him unpopular.

- He introduced arbitration committees to handle conflicts between industrial workers and their employers. He increased government spending on public works to try and increase job opportunities. He also tried to reform the army and reduce its budget.
- Increasingly unpopular, he stepped down on 28 January 1930.
- King **Alfonso XIII**, who was technically head of state during Primo de Rivera's dictatorship, but in practice wielded little power, now hoped to take advantage of this **power vacuum** and reimpose monarchical rule in Spain. An election was held on this issue, but the voters decided on a democratic republic. Embarrassed and defeated, King Alfonso XIII left Spain.

MULTICAUSAL EXPLANATIONS

Use the information on the page opposite and above to add examples to the right-hand column for each of the long-term causal themes for the Spanish Civil War.

Causal theme	Examples to support this causal theme
Economic	
Political	
Ideological	
Territorial	
Other causes	

WHAT WERE THE MOST SIGNIFICANT LONG-TERM CAUSES OF THE SPANISH CIVIL WAR?

Use the information on the page opposite, and your completed table above, to decide on the most important long-term causes of the Spanish Civil War. Write the causes in the box below. Place the more important causes higher up on the arrow. Include all of the causal themes from the table above: economic, political, ideological, territorial and any other causes you think are important. Add explanations next to the cause to explain why you placed it where you did in the box.

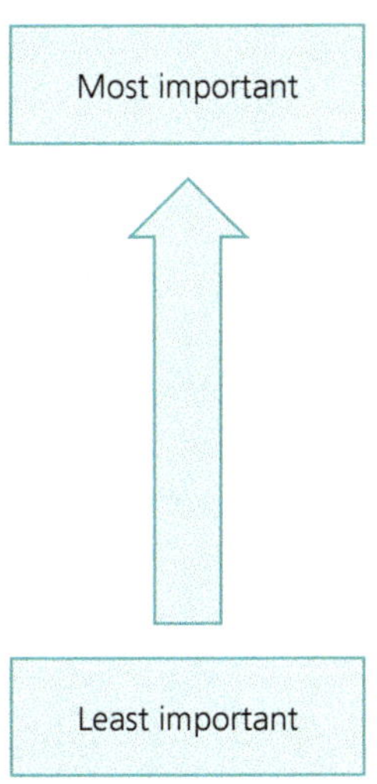

The short-term causes of the Spanish Civil War

Revised

The **Second Spanish Republic** faced serious social, economic and political problems from its inception. Successive governments were unable to find effective solutions to these problems to appease large enough sections of the Spanish people, and the result was that civil war began in July 1936. There were three major elections in these years, resulting in drastic swings between left- and right-wing coalition governments. These drastic swings demonstrated the divided nature of society, and contributed to further instability. The timeline below shows the changes in government during this period.

Date	Government
June 1931 to November 1933	Left-wing coalition government
November 1933 to February 1936	Right-wing coalition government
February 1936 to July 1936	Left-wing government, also called the Popular Front
July 1936	End of the Second Spanish Republic, and start of the Spanish Civil War

Left-wing coalition government 1931–3

The election of 1931 was a profound victory for the left, but not one political party gained enough seats to pass legislation, so a left-wing coalition was formed. Out of the 470 seats, the **Spanish Socialist Party (PSOE)** won the most, with 116. The right-wing parties only won 41 seats.

The reform package

The new government passed a radical set of left-wing reforms, which aimed to solve Spain's problems, but faced intense opposition from both ends of the political spectrum, and led to the defeat of the government in the November 1933 election. Some of the main reforms are listed below.

Urban worker reforms	• Urban workers were granted seven days of paid leave per year • An eight-hour working day was introduced, unless overtime was being paid • Urban workers were granted the right to strike without the fear of being dismissed
Agrarian reforms	• The Agrarian Reform Law of 1932 tried to break up *latifundia* estates exceeding 300 hectares (740 acres), or whose yield was in excess of 10,000 pesetas a year, and redistribute the land and resettle agricultural labourers • An eight-hour working day was introduced in 1931 for farm workers
Anti-clerical reforms	• Spain was redefined as a secular state, with the Catholic Church to receive no state financial support after two years • The display of religious images in public and teaching by religious orders were prohibited, to break the Catholic Church's control of education
Military reforms	• Army officer numbers were reduced and some with right-wing leanings were demoted to low-ranking positions • All officers had to swear an oath of loyalty to the Republic, or face discharge • The traditionalist military academy at Zaragoza was closed and high-level positions in the army were given to pro-Republicans
Separatist reforms	• The Catalan Statute of 1932 gave some autonomy to Catalonia, bringing one-third of Catalan taxation under local control • A Catalan parliament, the *Generalitat*, was given legislative authority over agriculture, transport, public health and poor relief in Catalonia

HOW DID LONG-TERM CAUSES INTERACT TO CAUSE THE SPANISH CIVIL WAR?

Read the example below which links long-term socioeconomic causes of the Spanish Civil War. Try to do the same for two other causes, completing the empty arrows and boxes.

Long-term cause	Interrelationship between causes	Long-term cause
For centuries, profound socioeconomic divisions between a small wealthy landowning elite and the vast masses of poor landless labourers created great tensions in rural Spain. Left-wing unions organized strikes and demonstrations against landlords. For example, the anarcho-syndicalist Confederación Nacional del Trabajo had over 700,000 members by 1918	**These long-term tensions in the Spanish countryside were mirrored in the cities, as there was a large exploited working class. This shared experience of suffering made it all the more difficult to de-escalate tensions** →	By 1930, 42 per cent of Spain's population lived in towns of at least 10,000 people and faced terrible living and working conditions. Trade unions increased in popularity, as did the idea of a social revolution similar to the October 1917 Bolshevik Revolution in Russia. When combined with unrest in rural Spain, there was a mass underclass becoming increasingly prepared to use violent means to change the unfair nature of Spanish society, increasing the likelihood of full-scale civil war
	→	
	→	

PLANNING AN IB ESSAY

Read the question and then plan your answer in the box provided below. Remember, you should spend about five minutes planning. A good plan will contain an argument (your prioritization of causes) and set out the structure of your essay, which will be designed to facilitate your argument.

Discuss the long-term causes of one 20th-century war.

Argument:

Paragraph 1 theme:

Paragraph 2 theme:

Paragraph 3 theme:

Paragraph 4 theme:

Opposition from the extreme left

The defeat of the left-wing government in the November 1933 election was largely a result of the extreme left withdrawing its support for the coalition, as it felt that the reforms did not go far enough to deal with Spain's socioeconomic problems.

- The Agrarian Reform Law only succeeded in resettling ten per cent of the 60,000 families it had aimed to help due to inadequate funding. Unemployment remained a huge issue in rural areas, accounting for 72% of those registered as unemployed in the early 1930s.
- Social security benefits for urban workers were limited, not covering those who were unable to find work, for example.
- Many urban workers and rural labourers wanted more dramatic reforms and voted for extreme left parties, or stopped voting.
- The PSOE fractured from within, as **Largo Caballero**'s extreme left-wing faction refused to cooperate with other left-wing parties, thus splitting the left-wing vote further.
- Protests and strikes proliferated. They were organized by the trade unions of the far left, such as the Federación Anarquista Ibérica and the **anarcho-syndicalist** union, the Confederación Nacional del Trabajo. These became increasingly violent. In 1933, in the village of Casas Viejas in Cadiz, nineteen agricultural labourers were killed by government assault guards.

Opposition from the conservative right

The reforms provoked great hostility from the conservative right, who saw them as a misguided attack on the traditional political, military, social and religious order. It disliked greater state intervention in the economy and feared that this was the beginning of more extreme socialist reform.

- The Confederación Española de Derechas Autónomas (CEDA), a union of right-wing opposition groups, which aimed to protect law, order, property and Catholicism, was founded in February 1933.
- CEDA grew in popularity and in the November 1933 election became the biggest single party with 115 seats.
- Military reforms upset the landowning officer class as it feared a purge of the entire traditional military hierarchy, leading to a failed military coup in August 1932 by General José Sanjurjo.

Right-wing Republican government 1933–6

CEDA, after becoming the largest party, worked closely with the Radicals, the second largest party, and established a right-wing government.

The reforms of the right-wing Republic

Once in power, the right-wing government set about undoing most of the reforms of the previous left-wing government.

- It refused to uphold the majority of the left-wing agrarian and industrial reforms.
- It allowed police searches of trade union premises and gave authorization for the authorities to break up strikes.
- It did not enforce the legislation that separated the Catholic Church from the State, and allowed the Church to play a significant role in education again.

The response of the left and the collapse of the right-wing Republican reforms

The extreme left became more active as left-wing protests proliferated. This pushed CEDA even further to the right, which lost it the support of the Radical Party, resulting in the collapse of the government.

- The most serious uprising took place in the **Asturias** mining region in October 1934. With high unemployment and poor working conditions, workers revolted and set up an independent workers' republic comprising over one-third of the province and 80 per cent of its population. The revolutionaries burned down 58 churches and killed 31 people. The right-wing government responded harshly, killing 1335 and wounding almost 3000, crushing the uprising.
- The government then lurched further to the right, increasing suppression of left-wing agitators and suspending Catalan autonomy.
- The more extreme right-wing position that CEDA appeared to be taking led to a breakdown in its coalition with the Radical Party.
- The coalition collapsed and President **Alcalá-Zamora** dissolved parliament, calling for fresh elections.

WHY WERE THE LEFT-WING REFORMS (1931–3) UNPOPULAR WITH BOTH THE RIGHT AND EXTREME LEFT?

Complete the table below explaining why the left-wing reforms (1931–3) alienated both the conservative right and the extreme left in Spain.

Reforms	Why did the conservative right dislike these reforms?	Why did the extreme left dislike these reforms?
Urban worker		
Agrarian		
Anti-clerical		
Military		
Separatist		

WHY DID THE LEFT-WING REFORMS (1931–3) CREATE SO MUCH TENSION IN SPAIN?

Complete the table below explaining why the left-wing reforms (1931–3) increased tensions in each of the following causal themes below.

Causal theme	Why did the left-wing reforms increase tensions in this area?
Economic	
Political	
Ideological	
Territorial	
Other causes	

Popular Front government, February to July 1936

The election of February 1936 saw the return of a left-wing coalition called the **Popular Front**. This was a broad-based coalition of left-wing groups including republicans, socialists and communists. The Popular Front held 286 seats, compared to the right-wing which held 132, yet the votes cast revealed Spain to be much more evenly divided, as 4,654,116 votes were for the left and 4,503,542 were for the right.

The reforms of the Popular Front government

The Popular Front resumed the left-wing agenda started by the left-wing coalition between 1931 and 1933.

- It resumed the agrarian and urban reforms that aimed to help the poorer rural and urban citizens.
- It restored Catalan autonomy and began discussions regarding Basque autonomy.
- It resumed the military reforms.

Opposition from the conservative right

The right-wing fiercely opposed these reforms and became increasingly militant and anti-democratic. Violence in Spain increased and several groups advocated for a right-wing military takeover of power. The right was drifting further towards extreme military solutions to their problems.

- There was an abortive right-wing coup involving Gil-Robles, the leader of CEDA, to stop the Popular Front from taking power.
- The membership of the fascist **Falange Party** drastically increased after the election of 1936. The Falange Party was overtly anti-democratic, and sought a military dictatorship.
- Increasing violence, including the assassination of prominent right-wing monarchist José Calvo Sotelo in July 1936, as well as street fighting between the left and right, led to calls by rightists to turn to violence to solve their problems.

Opposition from the extreme left

Left-wing militancy also drastically increased after the election of the Popular Front, further radicalizing the situation in Spain.

- Workers were encouraged by trade unions to take revenge on the right-wing for actions during the previous two years of right-wing government. This included the seizure of land, which was then legalized by the Popular Front.
- Largo Caballero, the leader of the extreme left-wing faction of the PSOE, called for a socialist revolution and refused to be part of the Popular Front, which he felt was not radical enough.

The military uprising and the start of the Spanish Civil War, July 1936

The Spanish Civil War began when right-wing members of the military launched an uprising against the Popular Front government in July 1936.

- The uprising was mainly planned by General **Emilio Mola**, and was very much the work of the army. He had established links with CEDA and monarchists, who supported the revolt.
- The Spanish Military Union, which was a secretive organization of over 3500 officers, was a key instigator of the revolt as it had established cells throughout the country. The majority of colonels and middle-ranking officers supported the uprising, and they brought their garrisons with them.
- Troops in Morocco were the first to revolt, on 17 July 1936, and this quickly spread throughout Spain.
- In response, the left-wing unions took up arms and mobilized civilians into militia units. The left were also supported by troops loyal to the Republic.
- As a result of this leftist response, the rebellious garrisons were unable to take control of all of Spain, and the civil war began.

USING HISTORIANS' INTERPRETATIONS TO HELP WITH THE PRIORITIZATION OF CAUSES

There are several conflicting interpretations that exist as to why the Spanish Civil War occurred. Engaging with the perspectives of historians in your essay can help you to develop your own argument, as you can argue whether you agree or disagree with their interpretation of events.

DIFFERENT INTERPRETATIONS OF THE CAUSES OF THE SPANISH CIVIL WAR

Nationalist interpretations

Pro-nationalist interpretations emphasize the extreme radicalization of the left as the primary cause of hostilities. They put great weight on the growth of militant unionism and events such as the Asturias Uprising, which, they argue, show that the right had to use military force to uphold order, property, law and religion against the dangers of socialist revolution. Ricardo de la Cierva, writing in the 1960s, was a main proponent of this view.

Republican interpretations

Pro-Republican accounts argue that it was in fact the extreme right that should be held more accountable for causing the Spanish Civil War. They focus on the ideologies and actions of the Falange and CEDA. The former was overtly anti-democratic, and the latter, according to this narrative, was never really a supporter of the democratic Republic. They also place emphasis on the role played by the right-wing military leadership as important in causing the war.

Socioeconomic interpretations

Other accounts tend to focus on the socioeconomic causes of the war and argue that long-term agrarian issues were the fundamental cause of conflict in Spain. This interpretation is held by historian Paul Preston and was evident in Gerald Brenan's *The Spanish Labyrinth*, published in 1943. According to this narrative, agrarian issues led to the growth of left-wing militancy and influenced the social reform programme of the left-wing governments. This left-wing radicalization antagonized the right, and ultimately pushed the country into war. Thus, the social and political divisions that pushed the country to war, and which democracy proved incapable of mediating, were caused by deep-seated agrarian problems.

Which interpretation of the causes of the Spanish Civil War do you find most persuasive?

Add examples from the opposite pages to support the three different interpretations of the causes of the Spanish Civil War. In the second column add examples to support this interpretation, then in the third column explain the extent to which you find this interpretation persuasive.

Interpretations	Examples to support this interpretation	Explain the extent to which you find this interpretation persuasive
Nationalist		
Republican		
Socioeconomic		

The course of the Spanish Civil War

Revised

When fighting began, the two sides could broadly be delineated as the forces of the conservative right, known as the Nationalists, and those who fought for the left-wing Republican government, called the Republicans. Eventually the Nationalists were triumphant, resulting in a right-wing military dictatorship that lasted for decades.

Initial positions of the Republican and Nationalist forces in July 1936

When war broke out, there was a rapid division of Spain into Nationalist and Republican controlled areas, as both sides scrambled for control of Spain. They each could claim some initial advantages. The map below shows the geographical division of Spain between the Nationalists and Republicans by the end of July 1936.

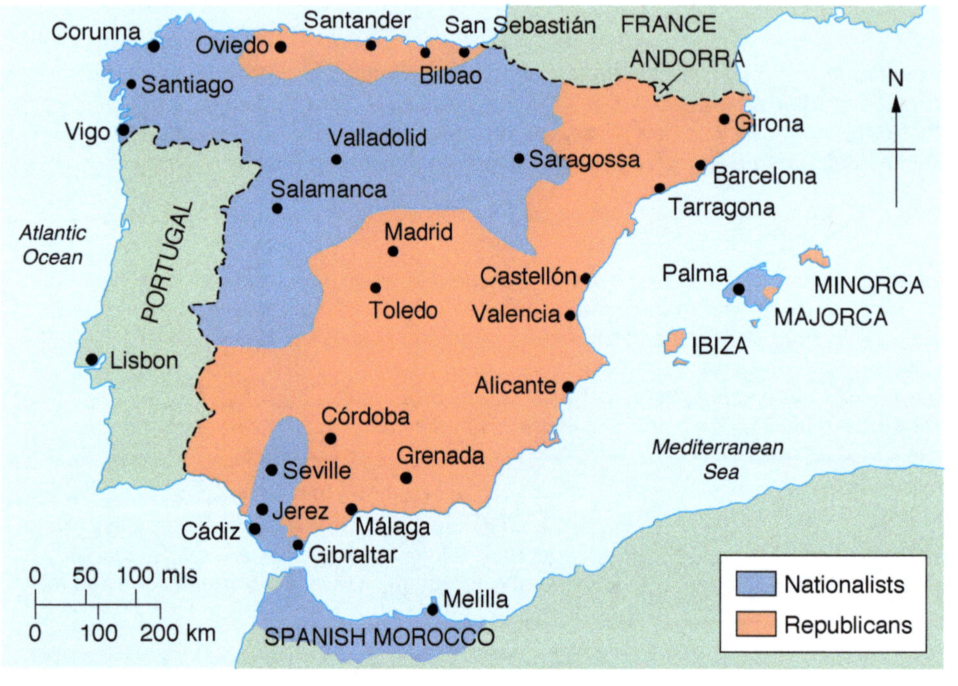

Nationalist position at the start of the war

- The agricultural north-west was controlled by the Nationalists, giving them food supplies.
- They controlled a small area of southern Spain around Seville, where 1500 elite troops from the **Army of Africa** were airlifted to by the German military from **Spanish Morocco**. They were led by **Francisco Franco**, who became the leader of the Nationalists.
- Two-thirds of army officers sided with the Nationalists, giving them the more experienced and professional leadership. They also had the more skilled troops at their disposal.
- They had international support from Italy and Germany.

Republican position at the start of the war

- Republican-controlled territory centred on southern and eastern Spain, and included Spain's largest and most important cities: Madrid and Barcelona. They also controlled the Basque country and Asturias, which were rich in industry and raw materials.
- The Republic had a larger army in the beginning and were supported by Spain's small navy and air force.
- They received support from the Soviet Union and volunteers from other countries called the **International Brigades**.

The war in 1936: the Nationalists advance to Madrid, but are held to a stalemate

The Nationalists aimed to take the capital city, Madrid, and made quick progress from Seville towards the outskirts of the city. However, by the end of 1936 a stalemate had been reached to the west of Madrid, as the Republicans put up a strong defence. Foreign aid proved to be decisive, even in these early battles.

- The Nationalist Army of Africa – transported in trucks, and given air cover by Italian and German aircraft – moved rapidly and reached the Republican-held city of Mérida, 320 km (200 miles) from Seville, within a week. The cities of Mérida and Badajoz fell to the Nationalists.
- As the Nationalists advanced on Madrid, Republican resistance was inadequate, as it was primarily composed of inexperienced and ill-equipped civilians. For example, the town of Talavera de la Reina fell in one day despite being defended by several thousand **militiamen**.
- The Republicans fared better in the Battle for Madrid as they were aided by the arrival of superior aircraft and tanks from the Soviet Union, as well as weapons from Mexico.
- Three and a half thousand members of the International Brigades arrived on 8 November to help Republicans defend the city, giving them superior manpower.
- A stalemate had set in to the west of Madrid by the end of November 1936, leaving the city in Republican hands.

COMPARING AND CONTRASTING THE INITIAL STRENGTHS AND WEAKNESSES OF THE TWO ARMIES

Using the information on the opposite page, complete the following table, noting down the strengths of the two armies across the three categories in the left-hand column.

Resources	Republican strengths in July 1936	Nationalist strengths in July 1936
Human resources		
Economic resources		
Foreign support		

WHY DID THE BATTLE FOR MADRID IN 1936 END IN A STALEMATE?

The battle for Madrid ended in stalemate in 1936. From the fighting there, we can learn a lot about what factors were going to be significant in determining the outcome of the Spanish Civil War.

For each statement below, explain whether you agree or disagree with it, and why.

Statement	Agree or disagree?
Foreign aid was the most significant factor in determining the outcome of the battle for Madrid in 1936	
The Republicans had access to the better technology in the battle for Madrid in 1936, and this was decisive in determining the outcome	
The Nationalists enjoyed no military successes in 1936 in the Spanish Civil War	
The Republicans were winning the Spanish Civil War by the end of 1936	

The war in 1937: the Nationalists in the ascendancy

The Nationalists made large territorial gains in 1937, and by the end of the year they controlled two-thirds of Spain, making a Republican victory less likely.

The Nationalists advance in the south and the north

The Nationalists made significant gains in the south and north of Spain during 1937, but Republican forces held firm in Madrid.

- The Málaga Campaign of February 1937 saw Nationalists achieve an important victory in southern Spain. Nationalist forces, alongside 10,000 Italian troops, employed ***guerra celere*** ('rapid war') tactics. Utilizing armoured vehicles and tanks, they relied on speed and air support to capture Málaga.
- In 1937, the Nationalists renewed their attacks on Madrid. In March, the Guadalajara campaign attempted to take the city from the north-east. The Republicans achieved a defensive victory, as they had larger numbers of troops and superior quality of weapons in Madrid, such as Soviet T-26 tanks. Fire from these tanks broke Nationalist infantry advances, and Madrid remained Republican.
- Due to their failure in Madrid, the Nationalists shifted their focus to northern Spain and the rich industrial regions of the Basque country and the Asturias. Nationalists achieved supremacy in this theatre of war through the support of the **German Condor Legion**, which was technologically superior to the Republican aircraft in this region. The Vizcaya campaign began with aerial bombing assaults on the cities of Ochandiano and Durango in March 1937. Both cities were first devastated from above, and then Nationalist troops occupied the towns with little resistance.
- In April 1937, perhaps the most infamous Nationalist attack of all occurred, as Guernica was devastated by Italian and German bomber and fighter aircraft. The town was of little strategic importance, but 27,000 kg (60,000 lb.) of incendiary bombs were dropped on it, and German fighters strafed streets packed with terrified civilians. Over 1500 people were killed in one of the first instances of deliberate targeting of a civilian area. Republican propaganda exploited these atrocities at home and abroad. The north was effectively won by the Nationalists when they took the Basque region's capital, the industrialized city of Bilbao. Heavy artillery and German aerial bombardment combined with a naval blockade to bring the city to its knees, and it surrendered on 19 June 1937.

Republican divisions and failed offensives

The Republican forces divided in Barcelona in May 1937. The extreme left wanted far-reaching social reform, the abandonment of conventional military strategies in favour of guerrilla tactics, and national labour strikes to cripple the Nationalists. The moderate left disagreed and fighting broke out in May 1937, which resulted in the defeat of the extreme left. The Republicans also launched two failed offensives during this period.

- To relieve the siege of Madrid, a military campaign was launched to capture Brunete in July 1937. It was initially successful, as Brunete was captured in two days. However, the Nationalists, supported by German aircraft, soon retook the city, ending the offensive.
- In an attempt to divert Nationalist troops away from Madrid, the Republicans captured Teruel, but it was retaken by Nationalists on 22 February 1938 after intense artillery fire and aerial bombardment.

THE KEY MILITARY BATTLES AND CAMPAIGNS OF 1937

The year 1937 was important in determining the outcome of the Spanish Civil War; by the end of it, a Nationalist victory had become the likely eventuality. Why did this happen?

Using the information on the page opposite, complete the following table to analyse which side won the key conflicts of the Spanish Civil War in 1937, and crucially, why they were able to.

Battle or campaign	Which side won? What was achieved?	Why did they win? Explain your thinking
Nationalist Málaga campaign		
Nationalist Guadalajara campaign		
Nationalist campaigns in the Basque country and the Asturias		
Republican Brunete offensive		
Republican Teruel offensive		

WHY WERE THE NATIONALISTS WINNING THE WAR BY THE END OF 1937?

Using the information on the page opposite, complete the spider diagram below, noting how the variables affected the outcome of the fighting in 1937. A key thing to consider is which side performed better in relation to each variable.

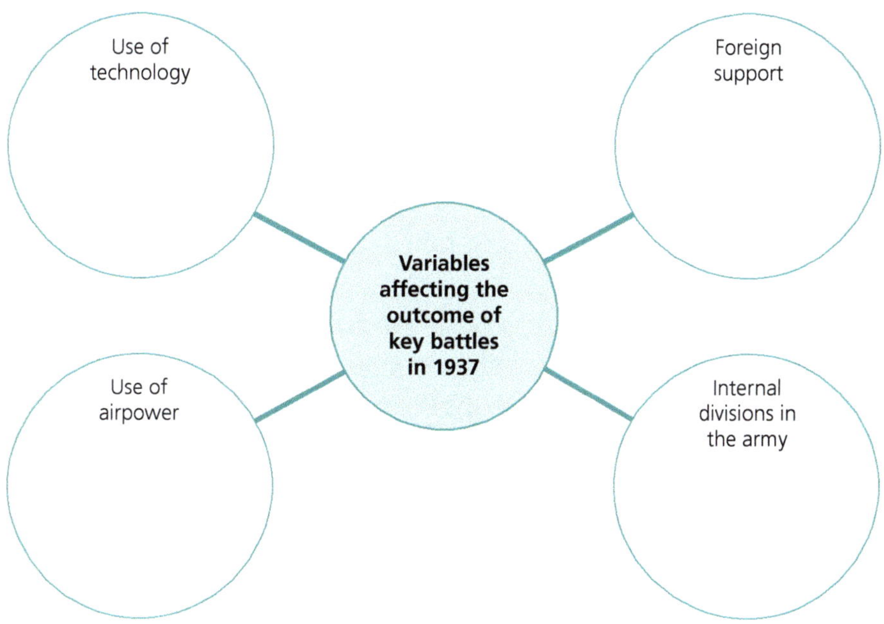

The war in 1938: the Nationalists advance into Catalonia

By 1938, the majority of Spain was controlled by the Nationalists and their army was now a third larger than that of the Republicans. The Nationalists now attacked Catalonia and took only six weeks to reach the Mediterranean Sea. The Republicans counterattacked at the Ebro River, but were beaten back decisively.

- The Republicans' Ebro Offensive aimed to divert Nationalist troops north and away from Valencia in Catalonia.
- It was a key element in Republican leader Prime Minister **Juan Negrín**'s plan to prolong the war. He felt that a general European war would break out soon between fascist and democratic states, of which the Spanish Civil War would be but a small part. He hoped that this would divert Italian and German resources away from Spain, and that ultimately the democratic side would win, to the great benefit of the Republicans in Spain, as the Nationalists would be defeated.
- Initially, the Republican advance across the Ebro River into Nationalist-held lands went well, and they took nearly 40 km (25 miles) of territory. However, the Republicans were unable to hold the land they had taken, as Nationalist resistance proved too strong. Again, aerial superiority proved decisive, as the Nationalists controlled the skies.
- Over the next three and a half months, the Republican forces were forced back, and by 16 November all of their territorial acquisitions had been reversed. The Republicans had gained no land, and lost 75,000 troops in the Ebro Offensive, as well as vast amounts of vital equipment. This meant that Negrín's plan to prolong the war was in ruins.

The war in 1939: Nationalist victory

By the start of 1939, the war was effectively won by the Nationalists. The key cities of Barcelona and Madrid did begin the year in Republican hands, but these would soon fall to the Nationalists.

- There was very little Republican resistance in Barcelona. The 2 million people in the city were cut off from what remained of Republican Spain, and faced severe food shortages. They were also subjected to brutal and continual aerial bombardment. Nationalists took the city on 26 January.
- With the fall of Madrid, the Republican president resigned and went into exile on 6 February. Then on 27 February, Britain and France recognized Franco as the legitimate leader of Spain, which was a bitter blow.
- There were only 500,000 Republican troops left in the Republican zone, and Negrín's plan to prolong the war lay in ruins. An internal rebellion established an anti-communist junta, which tried to negotiate a conditional surrender with Franco. Further violence led to Negrín fleeing to France.
- Franco had no interest in negotiating and occupied Madrid on 27 March. Spain was now fully under Nationalist control. The Spanish Civil War had ended.

THE COURSE OF THE SPANISH CIVIL WAR: HOW DID THE WAR DEVELOP EACH YEAR, AND WHY DID THE NATIONALISTS END AS THE VICTORS?

By the start of 1939 the Spanish Civil War was effectively over, as Nationalist victory seemed assured. From considering the fighting in each year we can learn a lot about what factors were going to be significant in determining the overall winner of the conflict.

Complete the table below, noting down the main successes of each army in each year using the preceding pages and your own knowledge. Then make an argument as to which side had the better of the fighting in each year, and why, in the right-hand column.

Year	Nationalist successes	Republican successes	Which side had the better of the fighting in that year, and why?
1936			
1937			
1938			
1939			

FROM 1936 TO 1939, WHAT WERE THE DECISIVE FACTORS DETERMINING THE OUTCOME OF THE WAR?

For each statement below, explain whether you agree or disagree with it, and why.

Statement	Agree or disagree?
The key theatre of war proved to be in the air. The army that controlled the skies over Spain had an insurmountable advantage	
Superior foreign support for the Nationalists was a vital factor in their ultimate victory	
Nationalist troops were more experienced and skilled than the Republican troops and this was very significant in their ultimate victory	

The practices of the Spanish Civil War and their impact on its outcome

Revised

Influence of foreign powers

The Spanish Civil War has been called the 'dress rehearsal for the Second World War', and this was in large measure due to the way that foreign powers used the conflict to test their forces to determine their capabilities. Some historians argue that these foreign powers played a decisive role in the outcome of the war. The Nationalist victory was in large measure due to the superior foreign aid that they received, in terms of both quantity and quality. The limited capacity of Spain to domestically produce armaments meant that both sides were largely dependent on foreign aid.

Foreign support for the Republicans

In 1936, the Republicans actually had superior foreign support, leading to their successful defence of Madrid. However, from 1937 onwards the international support they received paled in comparison to that received by the Nationalists, which proved to be a decisive factor in their eventual defeat.

- Republican France refused to support Republican Spain because that support would jeopardize its relationship with Britain, which was crucial in opposing German and Italian actions in Europe and Africa in 1936.
- Britain was anti-communist and therefore would not support the Republicans, who were in coalition with communists.
- France initiated the **Non-Intervention Agreement**, signed by Germany, the Soviet Union, Italy and Britain, along with many other countries, which pledged not to support the war in Spain, such as by sending or selling weapons and other materials, preventing the Republicans from being able to arm effectively or gain other assistance.
- The Soviet Union, a communist state, secretly supplied the Republicans with military equipment such as tanks and aircraft.
- Soviet-supplied Polikarpov I-15 and I-16 fighters gave the Republicans aerial control in 1936. Supplies, however, were limited and slowly dwindled. A total of 648 aircraft were supplied by the Soviets, far below the number supplied to the Nationalists by their allies (see below). In 1938 and 1939, the Soviets supplied no aircraft.
- Although initially supplied in large quantities, Soviet equipment lacked quality; rifles and machine guns were outdated and some weapons dated to the 1880s.
- The International Brigades contributed approximately 35,000 volunteers to the Republican side, but most were militarily inexperienced and had no effect on the outcome of the war.

Foreign support for the Nationalists

The Nationalists received a superior level of foreign support from 1937, which played a great role in their eventual victory.

- Germany and Italy supplied twice the amount of aircraft and artillery as the Republicans received from the Soviet Union.
- They also supplied 34,436 machine guns to the Nationalists, significantly more than the 20,486 supplied by the Soviet Union to the Republicans.
- German aircraft were especially significant in allowing the Nationalists to control the skies from 1937 to 1939. For example, the German Condor Legion played the decisive role in the conquests of the northern regions of the Basque country and the Asturias.
- In the opening week of the war, foreign transport was vital in mobilizing the Nationalist Army of Africa. The 1500 elite troops from the Army of Africa stationed in Spanish Morocco were airlifted to mainland Spain by the German air force. They were then transported in trucks and given air cover by Italian and German aircraft, helping them to reach the Republican-held city of Mérida, 320 km (200 miles) from Seville, within a week.

PLANNING ESSAYS IN TIMED CONDITIONS

Read the IB Paper 2-style questions and then plan your answers in the boxes provided. You should give yourself five to ten minutes to plan an essay to replicate exam conditions.

'Foreign intervention can prove decisive in determining the outcome of civil wars.' With reference to one 20th-century war, to what extent do you agree with this statement?

Argument:

Paragraph 1 theme:

Paragraph 2 theme:

Paragraph 3 theme:

Paragraph 4 theme:

Evaluate the importance of foreign support in determining the outcome of one 20th-century war.

Argument:

Paragraph 1 theme:

Paragraph 2 theme:

Paragraph 3 theme:

Paragraph 4 theme:

Discuss the reasons for victory in one 20th-century war.

Argument:

Paragraph 1 theme:

Paragraph 2 theme:

Paragraph 3 theme:

Paragraph 4 theme:

Technological developments: air, land and sea

A fundamental reason for the Nationalists' victory was their access to superior modern military technology, and in greater quantity than the Republicans. Aerial superiority proved to be of vital importance to the Nationalists, but the use of technological developments in the land and sea theatres of war were of limited significance to the eventual outcome of the conflict.

- A key component in all of the successful Nationalist campaigns after 1937 was the superior modern air force at their disposal.
- The arrival of the German Messerschmitt Bf 109 fighter aircraft in 1937 gave the Nationalists the advantage in the skies, as they were faster and had a longer range than any Soviet-supplied planes. The Soviet Polikarpov I-16 had a maximum speed of 489 km/h (303 mph) and a range of 700 km (435 miles), whereas the Bf 109 had a maximum speed of 640 km/h (400 mph) and a range of 850 km (530 miles).
- The Soviet Tupolev SB-2 bomber was the most powerful bomber aircraft deployed, but only a few were provided and they performed poorly, as they were slower moving than their German counterparts. Moreover, the German Heinkel He 111 bomber was also superior as it could generally take more damage, yet remain airborne, having better armour.
- Motorized combat vehicles were supplied in large quantities by foreign powers, but they were not used to their potential and did not significantly impact the outcome of battles. The Soviet T-26 tank performed better than the German Panzer I and Italian CV.33 and CV.35 tanks; however, it was mainly only used to support infantry instead of as the main weapon of combat. Tanks did help the Republicans successfully defend Madrid in 1936, but in later wars, such as the Second World War, tanks were effectively used in large formations to rapidly overrun enemy infantry, something which did not occur in the Spanish Civil War.
- War at sea played only a small part in this conflict. It was characterized by blockade and counter-blockade operations. An example of a successful naval blockade was around Bilbao in 1937, which starved the city of supplies. However, there were no major sea battles, and supplies were never completely cut off by blockades.

Mobilization of human and economic resources

Victory depended on maintaining an adequate supply of manpower, weapons and food. The Republicans held some initial advantages, but from 1937 onwards, the Nationalists dominated in all three of these areas, which contributed to their victory.

Military manpower

- The Nationalists had an army one-third smaller than that of the Republicans at the beginning of the war. However, this numerical balance shifted as the Nationalists conquered more territory from 1937 onwards. By the start of 1938, the Nationalist forces were one-third larger than the Republican army, and by 1939 they were twice the size.
- Nationalist troops were more experienced and skilled than the Republican troops as two-thirds of army officers sided with the Nationalists from the outset. The Nationalists operated 28 military academies to train lower-ranking commanders; there was no equivalent for the Republicans.
- Nationalist troops received orders from the military's Defence Council, which had complete authority over all Nationalist forces, including militias, which were merged with the army in December 1936, making central coordination easier.
- Republican zones were controlled by democratic politicians who had less authoritarian control. The Republican militias often came from labour unions and leftist political groups, which had a distrust of centrally controlled military hierarchies. They often operated independently, which made coordination challenging. Lack of experience and training was also a hindrance.

PLANNING ESSAYS THAT REQUIRE TWO CASE STUDIES

Many Paper 2 essays ask about two case studies. Follow the advice on page 11 of the 'Getting to know the exam' section.

Read the question below, and then the model plan provided. Then try to plan an essay in response to the question beneath in the box at the bottom of the page.

Compare and contrast the importance of technology in determining the outcome of two 20th-century wars.

Argument: In the Spanish Civil War, superior technology was of paramount importance in determining the outcome; after 1937 the Nationalists had access to a modern air force, which led to them winning the major battles. Conversely, in the First World War, aerial and land technology prolonged the conflict and bloodshed, but did not decisively alter the outcome of the war on the Western Front. Yet technology proved very important in determining the outcome of the First World War at sea. In both wars, new technology similarly contributed to the vast human and economic destruction in the countries involved.

Paragraph 1 theme: Aerial technological developments had a huge impact in determining the winner of the Spanish Civil War, but not in the First World War. Airpower was not developed enough in the First World War to have a decisive impact on the outcome.

Paragraph 2 theme: Technological developments on land, such as tanks and new types of machine guns, were deployed in both wars, yet had limited impact on deciding the outcome. They increased the death toll and prolonged the conflicts but did not decisively lead to victory.

Paragraph 3 theme: Technological developments at sea had little impact on the Spanish Civil War due to the predominantly land-based nature of the conflict, but in the First World War the naval blockade of Germany played a great role in causing its ultimate defeat.

Compare and contrast the importance of foreign intervention in determining the outcome of two 20th-century wars.

Argument:

Paragraph 1 theme:

Paragraph 2 theme:

Paragraph 3 theme:

Economic resources and food supplies

While domestic production only constituted a small proportion of the armaments used by each side, as international aid was of far greater significance, access to the industrial and mining regions of the Basque country and the Asturias gave the Nationalists a domestic production advantage after 1937. In contrast, the lack of raw materials in Republican-held areas hindered their war effort. For example, in Barcelona in 1939 industrial output was only one-third of the 1936 level.

The Nationalists' Defence Council controlled the supply and distribution of war materials efficiently in Nationalist-held areas, whereas the Republic's capacity to produce armaments was damaged by the establishment of worker collectives in many industries in 1936. Collectives allowed workers to decide what and how much to produce, instead of this being decided by the government or military based on overall needs.

Access to food supplies was vital and the Nationalists held the major agricultural regions of Spain. They also had efficient distribution methods, as the military Defence Council maintained tight control over the food supply, prioritizing the military.

The establishment of 2500 collectives in 1936 created problems, as farm labourers decided what to grow and in what quantities. This led to shortages and made central coordination impossible. Some collectives supplied food only to their militias and not to the Republican army.

Supplying food to Madrid and Barcelona was difficult, leading to rationing and massive inflation of food prices. In Barcelona, prices increased by 200%.

The effects of the Spanish Civil War

Revised

Just before the outbreak of war, Spain began moving in a left-wing, progressive direction. There had been attempts to undermine the traditional power bases of the rural landowning class, the conservative military and the Catholic Church. Increased political freedom for all Spaniards, including women, had been encouraged. The Civil War ended these hopes of left-wing reform, as a traditionalist right-wing dictatorship led by Franco assumed power. It could be argued that pre-war Republican Spain was the exception in Spanish history, and that Franco's Spain represented a great deal of continuity with pre-1930s Spain, as traditional culture and its values were once again emphasized, and government was once again in the hands of a conservative, right-wing elite.

Political impact of the war

The right-wing, conservative dictatorship that Franco established lasted until his death in 1975.

- On assuming power, Franco unleashed a large-scale round of persecutions on Republicans and left-wing elements that he saw as a threat to his regime, dividing society yet further. This terror saw tens of thousands of executions and hundreds of thousands of imprisonments. In 1933, the prisons of Spain contained 12,000 prisoners, but by the end of 1940 there were 280,000 prisoners.
- In July 1939, the foreign minister of Italy, Galeazzo Ciano, visited Spain and reported of, 'trials going on every day at a speed which I would call almost summary … in Madrid alone, between 200 and 250 a day, in Barcelona 150, in Seville 80'.
- Franco's power rested on the army, not his leadership of a political party. His regime was a military dictatorship where civil liberties were not respected.
- Franco's image as Spain's saviour was promoted. A cult of personality was constructed.
- His regime emphasized nationalism and did not entertain any tolerance for regional autonomy as the Basque country and Catalonia were kept under Spain's control. As part of this nationalism, economic autarky was encouraged.
- He promoted conservative values. The power and influence of the Catholic Church were re-established, and traditional attitudes towards women and the family were espoused.
- The Spanish Civil War had limited impact on international politics, as Spain remained on the periphery of the geopolitical power games being played out in Europe in the late 1930s.

THE RELATIVE SIGNIFICANCE OF DIFFERENT VARIABLES IN EXPLAINING THE OUTCOME OF THE SPANISH CIVIL WAR

For each of the following variables, explain the impact that it had on the outcome of the Spanish Civil War, and then decide on the significance of the variable. Complete the blank sections.

Variable	Explain the impact that this variable had on the outcome of the Spanish Civil War	How significant was the impact of this variable on the outcome of the Spanish Civil War?
Technological developments		
Land war		
War in the air		
War at sea		
Human resources		
Economic resources		

Economic impact of the war

The Spanish Civil War devastated Spain's economy, with homes, businesses, agricultural land and industry all severely damaged. The country was also in debt to other countries, and repayment drained much-needed resources.

- War had destroyed cities and infrastructure, so that by 1939:
  - industrial production was only 25% of 1929 levels
  - just half of the railways were operational
  - livestock numbers were 33% less than they were before the war.
- $700 million was owed to other countries, with repayments made in food and industrial raw materials, which represented a significant drain on the Spanish economy. These repayments continued for decades. For example, Spain was still paying back debts to Italy in the 1960s.
- The task of rebuilding Spanish industry and agriculture took considerably longer than it might otherwise have done as the result of losing 500,000 workers in the war.
- Pre-war gold reserves were spent by the Republican government, leaving the government no funds to pay for rebuilding.

Social impact of the war

Spain was left socially devastated and divided by the war. The human trauma from the war was vast, and the divisions between Nationalists and Republicans, right-wing and left-wing, conservatives and progressives, ran deep. Franco's post-war repression campaigns and heavy-handed policies that greatly favoured Nationalists did little to heal the wounds of the civil war.

Casualties and social divisions

The social impact of the Spanish Civil War was vast as casualties were high, and there was long-lasting mistrust and bitterness between the two sides.

- 350,000–500,000 were killed during and just after the war. These deaths were from combat, executions and murder, and represented about two per cent of the population. About 100,000 people were permanently disabled.
- After the war, wounded Nationalists were given jobs and pensions, but there were no such provisions for wounded Republicans.
- 400,000 people fled Spain as the Republic was defeated, with 250,000 permanently remaining outside Spain.

THE EFFECTS OF THE SPANISH CIVIL WAR

Using the information on the preceding pages and your own knowledge, complete the Venn diagram below, noting down the main political, economic and social impacts of the Spanish Civil War, deciding which are distinct and which overlap across these three conceptual areas.

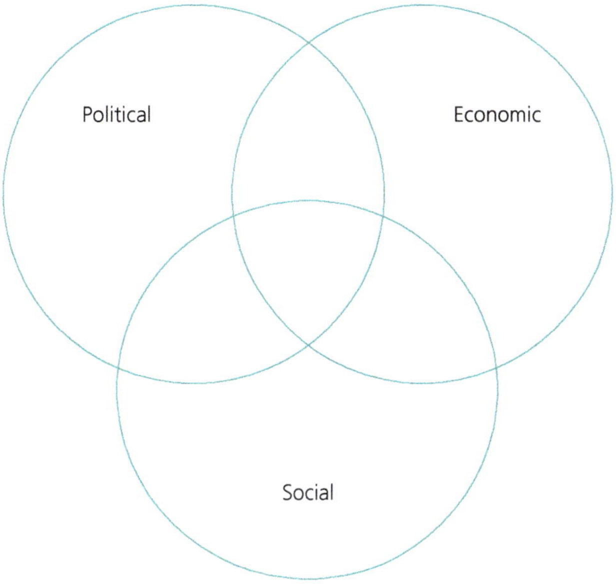

BODY PARAGRAPH

Read the IB-style question below on the effects of war, and plan an answer in the box provided, staying focused on the political and economic repercussions of the Spanish Civil War. You should give yourself five to ten minutes to plan an essay to replicate exam conditions.

Evaluate the political and economic repercussions of one 20th-century war.

Thesis:

Paragraph 1 theme:

Paragraph 2 theme:

Paragraph 3 theme:

Paragraph 4 theme:

Impact of the war on women

During the war, women in Republican-held areas had liberal freedoms and greater equality with men, but this came to an end with Franco's victory. The Franco regime stressed conservative, traditional ideas of the family, such as women living primarily as housewives and mothers. The prominent role accorded to the Catholic Church in post-civil war Spain further emphasized the return to traditionalism in Spanish life that the Nationalist government demanded.

Women in Nationalist Spain

- In Nationalist-controlled areas during the war, women were expected to fulfil traditional roles as housewives and mothers. They also had to conform to traditional expectations of dress and appearance which were supported and emphasized by the Catholic Church.
- Even with the needs of the war economy, women in Nationalist-held areas were confined to traditional female jobs, such as health services and food preparation. Other forms of work were strongly discouraged, and the Labour Charter passed in March 1938 stated that it would 'liberate' married women from paid work in workshops and factories.
- The ruling Defence Council in Nationalist-held lands enshrined this conservative view of women with decrees that banned divorce, civil marriage and mixed-gender classrooms. Another decree stated that education in schools for girls was to be primarily focused on domestic work and motherhood. Franco enforced these policies across the country at the war's end.

Women in Republican Spain

- During the war, women living within the Republican-held areas had greater freedom than those in the Nationalist zones. In Catalonia, a marriage law was passed that gave women equal rights in issues of marriage and divorce.
- Republican Spain was the first European country in which a woman held a cabinet position in the national government when Federica Montseny became minister for public health and assistance in 1936. In theory, complete political equality existed with men in Republican Spain. **Dolores Ibárruri** was another woman who wielded significant influence as she was a high-ranking Communist Party member who was famed for her speeches and leadership of organizations trying to help victims of the war.
- However, while they made a name for themselves in politics, which was progressive for the time, even these famous examples of powerful women operated in spheres associated with traditional female concerns, such as public health and welfare.
- Some women in Republican Spain did enter a sphere that was far from traditional and participated in the fighting. They were referred to as ***milicianas***. A few became very famous, such as **Lina Odena**, leader of the communist youth movement, who killed herself rather than be captured near Granada. Yet, women's participation in combat was not the norm and the Republican government passed a decree calling for them to be banned from fighting in the Popular Army.
- Women did begin working in war-related industries during the war, such as factories, as men were absent fighting. Yet, they were often confronted with hostility from male employers with traditional mindsets. Indeed, even in Republican areas, the great majority of women remained in the home during the war in traditional roles, struggling to feed their families.
- Any non-traditional roles that women did fulfil during the war were taken away from them after the Nationalist victory as traditionalist values were reimposed across the entirety of Spain.
- Although women in Republican Spain were more equal and participated in political, military and work life more than women in Nationalist Spain, they faced opposition and some hostility.

THE EFFECTS OF THE SPANISH CIVIL WAR

Read the definitions below and add relevant examples for each area from the preceding pages.

Prescribed content	Definition	Examples from Spanish Civil War
Peacemaking	The attempts to uphold peace after a war. Major aims include trying to prevent further loss of life and conflict, trying to rebuild a nation by ensuring civilians are protected, and rebuilding infrastructure. However, often peace terms are decided by the victors alone who have other motives, such as revenge and gain for their nation. These motives may result in unsustainable peace terms	
Territorial changes	Changes to who governs areas of land. These can involve the creation of new countries and empires, and the end to others. The implications for the populations of these areas are often significant	
Political repercussions	Repercussions of war for political systems. War can often lead to significant upheavals to the governing classes of countries, and result in regime changes and new ideologies taking precedence. Sometimes these include greater rights for people, other times the complete opposite occurs	
Economic impact	Warfare can impact on the economy in areas such as gross domestic product and employment levels. It can also leave countries facing huge war debts in the form of reparations. The reconstruction of an economy after a war can be a tricky, protracted process	
Social impact	Warfare can impact on society in areas such as culture, religion, familial relations, relations between different groups in society, lifestyle changes, wealth and living conditions	
Demographic impact	Demographic studies attempt to measure quantifiable characteristics of a given population. War may impact the number of people left alive, the average age in a country, the ethnic makeup of a country and the gender balance, to name a few of the most common indicators	
Changes in the role and status of women	War may have a big impact on the role and status of women as the demands of war may require greater numbers of women to enter the workforce or join the army. This can lead to the enfranchisement and empowerment of women	

CHAPTER 2 Exam focus

Sample question and answer

Consider the response to the essay question below. Read it and the examiner's comments around it.

Compare and contrast the importance of aerial technology in determining the outcome of two 20th-century wars.

Superior technology was of paramount importance in determining the outcome of the Spanish Civil War. Starting in 1937, Nationalists had access to a deadly modern air force. This led to victory in all major battles as they coordinated air and land attacks on Republican forces. Conversely, aerial technology did not decisively alter the outcome of the First World War, as the technology was not deadly enough, nor was it utilized effectively in conjunction with tactics involving ground troops. The first section of this essay will argue that in the Spanish Civil War there was a technological imbalance, as the Nationalists had a deadlier air force than the Republicans, which helped them attain victory. Secondly, it will be contended that in the First World War, aerial technology was in its infancy and was therefore slow and inefficient, so did not alter the outcome. Finally, we will turn to consider how the Nationalists in Spain developed their tactics to take full advantage of developments in aerial technology as they coordinated land and air attacks, something that did not happen in the First World War, meaning aerial technology had far less of an impact on the outcome.

This part of the introduction sets out the structure of the essay, which makes it clear to the examiner how the arguments will be organized.

In the Spanish Civil War, superior aerial technology determined the outcome of the conflict. The Nationalists had at their disposal a more technologically advanced air force than the Republicans from 1937 onwards and this was a key component in all Nationalist campaigns after 1937. For example, the arrival of the German Messerschmitt Bf 109 in 1937 gave the Nationalists the advantage, as these planes were faster and had a longer range than any Soviet-supplied fighter planes. The Soviet Polikarpov I-16 had a maximum speed of 489 km/h and a range of 700 km, whereas the German Messerschmitt Bf 109 had a maximum speed of 640 km/h and a range of 850 km. The effectiveness of this technology in deciding the outcome can be seen in the supremacy the Nationalists achieved in the Basque country and Asturias through the support of the German Condor Legion.

There are strong examples used as evidence in these lines that show how the Nationalists had superior aerial technology compared to the Republicans.

In contrast, this was not the case in the First World War where aerial technology was not deadly enough to decisively alter the outcome of a single battle, much less the entire conflict. Starting with German Zeppelin airships being used for spying and bombing in 1915, through the development of fighter and bomber aircraft by both sides by the end of 1918, aircraft instilled terror in troops through the use of bombs and machine guns. Nevertheless, aircraft were unable to affect the warfare on any front, including the Western Front where troops were entrenched.

This is a focused first line to a paragraph that sets out the argument that will be made in the paragraph, and is focused on the question.

Furthermore, the greater importance of aerial technology in the Spanish Civil War in determining the outcome is in part a reflection of the fact that air warfare was a new development in the twentieth century. As the century progressed, so did the use and effectiveness of aircraft in warfare. During the First World War, aircraft, including the Zeppelin, as well as fixed-wing aircraft, were primarily used initially for spying on and terrorizing entrenched enemy troops. They were not used in cooperation with any land offensives, and were ineffective as the result of low production numbers. This limited

This well-developed point extends the range of the essay, and highlights an important contrast between the use of technology in both wars. It is focused on the question and analytical.

the range of tactics and aircraft were therefore ineffective in determining the outcome of the war. By 1936, and the Spanish Civil War, tactics had changed so that aircraft bombed cities and infrastructure in support of rapidly advancing ground troops. The Vizcaya Campaign, for example, began with aerial bombing assaults on the cities of Ochandiano and Durango in March 1937. Both cities were first devastated from above, and then Nationalist troops occupied the towns with little resistance. This change in tactics made aircraft more important. Additionally, they were now used for transporting troops and equipment so that offensives could be more effectively supplied with troops and equipment. As a result, aircraft were critically important for determining the outcome of the Spanish Civil War, especially for the Nationalists who used these more effective tactics and who were supported by Germany and Italy, with twice the number of aircraft held by the Republicans.

To conclude, aerial technology was vitally significant in affecting the outcome of the Spanish Civil War, but it had little effect on the outcome of the First World War. In Spain, the Nationalists won primarily because of their domination of the skies, which was a result of having more advanced planes, and larger numbers of them, in combination with well-judged tactics that saw devastatingly effective land and air coordinated attacks. Conversely, in the First World War, such tactics were not deployed, as the warring parties grappled with understanding the full applications of new aerial technological developments. Moreover, the technology they had at their disposal from 1914 to 1918, such as the cumbersome Zeppelins, was simply not deadly enough to significantly alter the outcome of the war. As such, technology was decisive in impacting the outcome of the Spanish Civil War, but not the First World War.

This is a good conclusion because it is consistent with the rest of the essay, and draws out the main comparisons and contrasts made in the essay.

A well-written response that stays focused on comparing and contrasting the importance of aerial technology. It develops a reasoned line of argument that is well supported by evidence. The structure is clear and a variety of technology in relation to these wars is considered, and its contribution to the outcome examined. The conclusion is consistent with the rest of the essay.

Exam practice

Now either attempt the above essay question or try one of the following questions, with reference to the Spanish Civil War.

1 Discuss the long- and short-term causes of one 20th-century war.

2 'Technological superiority was vital in determining the outcome of 20th-century wars.' With reference to two 20th-century wars, to what extent do you agree with this statement?

3 Compare and contrast the impact that two 20th-century wars had on women.

3 Second World War in Europe and north Africa 1939–45

On 1 September 1939, Germany invaded Poland. Britain and France quickly entered the conflict against Germany, turning a limited war into a regional conflict. By the end of 1941, the war was a global one of great significance for most countries involved. It ended in 1945, but there were decades of repercussions.

The long-term causes of the Second World War in Europe and north Africa

Revised

Historians still debate what caused the Second World War, with many initially placing the blame solely on the actions of **Adolf Hitler**, Germany's leader. However, as with all conflicts, the causes are complex and multilayered. While there is no historical consensus as to what led to war, the causes discussed in the following pages all played a role.

First World War peace treaties

Treaty of Versailles

The Treaty of Versailles, signed in 1919, was the peace agreement imposed on Germany after its defeat in the First World War. Its terms were considered by most at the time (and since) to be very harsh on Germany. As a result of the treaty, Germany:

- was forced to pay reparations to the Allied powers (later agreed to be £6.6 billion)
- had to accept full blame for causing the war
- had its military severely reduced
- lost its colonies and some territory to neighbouring countries, including Poland, Belgium and France
- was not allowed to join the newly created League of Nations.

Other peace treaties

Along with Germany, the remaining countries that formed the Central Powers were forced to sign peace agreements in the years 1919–20, which also had significant repercussions:

- The Austro-Hungarian Empire was dissolved and smaller states were created.
- The Ottoman Empire was also dissolved, with Middle Eastern **mandates**, or semi-autonomous states under the supervision of a European power, being created, such as Palestine, Jordan, Iraq and Syria.
- Bulgaria lost territory.
- Armies were reduced, and reparation payments were enforced on Austria, Hungary, Bulgaria and Turkey.

Impact of the peace treaties

The end of the First World War and the peace treaties which followed had long-lasting effects on Europe:

- Germans felt resentment that their country had been weakened and made to accept blame for the war.
- The German people were angry that the new German government, called the Weimar Republic, had signed the Treaty of Versailles.
- It was unfair that Germans were not allowed to live in one state, unlike Poles, Czechoslovaks, Hungarians and others; Austria and Germany were not allowed to merge or ally with each other and millions of Germans were now minorities living in Czechoslovakia and Poland.

The government faced political challenges, with attempts at revolution from the political left and right, indicating that extremists on both ends of the political spectrum were not willing to cooperate with the government, adding to its instability.

While Germany lost land, it remained the largest country in central Europe, surrounded by nations that lacked the necessary infrastructure to modernize rapidly. Germany soon began to reassert its dominance over Europe through its economic strength.

SOURCE ANALYSIS

Review the following source on the Treaty of Versailles and answer the questions that follow.

1 What can you learn from this source about the peace treaties after the First World War?

2 Using the source and the information on the previous page, why do you think the First World War peace treaties were a cause of the Second World War?

SOURCE 1

A cartoon by the artist Will Dyson, first published in the *Daily Herald*, 13 May 1919. The '1940 class' represents the children born in the 1920s who might die in a future war resulting from the treaty.

CONSEQUENCES OF THE FIRST WORLD WAR

Complete the spider diagram, organizing the consequences of the First World War into the following themes: political, economic and social.

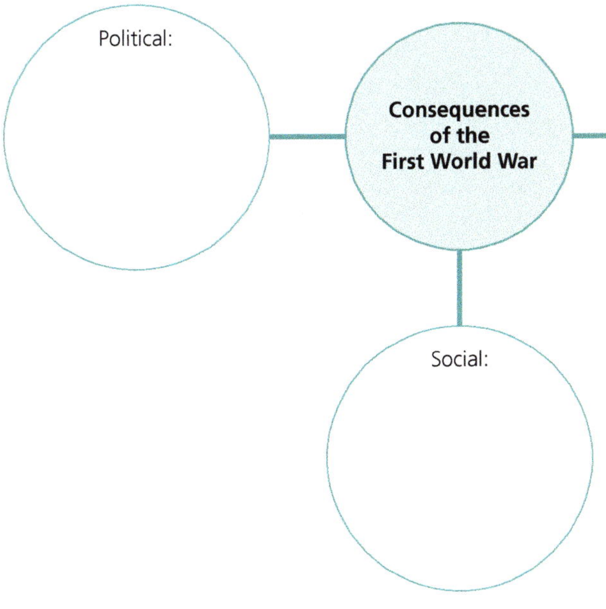

Post-war economic problems

Germany faced a number of economic problems after the First World War, which contributed to the failure of democracy and the rise of an authoritarian leader. Germany failed to pay its 1923 instalment of reparations, causing France and Belgium to occupy the industrialized Ruhr Valley until Germany paid. This, along with other economic problems that Germany was suffering, led to a period of hyperinflation, during which the German government printed vast quantities of money, causing its currency to lose value rapidly.

France and Belgium eventually agreed to leave the Ruhr Valley in 1924 and Germany accepted loans from the USA. Both of these actions brought an end to hyperinflation; however, Germany remained economically vulnerable and much of the population blamed this on the reparations it had to pay.

The Great Depression

In 1929, the US stock market crashed, causing a global economic crisis:

- The USA recalled loans to Germany, bringing a quick and dramatic end to the '**golden years**' that Germany had enjoyed in the mid to late 1920s, indicating Germany's dependence on the US economy.
- States throughout the world, including Britain, France, Japan and Italy, reduced trade as the result of lower US investment and a fall in consumption.
- In Germany, unemployment rose, businesses closed and high import tariffs were imposed, reducing trade opportunities and causing unemployment to rise to 6 million by 1933, with the government unable to take effective action.

National Socialist German Workers' Party (Nazi Party)

The Nazi Party assumed power in Germany in 1933 and pursued an aggressive economic policy that included building a large military. The actions of the Nazi Party prior to 1933 included:

- an attempt to take over Bavaria, a southern German province, in 1923 that led to Hitler, the party's leader, being sent to prison
- the creation of paramilitary units to harass and attack opponents before and during the Great Depression, as well as the establishment of an effective system of propaganda, leading to gains in the German parliament, the *Reichstag*
- the development of a set of political beliefs, or platforms, that included:
  - the Treaty of Versailles should be voided
  - Germany should become a self-sufficient nation
  - Germany required more ***Lebensraum***
  - communism was evil and its growth must be stopped
  - Germans were a master race and all other races (Jews, Roma, Slavs, Sinti and others) were inferior, and those who weakened the German race should be removed, including homosexuals, handicapped and mentally ill people, and others.

National Socialists into power

By the beginning of 1933, the Nazi Party was the largest party in the *Reichstag* and Hitler was offered the role of chancellor. Over the following two years, Hitler and the Nazi Party effectively removed all opposition, including potential opposition from within the Nazi Party itself, enabling Hitler to declare himself *Führer* of Germany.

WEIMAR GERMANY'S DOMESTIC PROBLEMS

Below are some key events that the short-lived German democratic government faced in the 1920s.

For each one, identify whether it was a political, economic or social event and how it contributed to the rise of an authoritarian leader who would guide Germany towards war in the 1930s.

Problem	What kind of event?	Why was it a cause of war?
French and Belgian invasion of the Ruhr		
US stock market crash		
High unemployment		
Rise in popularity of the Nazi Party		

CATEGORIZING THE LONG-TERM CAUSES OF WAR

Sort the following long-term causes into priority order by writing them in the hierarchy pyramid. Place the cause which you think is most significant at the top of the pyramid, down to the least significant at the bottom. Use the lines underneath the pyramid to explain why you have chosen that priority order.

- First World War peace treaties
- German economic problems before the Great Depression
- Great Depression
- Rise of Hitler and the rise of the National Socialist German Workers' Party

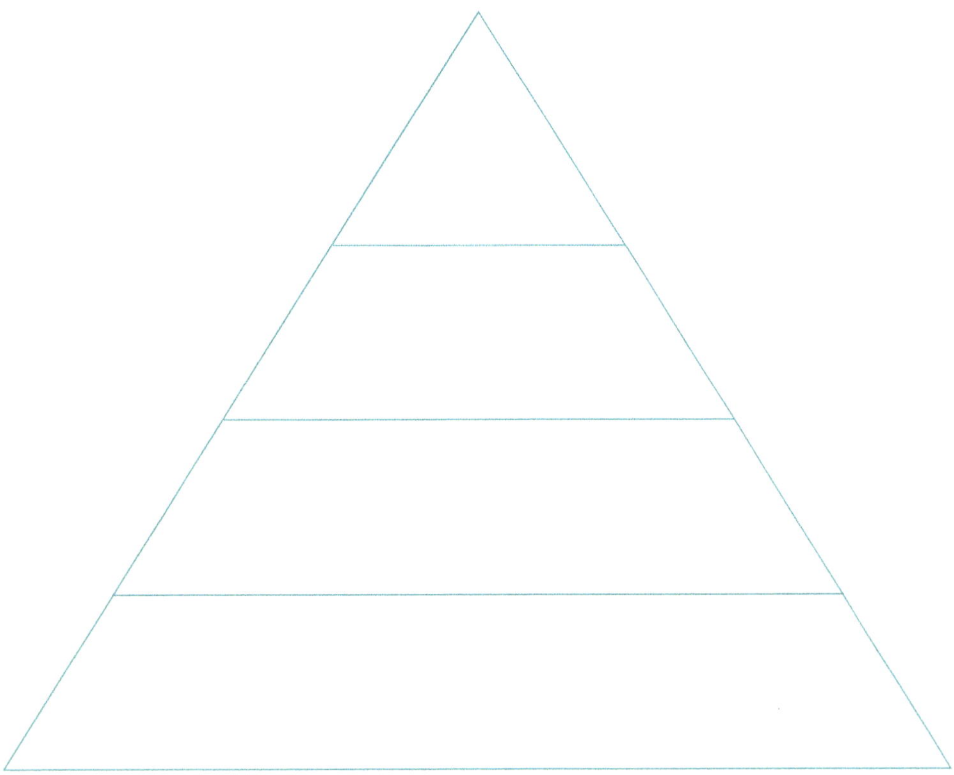

The short-term causes of the Second World War in Europe and north Africa

Revised

German economic recovery

The Nazi economics minister, Hjalmar Schacht, created the 'New Plan', which attempted to pull Germany out of economic depression and towards self-sufficiency. By 1935, Germany was exporting more than it was importing, leading to an increase in hard currency that could be invested in important raw material imports such as iron and oil. Economic recovery pleased the German population, with official statistics reporting unemployment at zero by 1938, and enabled the Nazi Party to embark on rapid military expansion.

German rearmament

In the 1930s, Germany began to rapidly rearm, readying itself for war:

- Germany withdrew from a World Disarmament Conference in 1932, declaring that if France would not disarm then Germany would no longer maintain its reduced military force as stipulated by the Treaty of Versailles.
- In 1934, Germany signed the Polish–German Non-Aggression Pact, which stated that neither Germany nor Poland would attack the other for ten years.
- In 1935, Germany introduced conscription (banned by the Treaty of Versailles) and by 1939 the German army had increased to 700,000 men.
- In the same year, Germany signed an agreement with Britain which enabled it to increase its navy; proportionate to 35% of Britain's.

The Stresa Front and the Abyssinian Crisis

In the 1930s, many European nations were focused on meeting the needs of their own citizens and failed to act effectively on the growing German threat:

- Britain, France and Italy formed the Stresa Front in 1934, an agreement which aimed to keep Germany isolated in Europe.
- The Abyssinian Crisis effectively destroyed this agreement, however, as Italy invaded the east African nation despite being a permanent member of the League of Nations.
- Britain and France, the only remaining permanent members of the League, placed limited economic sanctions on Italy but did not threaten military action.
- Rather than withdraw from Abyssinia, Italy withdrew from the League and signed the Rome–Berlin Axis with Germany, developing a new relationship between Italy and Germany and ending German political isolation in Europe.
- Germany followed this by signing the **Anti-Comintern Pact** with Japan in November 1936.

German foreign policy successes

Germany's improved economic, military and diplomatic situation enabled it to develop a more aggressive foreign policy in the 1930s, leading to the invasion of Poland and the outbreak of war in 1939. Germany had a number of foreign policy successes during this time:

- Under the terms of the Treaty of Versailles, the Saar region could hold a **plebiscite** in 1935 to determine the future of the land. The population voted overwhelmingly in favour of rejoining Germany.
- In 1936, Hitler sent troops into the Rhineland, which was a **demilitarized zone** on the border with France. Hitler ordered his troops to retreat if they were met with any resistance; however, Britain and France were busy with the Abyssinian Crisis and reluctant to engage in conflict with Hitler.
- In 1938, the Nazi Party helped to enable a situation where Austria held a plebiscite on whether to unify with Germany. The results of the vote were overwhelmingly in favour of *Anschluss* and as there were no serious protests internationally, the two countries united.
- The Sudetenland, a region of Czechoslovakia, was home to 3 million German-speaking people who wanted to reunite with Germany. Britain, France, Italy and Germany met in Munich in 1938 and agreed to this request, so long as German territorial ambition did not extend further (known as the Munich Agreement).
- In March 1939, Germany violated the Munich Agreement and invaded Czechoslovakia, ending any remaining hopes that countries had about effectively negotiating with Hitler.

HOW RESPONSIBLE WERE DIFFERENT COUNTRIES FOR WAR?

Reflect on the information that you have read so far and consider how responsible different countries were for the outbreak of the Second World War. In the box next to the country, write down any evidence that suggests the country was in some way responsible. In the final column, score each country out of 5 for how responsible you think it was based on the information.

Country	Responsibility for the outbreak of war	Level of responsibility (score out of 5)
Germany		
Britain		
France		
Italy		

SOURCE ANALYSIS

The following cartoon was drawn during the Abyssinian Crisis.

Study the source and then answer the questions below.

SOURCE 2

A cartoon from *Punch*, 1935. *Punch* was usually very patriotic towards Britain. It rarely criticized British politicians over foreign policy.

THE AWFUL WARNING.

FRANCE AND ENGLAND (*together?*). "WE DON'T WANT YOU TO FIGHT,
BUT, BY JINGO, IF YOU DO,
WE SHALL PROBABLY ISSUE A JOINT MEMORANDUM
SUGGESTING A MILD DISAPPROVAL OF YOU."

3 Who does the cartoonist suggest is to blame for the Abyssinian Crisis? How does it suggest this?

____

____

4 How did the tensions between Britain and France and Italy, as shown in this cartoon, contribute to the outbreak of the Second World War? Use the source, the information on the opposite page and your own knowledge to answer.

____

____

____

____

Poland 1939

Germany stated its intent to gain Polish territory in early 1939, leading to a series of events which ended in the outbreak of war:

- The British and French public realized that Hitler had no intention of sticking to the promises he had made in Munich the year before.
- The British and French governments publicly assured Poland that they would intervene militarily if it was attacked.
- Britain and France increased rearmament efforts at home and Britain introduced conscription; the first time ever in peacetime Britain.
- Britain and France attempted to gain the support of the USSR against Germany, but as it was clear to the USSR that neither Britain nor France intended to create a meaningful alliance, it refused.
- Instead, the USSR entered into an alliance with Germany. The Nazi–Soviet Pact stated that neither country would invade the other and secretly agreed to dismantle Poland and share the spoils.
- One week later, Germany invaded Poland.

Appeasement

Appeasement was the strategy followed by Britain through much of the 1930s. The policy aimed to negotiate with Hitler and allow some concessions, in order to satisfy Germany's territorial demands. This policy appeared to be reasonable to many, as Germany's actions initially seemed to be about removing the terms of the Treaty of Versailles, which many also thought were too harsh on Germany.

The policy was criticized by some at the time for being too lenient on Germany and encouraging Hitler to become more ambitious. The British and French public were keen to avoid another war; however, this opinion quickly changed when Germany invaded Czechoslovakia in March 1939.

The role of Hitler

There are various interpretations regarding the importance of Hitler as an individual in the outbreak of war:

The 'Great Man Theory', the belief that history can be explained by the actions and impact of individuals, is still ongoing in historical debate.

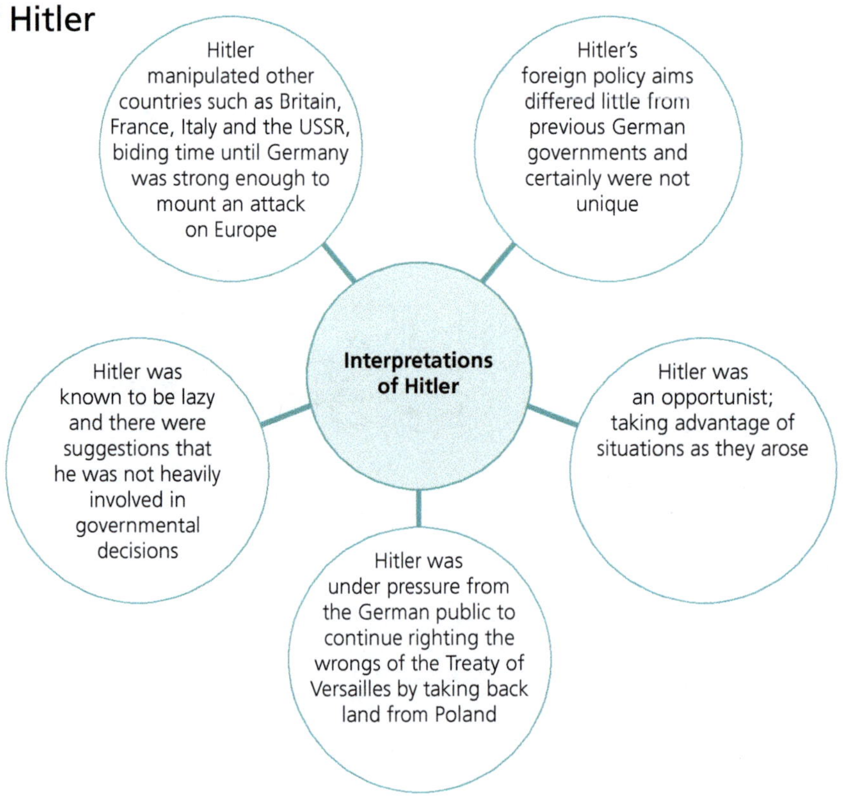

The economic argument

Some historians believe that war became a necessity for Germany in order to protect its economy. German industry shifted heavily towards armament building in the later 1930s, meaning lower consumer exports and therefore less hard currency to purchase raw materials from abroad. War provided Germany with an opportunity to seize land rich in raw materials and gain access to larger populations to join the expanding workforce.

SOURCE ANALYSIS

Read the source below and answer the questions that follow.

SOURCE 3

Winston Churchill speaking after the Munich Agreement in 1938:

We have suffered a total defeat … I think you will find that in a period of time Czechoslovakia will be engulfed in the Nazi regime.

5 What is Churchill's opinion of the British policy of appeasement?

6 To what extent do you agree with Churchill's analysis of the policy of appeasement made in 1938?

HISTORIOGRAPHY OF HITLER

Read the following summaries of the orthodox and revisionist views of Hitler's role in causing the Second World War. Decide where your interpretation lies in the debate and explain which viewpoint you agree with more, and why, using the information on the previous pages.

Views on Hitler

Orthodox view: Hitler maintained a consistent programme of aggression and had such a strong desire for German expansion that he was happy to go to war to achieve it.

Revisionist view: Hitler was not an all-powerful leader in Nazi Germany and did not have complete control over German domestic and foreign policy. Leaders within the Third Reich often disagreed on key matters and Hitler was indecisive.

Your interpretation:

____

____

____

____

____

BODY PARAGRAPH

Write a body paragraph in response to the question below. The question is a 'compare and contrast' style question which means that you need to select another war to compare with the Second World War. The response should be comparative throughout, examining how the short-term causes between these two wars were both similar and different.

Compare and contrast the short-term causes of two 20th-century wars, each chosen from a different region.

The course of the war in Europe from 1939 to June 1941

Revised

The invasion of Poland

Germany invaded Poland on 1 September 1939 and had successfully captured it within one month of fighting. This success was due to the following:

- The Polish army rushed to defend its border, believing that French and British support was imminent; both Britain and France declared war on Germany on 3 September, but neither made any meaningful efforts to help defend Poland.
- Poland had 1 million soldiers compared to Germany's 1.5 million.
- Germany had superior tanks and aircraft. German tanks outflanked the Polish army while aircraft were used to bomb strategic targets.
- The USSR invaded Poland on 17 September and captured key cities with relative ease as Polish forces were busy fighting the Germans.

The remaining Polish forces retreated to Romania before being moved to France, where the Polish government-in-exile was established on 30 September. Poland was divided between the USSR and Germany. Poland lost 65,000 soldiers during the fighting, with a further 660,000 being captured by German and Soviet forces.

The Phoney War 1939–40

Britain and France were involved in little fighting for the first nine months of the war and this period became known as the Phoney War. France used this time to strengthen its defences along the border with Germany and Britain began to mobilize the troops in its empire. The USA altered its neutrality acts to enable Britain and France to purchase war-related goods. The increase in trade with America led to naval clashes in the Atlantic, with both Britain and Germany trying to blockade the other.

The Winter War 1939–40

The USSR expanded its territory over the winter of 1939–40:

- Finland was invaded in November 1939 by hundreds of thousands of Soviet troops, supported by thousands of tanks and aircraft.
- Finland resisted effectively but had a much smaller army, and an agreement was signed in February 1940, allowing Finland to remain independent but surrender eleven per cent of its territory.
- The USSR went on to annex Estonia, Latvia, Lithuania and Bessarabia in 1940.

The invasion of Denmark and Norway, April 1940

Germany needed to secure its supply of iron ore from Sweden, which was a challenge due to British attempts to blockade the Swedish ports and the ports freezing over in the winter. To solve the problem, Germany invaded Norway via Denmark on 9 April 1940. By June, Germany had conquered all of Norway, including the port of Narvik which was then used to ship Swedish iron ore.

The invasion of western Europe, May 1940

Germany launched its first major offensive against France in May 1940 and had successfully captured its capital by 13 June 1940. The invasion proceeded as follows:

- Germany sent 3.3 million troops to fight, being slightly outnumbered by the Allied forces, which totalled almost 3.5 million.
- The Germans had superior equipment and tactics.
- The Netherlands fell to the Germans just four days after being attacked.
- Luxembourg failed to mount any meaningful resistance and was quickly captured, leaving Belgian and French borders more exposed.
- Belgium put up a stronger resistance as it received support from both the French and the British; however, the German army managed to surround enemy forces by successfully invading France through the Ardennes Forest.

- France had put a great deal of effort into reinforcing the **Maginot Line**, believing the region in the north of the country would be impassable to German tanks.
- The French were wrong, however, and Germany managed to access the English Channel through the forest and cut off troops both in and travelling to Belgium.
- Belgium surrendered on 28 May, causing a mass evacuation of British and French soldiers.
- The evacuation of Dunkirk rescued around 330,000 soldiers, but all equipment had to be abandoned to the Germans and 20,000 French soldiers were captured by the German army.
- Germany was now able to focus its efforts on France, capturing its capital on 13 June after an Italian invasion to the south of France helped to weaken its defence.

WAR ESCALATION

Consider the responsibility of each country below for escalating the war in its first year. Summarize the actions of each country in the middle column and rank the countries in terms of responsibility in the final column (1 = most responsible to 5 = least responsible).

Country	Evidence of war escalation	Ranking of responsibility
Germany		
USSR		
France		
Britain		
USA		

MAP ACTIVITY

Below is a blank map of western Europe.

Using the information on the previous page, annotate the map to show the key events in the invasion of western Europe.

The invasion of the Balkan peninsula, October 1940 to June 1941

Italy successfully conquered Albania in April 1939. In October 1940, Italy launched an attack on Greece from Albania, but the attack failed and Greece was able to push Italy back and occupy territory in Albania.

Germany, with the support of Bulgaria, invaded and conquered Yugoslavia in April 1941, dividing it among Germany, Italy, Bulgaria and Hungary. Greece was invaded in the same month and, despite support from British troops, the capital Athens was captured by 27 April and Greece surrendered soon afterwards.

The course of the war in Africa and Italy 1940–5

Revised

Italy joined the war on the side of Germany in 1940 and was quickly engaged in battles with Britain on the African continent.

East Africa, January to November 1941

In January 1941, Britain launched a three-pronged attack on Italy's east African empire. By November 1941, this area had been conquered and the states were either granted independence or placed under British control.

North Africa 1940–3

Egypt

Italy wanted to gain control of the Suez Canal to improve access to its east African colonies and Egypt. This was in order to access the valuable raw materials in the region. Italy invaded Egypt on 13 September 1940 but was met by strong British resistance, which successfully pushed Italian troops out of the country by December.

Libya

British forces, made up of mostly Australian troops, successfully invaded and captured eastern Libya in February 1941, marking Britain's first proper successful campaign in the war. Germany responded by sending troops to assist Italy in the region and British forces were pushed out of all of Libya bar the city of Tobruk by April 1941.

Britain launched Operation Crusader in November 1941 in an attempt to recapture Libya and help the troops left in Tobruk. The campaign was successful initially, with eastern Libya falling under British control again; however, the success did not last and by May 1942 Libya was once again under German and Italian control.

El Alamein

The Axis powers attempted to break through the British line in Egypt in June 1942. Britain resisted the attack, in part through the efforts of the British navy and air force, which targeted supply convoys heading for north Africa. While German forces were exhausted and struggling for supplies, Britain had been able to resupply its forces through the Suez Canal. On 23 October 1942, British, Polish and Greek forces relaunched an attack against the Germans at El Alamein, causing the tired German soldiers to retreat into Libya.

Britain, now with the support of the USA, which joined the war in December 1941, continued to fight the Axis powers in Tunisia and Libya. By the end of May 1943, all Axis powers in northern Africa had been defeated.

REASONS FOR ALLIED SUCCESS IN NORTH AFRICA

Using the information on the previous page, create a mind map of the reasons why the Allies were able to defeat the Axis powers in north Africa.

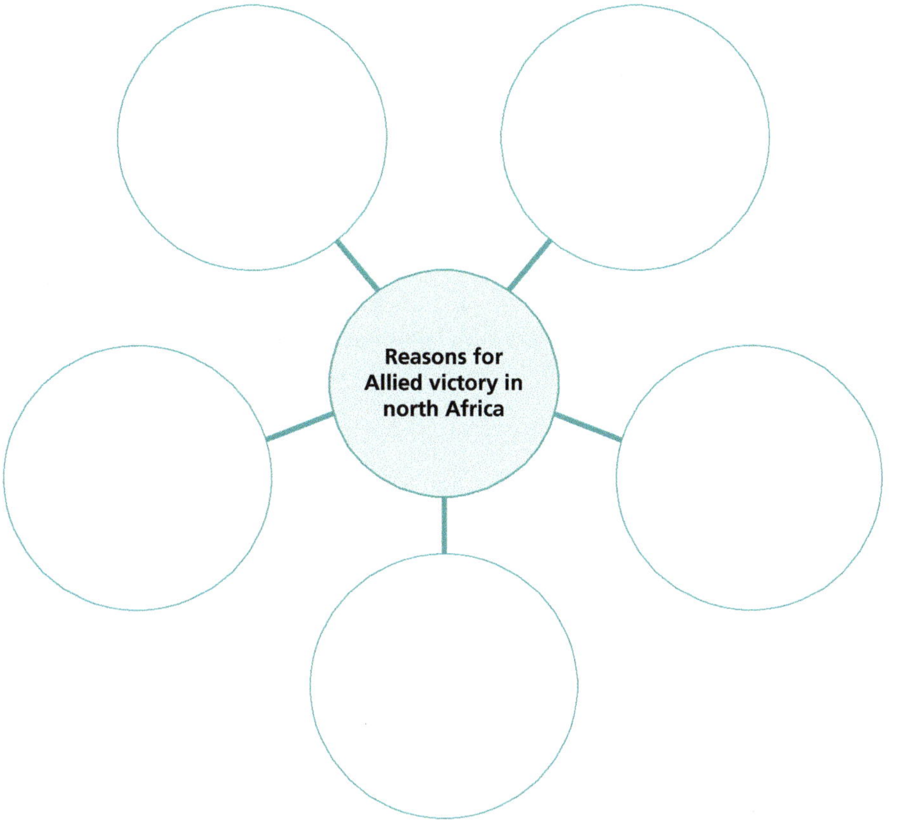

COMPLETE THE BODY PARAGRAPH

Fill in the body paragraph below to practise your writing on land as a theatre of war.

Land proved to be an important theatre of war in the years 1939–43 for both the Allied and Axis powers.

The Italian Front 1943–4

Battles on the Italian Front in the years 1943–4 resulted in Allied victory and were important to the Allies' overall success in the war for the following reasons:

- 500,000 Allied troops launched an attack on Sicily on 9 July 1943, defeating the 300,000 Axis troops stationed there by 17 August 1943.
- During the battle for Sicily, the Italian king deposed and arrested Italy's fascist dictator Benito Mussolini.
- Italy, realizing an Axis defeat was likely and hoping for favourable peace terms, agreed a secret armistice with the Allies on 3 September. Italian troops subsequently surrendered when confronted by Allied forces.
- German troops continued to fight in Italy and launched an attack on the whole Italian peninsula on 8 September 1943.
- The Allies managed to gain control of southern Italy by November 1943 but struggled to break through the German defensive line north of this.
- Rome fell to the Allies in May 1944, forcing the Germans further north but not defeating them.
- Italy fell into civil war in late 1944, with the north being controlled by Mussolini, who had been rescued from prison.
- The Allies made small territorial gains in northern Italy in early 1945 but the fighting did not stop until the German surrender on 2 May.

The course of the war at sea 1939–45

Revised

Naval power had been a decisive factor in the outcome of the First World War, with Britain imposing a naval blockade on Germany that led to starvation and lack of raw materials for war production. The Germans feared the same at the start of the Second World War as their naval power was greatly inferior to that of Britain and France. This fear was not to play out, however, as Germany quickly conquered Norway and most of continental Europe, giving it access to food and supplies, as well as ports.

Battle of the Atlantic 1939–45

The Battle of the Atlantic was ongoing for most of the war between German submarines and aircraft and British and US merchant and battle ships. The battle proceeded as follows:

- German submarines, organized into groups called wolf packs, launched attacks against increasing numbers of merchant ships carrying supplies from the USA.
- German aircraft supported the attacks, meaning that British ships had to face the enemy from below and above.
- Germany was very successful initially as it deciphered British naval codes, allowing its wolf packs to locate large convoys of British ships.
- 848 Allied ships had been destroyed by July 1941, compared to just 43 German submarines.
- To counteract Germany's initial success, the Allied ships travelled in large convoy systems and aircraft were used to patrol the sea.
- The Allies developed various weapons to destroy German submarines, including **depth charges**, **ASDIC** or sonar, **radar** and **high-frequency direction finding**.
- In 1941, Britain decrypted the German naval codes, enabling it to locate German submarines.
- The Allies were victorious in the end, their naval technologies and intelligence being too much for the Germans to counter while building large numbers of submarines.

Mediterranean Sea 1940–3

In July 1940, Britain attacked French warships while they were in port in Algeria. Britain feared that if French ships fell into the hands of the Axis powers, it could prove decisive in the conflict in north Africa. Control of the Mediterranean Sea would make it easier for the Axis powers to access and send supplies to Africa. British ships also battled Italian ships, proving victorious in November 1940 after three of Italy's six battleships were torpedoed while in port at Taranto. As in the Battle of the Atlantic, Axis and Allied submarines continued to seek out and destroy enemy ships in the Mediterranean, which were there to protect supply routes into north Africa.

CONSIDER THE SIGNIFICANCE

Review the land battles and invasions that have already been covered in this chapter. For each one, consider its significance in the overall outcome of the war.

Land battle	Significance
German invasion of Poland	
German invasion of western Europe	
Axis invasion of the Balkan peninsula	
Battles of El Alamein	
The Italian Front	

HOW CLOSE WAS THE WAR AT SEA?

Weigh up both the Allied and Axis strengths during the war at sea. Note the key successes of each side in the table below.

Allied strengths/successes	Axis strengths/successes

WHY DID THE ALLIES WIN THE WAR AT SEA?

Reviewing the information you have placed in the table above, complete the paragraph below.

The key reason why the Allied forces won the war at sea was ...

This proved crucial to the Allied victory because ...

The course of the air war 1939–45

Revised

The use of aircraft was a prominent feature of the Second World War, highlighting the extent to which warfare was changing in the twentieth century.

Britain attacked, July 1940 to July 1941

Germany began bombing Britain in July 1940, causing serious damage to cities and industrial areas across the country. Up to 60,000 people had died by July 1941 as a result of the bombs. Germany hoped either to force the British government into negotiating a peace settlement, in order to prevent such high civilian casualties, or to weaken Britain enough to enable German ships to safely cross the English Channel. Germany was not successful and the Allies responded by bombing Germany.

Bombing Germany 1940–5

Initial campaign

Britain began bombing German industrial sites and railways in May 1940 with the aim of slowing down the German invasion of France. British bombers struggled to hit targets accurately, with only 30% of bombs dropped landing within eight kilometres (five miles) of their intended target.

Area bombing 1942–5

Britain changed strategy to area bombing, or targeting a larger area to negate the need for precision, with mixed success. The aim was to both destroy industrial areas and lower morale, as citizens would get caught up in the bombing. The bombing raids would take place in waves, with the first wave destroying the roofs of buildings before a second wave caused fires within the buildings. The German city of Lübeck was bombed in this manner in March 1943, with 62% of the city being destroyed. In May 1942, Operation Millennium was launched, involving over 1000 British bombers which attacked the German city of Cologne, destroying 3300 houses and 36 factories. The strategy continued to be used throughout the war, assisted by US planes once the USA joined the Allies in 1942.

Other bombings

It was not just Germany that was attacked by British and US bombers, but also Romania's oilfields and parts of Italy. The Germans also continued to use aerial bombing as a strategy, targeting Soviet cities and areas of north Africa.

It is debatable how important bombing campaigns were to the war effort and the eventual Allied victory. Improvements in Allied air attacks had significantly harmed Germany by the end of 1944 due to repeated campaigns on its oil installations and railways. However, targeting civilians seems to have increased rather than decreased their morale and Germany managed to repair damage to industrial areas at rapid speed. The cost of the campaigns was also incredibly high, with an estimated 600,000 civilians killed in Germany and many more injured or made homeless as a result of the bombings. The campaigns also led to the death of 160,000 Allied air crew.

HOW EFFECTIVE WAS STRATEGIC BOMBING?

Using the information on the previous page, summarize the key evidence that suggests that strategic bombing was or was not effective.

Evidence that strategic bombing was effective	Evidence that strategic bombing was ineffective

REVIEWING A STUDENT RESPONSE

Read the body paragraphs below, which are parts of an answer written by a student to the following exam-style question:

Examine the impact that aerial warfare played in the outcome of one 20th-century war.

Aerial warfare played an important role in the outcome of the Second World War because it damaged both civilian and industrial properties. The Allies bombed cities across Germany such as Cologne, where over 3000 homes were destroyed. These campaigns killed many civilians and caused many more to be homeless. This lowered morale in Germany. The Allied bombing campaign became particularly important towards the end of the war when the USA had joined and German supplies were running low. The Allies were able to repeatedly bomb key strategic targets such as railways which made it very difficult for the Axis powers to keep its supplies and soldiers moving.

Aerial warfare did not play a crucial role in the outcome of the Second World War, however. While the Allied bombing campaigns destroyed cities and homes, there is little evidence that German morale was lowered, particularly at the beginning of the war. Similarly, the high number of civilian casualties did not seem to do much to alter the direction of the war and many historians now consider it to be a great waste of life. Finally, the aerial campaigns were often inaccurate, and bombs did not consistently hit the targets which they were intended to hit. For example, when Britain first began bombing Germany, only 30% of its bombs landed anywhere near the intended target. This highlights how aerial warfare did not play a crucial role in determining the outcome of the war.

What are the strengths of the response?

What do you think could be improved in the response?

Have a go at rewriting the response including the improvements you suggested above.

The course of the land war in Europe, June 1941 to May 1945

Revised

World war in Europe 1941–3

By mid-1941, Germany controlled much of northern, central, western and south-eastern Europe. The next step was to eliminate the threat from the USSR.

Operation Barbarossa 1941

Germany launched the largest invasion in history against the world's largest country in June 1941. The operation proceeded as follows:

- Three million German troops, 3500 tanks and 2000 aircraft invaded the USSR.
- The USSR was caught by surprise and Germany quickly advanced, capturing large areas of land, armies and equipment.
- German tanks advanced 80 km (50 miles) a day to begin with, and by mid-November German troops were just 32 km (20 miles) from Moscow.
- The Soviets launched a counterattack that was able to save Moscow and brought an end to Operation Barbarossa.
- An estimated 3 million Soviet troops were killed and a further 3.5 million captured.
- While the Soviets were initially overwhelmed and suffered massive losses in terms of both human casualties and machinery, they continued to put up resistance for longer than the Germans had prepared themselves to fight for.
- The Soviet government understood the importance of saving its workers and evacuated as many personnel as it could from industrial areas, ensuring that they did not become German prisoners.

German offensives in the USSR 1942

- Early 1942 – the Soviets launched various counterattacks against the Germans, all of which were unsuccessful.
- June 1942 – Germany launched Operation Case Blue against Stalingrad, with the aim of capturing the oilfields.
- Mid-August 1942 – the Germans had advanced a further 600 km (375 miles) and successfully captured the USSR's western oilfields.
- Mid-September – Germany occupied most of Stalingrad. Effective capture of this city had the potential to completely halt the Soviets' oil supply lines.

Operation Uranus, November 1942 to January 1943

Soviet armies launched a counterattack on German forces in Stalingrad on 19 November. It was successful due to the following:

- The German army were taken by surprise and many were trapped in the city and cut off from supplies.
- German soldiers struggled in the freezing temperatures and surrendered on 31 January 1943.

The German loss in the Battle of Stalingrad was the first major German defeat of the Second World War.

Soviet offensives 1943

The Soviets also launched additional attacks against German troops which led to the recapture of Kursk, Rostov and Kharkov by mid-February 1943. The offensives proceeded as follows:

- Kharkov was recaptured by the Germans in March.
- Germany launched Operation Citadel in July 1943 to try to recapture Kursk. The Battle of Kursk involved a close-range tank battle that left thousands dead, hundreds of tanks destroyed and no clear victory for either side. What the battle did prove, however, was that Germany had failed to mount a successful offensive against the Soviets.
- The Soviets launched Operations Kutuzov and Rumyantsev against the Germans in July 1943, successfully capturing hundreds of thousands of German soldiers and the cities of Kharkov, Kiev and Briansk, among others.

The Germans failed to win any major offensive operation on the Eastern Front after July 1943.

DRAWING ACTIVITY

In the blank boxes below draw a series of images to illustrate the German offensives into the USSR in the years 1941–2.

TURNING POINTS

A turning point is considered to be a significant moment that leads to change. Many historians consider the Axis defeat in the Battle of Stalingrad to be a turning point in the Second World War.

Explain below why you think the Battle of Stalingrad can be considered a turning point. To do this effectively, you should show an understanding of the situation in the war prior to the battle, give details of the battle itself and explain how the battle led to change.

The war in Europe 1944–5

Soviet offensives 1944

The USSR continued to make advances on the Eastern Front and in the Balkans. Soviet forces successfully drove German armies out of Ukraine early in 1944, causing them to retreat west and south-west.

In June 1944, the Soviets launched Operation Bagration: a highly successful operation in which Soviet armies advanced 160 km (100 miles) into German-held territory. By August, Soviet forces controlled eastern Poland.

Balkan campaign 1944–5

In August 1944, the USSR launched an attack on German and Axis troops in Romania, causing Romania to switch sides in the war and giving the Soviets control of oilfields. Bulgaria subsequently left the Axis powers and joined the Allies in September 1944. In October 1944, Soviet troops captured Yugoslavia's capital, Belgrade.

Baltic campaign, June 1944 to January 1945

Soviet troops launched a large-scale attack on German and Finnish troops in Leningrad. Finland's army was driven out of the city by the end of June. By September, Soviet troops had successfully captured Tallinn, Estonia's capital, which Germany had been occupying. By the end of January 1945, the Soviets had also captured the Latvian capital, Riga, and Memel, which was a German territory.

Battle of Berlin, 20 April to 2 May 1945

On 16 April, Soviet forces entered Germany bound for Berlin. Hitler continued to direct operations from a bunker in Berlin until he killed himself on 29 April. By 2 May 1945, Soviet forces had captured Berlin.

The Western Front 1944–5

The leaders of USA, Britain and the USSR met in Tehran, Iran, in 1944 and agreed to open a second front against Germany in the west. Activity on this front proceeded as follows:

- The invasion, Operation Overlord, was launched in June 1944.
- 160,000 British, Canadian and US troops landed on the beaches in Normandy, northern France, supported by 1200 warships and bombers which attacked German defences.
- All five beaches were captured by the end of the day and by 4 July there were over 1 million Allied troops in France.
- Operation Dragoon was launched in August 1944, in which Allied forces successfully drove German troops out of southern France.
- Allied troops captured Paris on 25 August, and by December German troops had retreated from most of France and Belgium.
- Germany counterattacked in December 1944, launching attacks against Allied forces in the Ardennes Forest in what became known as the Battle of the Bulge.
- The German troops took Allied forces by surprise and made initial territorial gains, but these had been lost by the end of January and Germany lost valuable weaponry and supplies which it could not replenish.
- Allied troops entered Germany early in 1945, capturing key territory. Berlin was not invaded by Allied forces as it had been agreed that the USSR would capture the city.

Germany surrenders, May 1945

Grand Admiral Karl Donitz assumed authority in Germany once Hitler had killed himself. On 4 May, German troops in the Netherlands, Denmark and north-western Germany surrendered. In the official German surrender, signed on 7 May 1945, Germany agreed to unconditionally surrender on 8 May 1945.

WHAT ROLE DID DIFFERENT COUNTRIES PLAY IN GERMANY'S DEFEAT?

Using the information on the previous pages, summarize the roles of the USSR, the USA and Britain in causing Germany to surrender in 1945. In the final column rank the three countries in terms of their contributions to Germany's surrender.

Country	Role in causing German surrender	Rank
USSR		
USA		
Britain		

SOURCE ANALYSIS

Carefully look at the image and answer the questions below.

SOURCE 4

Soviet military forces at the German *Reichstag* during the Battle of Berlin, 1 May 1945.

7 What does the source suggest about the reasons for Germany's surrender in 1945?

8 How useful is this source to a historian studying the Allied victory in Europe in 1945?

Reasons for Germany's defeat

Revised

Weak Axis partners in Europe

Germany did not have strong war allies in Europe. Italy failed to conquer Greece without assistance from Germany and was not successful in its invasion of Egypt. Italy did not assist Germany in any European campaigns of any significance. While Slovakia, Hungary, Bulgaria and Romania all provided troops for the Eastern Front, they were poorly equipped and not instrumental in German success.

War production

Germany was weakened as the result of problems in war production. German industry was not fully mobilized until 1943. Germany produced a wide variety of weapons, causing funds and resources to be channelled into experimentation rather than mass production.

The Allied nations, on the other hand, were well-resourced, well-manned and well-organized. The USSR had improved its industrial capabilities through a series of **Five Year Plans** in the 1930s and the USA was the world's largest economic power.

Failed strategy

- Germany's ***Blitzkrieg*** tactics were successful in the beginning stages of the war on mainland Europe; however, Germany struggled once it was required to adapt its tactics.
- Britain, as an island, was difficult to invade, and German aircraft, which were designed to work alongside land forces, failed in the attempt to do so.
- Germany's invasion of the USSR was initially successful, but the speed at which troops advanced left them overextended and vulnerable.
- Germany also struggled in the USSR once it became clear that victory would not be achieved rapidly and the German forces would be required to fight through the winter months.

Hitler's military decisions

Hitler could be held responsible for Germany's defeat. As head of the armed forces he had little experience. Hitler often refused to take advice from his generals, including the recommendation to retreat in order to preserve men and equipment for key battles. Some of Germany's best soldiers and key weaponry were lost in important battles, including in Stalingrad and Kursk, in relation to which Hitler refused such advice.

USSR as the cause of German defeat

The USSR was very difficult to conquer for a number of reasons:

- Its size, climate and challenging terrain, and its enormous population who were willing to work and fight exceptionally hard for their country.
- The Soviet government was prepared to sacrifice its people in its defence of land.

Soviet forces were responsible for around 80% of all Germans killed or wounded.

The role of the USA and Britain in defeating Germany

US war production assisted the USSR greatly in its prolonged campaign against Germany. The US, British and Canadian invasions of France in 1944 helped to occupy German forces which would have otherwise been sent to the Eastern Front. However, the bombing of Germany had little significant impact on the war effort until later in 1944 when the Soviets had almost advanced into Germany.

WHAT WAS MOST RESPONSIBLE FOR GERMANY'S DEFEAT IN EUROPE IN 1945?

Using the information on the previous page, complete the bar chart. Consider how much responsibility each factor should have in Germany's defeat and draw a bar accordingly. Once the bar chart is complete explain your decisions by writing a brief summary inside each of the bars.

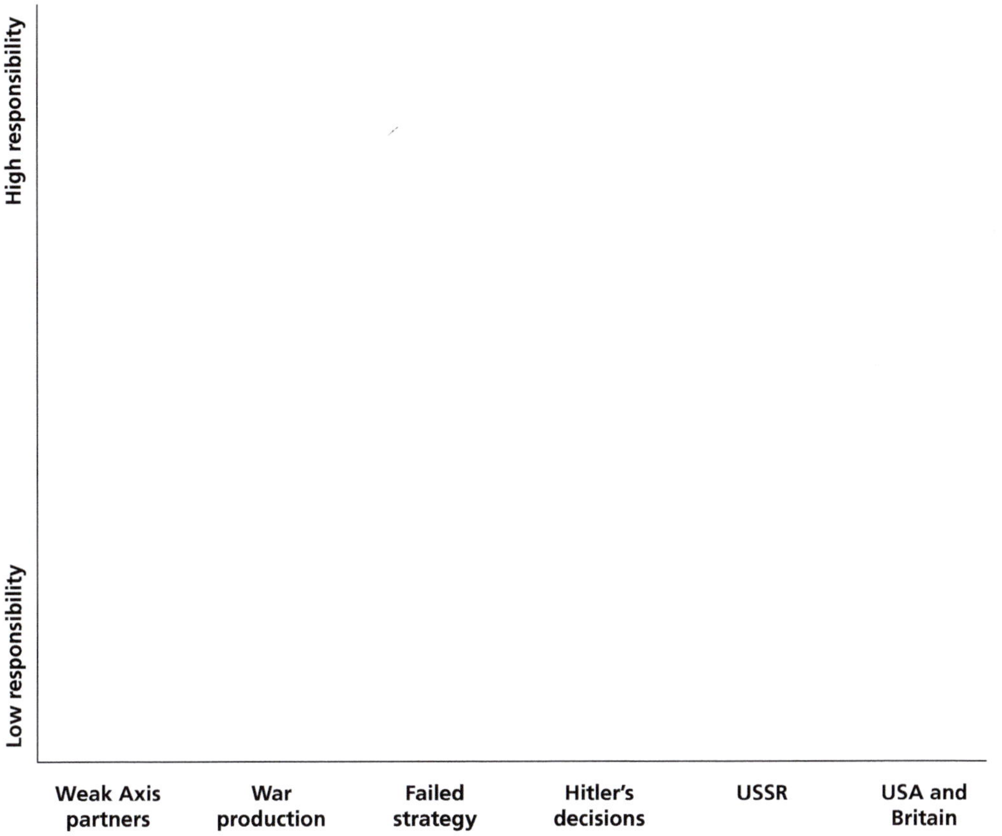

The home front and occupied Europe

Revised

Civilians were affected greatly by the Second World War. Millions took up active service or support roles for the war effort and all nations were affected by the impact of food and fuel shortages.

Women in war

Women's roles varied from nation to nation, with women in the USSR taking on combatant roles, women elsewhere taking on support roles in the armed forces and almost all nations involving women heavily in war production.

Germany

Women did not become heavily involved at the beginning of the war as Nazi ideology believed that women should remain in the home. By the end of 1939, however, women made up 37% of the workforce. German women were never allowed to be involved in military service.

Britain

In 1941, all women aged between 18 and 60 were registered ready for conscription into the industrial workforce. By the end of the war, 6.5 million British women were employed in factories or shipyards.

Women also took up non-combatant military roles, joining organizations such as the Women's Auxiliary Air Force, the Women's Royal Naval Service (WRNS) and the Women's Land Army. In 1945, 460,000 women were employed in non-combat work for the military.

USSR

Tens of millions of women were conscripted for military service, with over 800,000 women serving in the Soviet armed forces over the course of the war. Women took up roles as pilots, mechanics, agricultural labourers and soldiers. By 1945, over 40% of Soviet doctors were women.

Rationing

Rationing was a major part of the war effort by all combatants:

- Britain began rationing oil-based products at the start of the war, followed by food such as butter and sugar in 1940, and eventually almost all food products.
- In the USSR, rationing was severe, with children and older people allowed 700 calories of food daily, while adult workers received around 1500 calories. Almost all of the entire population was on the verge of starvation through most of the war.
- Italy introduced rationing in 1939, prior to joining the war. The purchase of petrol was banned and most urban civilians survived on 1000 calories of food daily.
- Germany introduced limited rationing prior to the invasion of Poland in 1939 and added further restrictions as the war went on. German civilians had better access to food products than most warring countries; by the end of the war, however, shortages were apparent in all areas.

War production

The table below shows the war production of the major powers in the Second World War in Europe and north Africa.

Output	USA*	Britain	USSR	Germany	Italy
Tanks	88,500	30,000	105,000	67,000	2,500
Aircraft	300,000	130,000	145,000	120,000	11,000
Artillery units	257,000	125,000	500,000	160,000	7,200
Trucks	2,400,000	480,000	200,000	345,000	83,000
Machine guns	2,700,000	–	1,500,000	675,000	–
Submarines	200	170	–	1,100	28
Surface warships	1,200	730	–	42	15
Merchant shipping (tons)	34,000,000	6,300,000	–	–	1,500,000
Coal (tons)	400,000,000	120,000,000	71,000,000	240,000,000	4,000,000
Iron ore (tons)	400,000,000	120,000,000	71,000,000	240,000,000	4,000,000
Oil (tons)	830,000,000	91,000,000	110,000,000	33,000,000	0

*Production for the simultaneous war in Asia and the Pacific. –, Not available.

US military production was crucial to the Allied war effort even before the USA became a belligerent nation. Under the terms of the **Lend–Lease** agreement, Britain and the USSR were sent vast amounts of goods and supplies.

German production proved problematic at first; however, industry was reorganized in 1942 to give the German government control, and subsequently production levels increased. Italy's industrial production output was the second highest of the Axis powers in Europe, although it was significantly behind the output levels of Germany.

WOMEN'S ROLE IN WAR

Review the varying roles that women played in the war. For each country tick the appropriate boxes in the table.

Country	Combatant roles	Military support roles	War production
Britain			
Germany			
USSR			

IMPACT OF RATIONING

Explain in the space below what the impact of rationing would have been on the civilian populations. Try to consider men, women and children.

Imprisonment and extermination

The Holocaust

Germany introduced a series of anti-Jewish laws in the 1930s that removed the majority of freedoms from the one per cent Jewish population. Discrimination and violence against Jewish people worsened in the late 1930s and the German government actively encouraged emigration.

As the Second World War progressed and Germany began to control more land in Europe, its policy against Jewish people evolved. When Germany invaded the USSR in June 1941, the German government ordered the immediate execution of Jewish people in occupied areas, leading to 500,000 Soviet Jewish people being killed in the winter of 1941–2.

In 1942, Germany introduced the **Final Solution** policy for Jewish people in Europe. Jewish people capable of labour would be worked to death and those not deemed capable would be exterminated. Hundreds of labour and death camps were set up across Europe, including Auschwitz-Birkenau in Poland, the largest camp, which was responsible for the death of an estimated 1.5 million people. It is thought that around 6 million Jewish people were killed during the Holocaust; 60% of Europe's Jewish population. Concentration camps are also estimated to have killed 5 million non-Jewish people, including Roma, Sinti, Slavs, priests, gay/lesbian people, people with mental illness and prisoners of war.

Prisoners of war

Millions of Allied and Axis soldiers were captured over the course of the Second World War:

- Germany: the treatment of Allied prisoners in Germany varied depending on nationality. White British and US prisoners were mostly imprisoned, but not sent to labour camps. An estimated 250,000 British and US soldiers were captured by Germany during the war, with fewer than 10,000 dying while captive. Soviet prisoners were treated poorly, however, with around half of the 6 million Soviet and Polish prisoners dying while in prison camps.
- USSR: Soviet troops captured around 3 million German soldiers during the war. Most of these died as the Soviet population was struggling to keep its own people alive. German prisoners were sent to labour camps, where harsh treatment was common.
- Britain, Canada and the USA: Britain initially sent most captured enemy soldiers to Canada, as it feared a German invasion. As the threat of a German invasion decreased, Britain held more German prisoners, who had the choice of detention or agricultural and construction work. The USA held over 500,000 German prisoners, who were treated similarly to those in Britain.

Internment of foreign nationals

Hundreds of thousands of civilians who were living in countries that were at war with their homelands were arrested and imprisoned. France arrested all German males at the outset of the war, while the USA imprisoned thousands of Germans and Italians (including those who were US citizens of German or Italian descent). Thousands of civilian prisoners died over the course of the war due to overwork in labour camps or from contracting deadly diseases.

IMPACT OF THE SECOND WORLD WAR

Reflect on how the Second World War impacted different groups of people. Summarize the events and your thoughts in the spider diagram below.

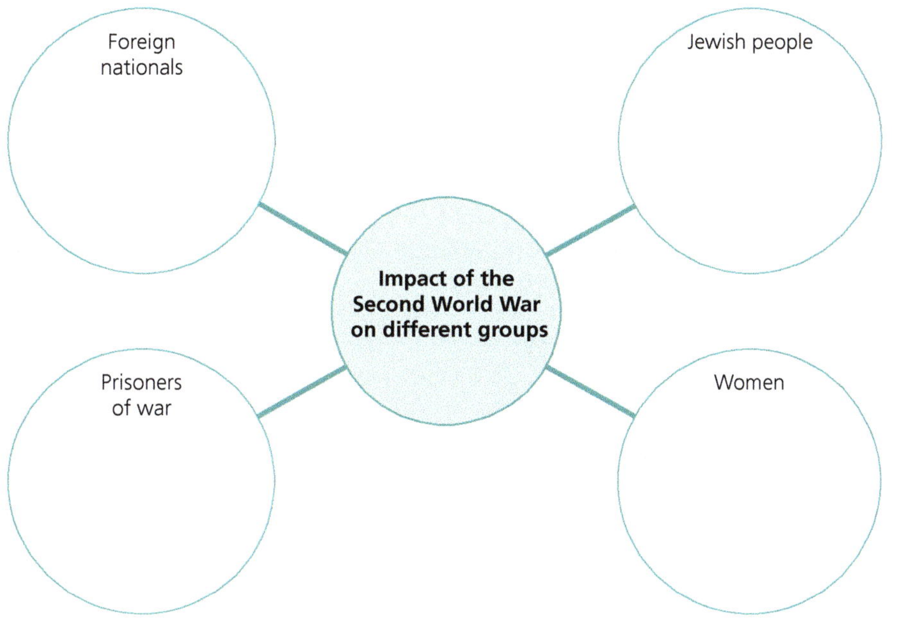

SOURCE ANALYSIS

Study the source below.

SOURCE 5

A photograph taken of concentration camp prisoners shortly after the camp's liberation.

9 How useful is this source to a historian studying the treatment of Jewish people during the Second World War?

Resistance movements

Opposition to foreign occupation was evident across Europe, ranging from passive actions to organized armed resistance groups.

Poland

There was very active resistance against German and Soviet occupation in Poland:

- The largest Polish resistance group was the Polish Home Army (AK).
- It was allied with the Polish government in exile and had a spy network which provided the Allies with information on German military operations.
- German supply convoys that were travelling through Poland and railways were targeted, slowing down the transportation of German supplies to the USSR.
- In 1944, the AK began leading uprisings in cities across eastern Poland, including an uprising in Warsaw in August that saw AK members take control of most of the city.
- Jewish resistance groups were also organized in Poland during the war, such as the Jewish Combat Organization (ZOB) and the Jewish Military Union (ZZW).
- The ZOB joined forces with the AK in 1942 and the ZZW had small cells in major cities across Poland.
- Members of the AK, ZOB and ZZW revolted together against Germany's attempt to remove remaining Jewish people from the **Warsaw Ghetto** in April 1943.

Yugoslavia and Albania

Yugoslavia was not a very united country prior to the war and was engaged in civil conflict from its invasion in April 1941 through to the end of the war:

- Ultra-nationalist Serbs formed groups called *Chetniks*, which fought against various groups including Italians, Germans and Croats.
- An Albanian nationalist group called *Balli Kombëtar* formed and battled *Chetniks*, Croats and communists in an attempt to expand Albanian territory.
- **Josip Broz (Tito)** led a large communist resistance movement known as Partisans. These communist fighters, supported by Britain and the USSR, led guerrilla campaigns against all other groups in Yugoslavia.
- The Partisans had a membership of 225,000 by 1943, and by October 1944 had taken control of Yugoslavia's capital, Belgrade. At the time of Germany's surrender the Partisans controlled all of Yugoslavia and Albania.

France

Several resistance groups formed in France and carried out acts of sabotage to disrupt military production and the transportation of goods. French groups provided information to Britain and the USA and assisted in the Allied advances which took place in 1944.

USSR

Tens of thousands of people, known as partisans, had been ordered by the Soviet government to remain behind (rather than flee east) after the German invasion in June 1941. By the end of 1942, there were around 300,000 partisans operating in German-occupied Soviet territory. They carried out various acts, such as assassinating German soldiers and destroying transportation routes.

Ukrainians formed the Ukrainian Nationalist Organization (UNO) to battle both Germans and Soviets. UNO membership reached 300,000 by 1943; however, most were captured and executed by the Soviet military in 1944.

RESISTANCE GROUPS MATCH-UP

Below are the names of different countries and information about resistance groups within them.

Match up the country with the information.

Country	Information
Poland	Carried out acts of sabotage and sought information to send to the Allied forces
Yugoslavia	Formed of people who had remained in German-occupied territory. Assassinated German soldiers and disrupted transportation routes
France	Various nationalist groups were formed which engaged in civil war. The largest resistance group was formed of communists
USSR	Various groups formed, some of which were Jewish resistance groups. The largest resistance group had a spy network which provided information to the Allies

EXTENDED WRITING

Read the question below and write a two-paragraph response. In the first paragraph explain why you might agree with the opinion in the question and in the second write why you might disagree.

'Resistance movements in Poland were the most disruptive.' To what extent do you agree with this statement?

The statement can be seen as accurate because ...

However, the statement has limitations because it hasn't considered ...

The effects of the Second World War in Europe and north Africa

Revised

The Second World War had profound and long-lasting impacts for all nations involved; millions were dead, infrastructure was destroyed and political systems had been dismantled.

Post-war trials

German political and military leaders were imprisoned and prosecuted for war crimes. The Nuremberg Trials began in November 1945, beginning with the trial of 24 men, most of whom were found guilty and executed, and continued until 1949.

Poland tried German officials for the Holocaust in 1947 and the USA held the Dachau Trials between 1945 and 1948, finding over 1400 Germans guilty.

Effects on civilians

Casualties

Civilians died in numbers greater than in any other modern war. This included:

- over 11 million people dying in concentration camps
- close to 17 million people dying in the USSR
- 2 million people dying in Germany.

It is difficult to comprehend the sheer volume of life lost as a result of the war.

Destruction

Major cities across central and eastern Europe had been destroyed, leaving millions homeless. Destruction of infrastructure made it difficult for civilians to get access to vital supplies even once the war had ended, hindering a return to any economic normality.

Population transfer

Millions of civilians had been forced to move to occupied areas of Europe to support the German war effort. The Soviet government removed people from their home regions if they were suspected of being pro-German or not fully committed to the Soviet war effort. This resulted in millions of Chechens, Koreans, Finns, Poles and many more groups being moved to central Asia or Siberia. Those who survived the war were unable to return home immediately.

After the war, some countries, such as Poland, expelled Germans, regardless of how long they had been living in the country. Most surviving Jewish people left Europe and settled in the USA and the British mandate of Palestine, part of which later became the Jewish state of Israel in 1948.

Military casualties

The table below shows the numbers of military deaths incurred by the major powers in the Second World War.

Nation	Soldiers mobilized	Military dead	Percentage who died
USSR	20,000,000	8,700,000	43
USA	16,400,000*	292,000†	2
Germany	10,800,000	3,250,000	30
Britain	8,850,000‡	383,000	4
France	5,000,000	250,000	5
Italy	4,500,000	380,000	8
Poland	1,000,000	600,000	60
Others	5,660,000	445,000	7
Totals	72,210,000	14,300,000	20

*Totals are for soldiers who fought in both Europe and Asia. †Approximately 100,000 were killed in Asia.
‡Total includes soldiers from British Dominions, who made up 4,150,000 of this number.

Millions of soldiers died during the Second World War. Many died fighting, but many died from disease or starvation or as a result of dire conditions, such as freezing temperatures.

Border changes

Territorial boundaries were adjusted after the war, causing some populations to be forcibly moved and some nations to be completely absorbed into other states. This included the following changes:

- The USSR acquired the eastern regions of Poland, which was compensated by being given land in Germany, including a sizeable amount of the German province of East Prussia and the port of Danzig.
- Germany lost all the territory it had annexed after 1937, which included Czechoslovakia, Austria and parts of France.
- The Saar region of Germany was placed under French administration.
- Germany was occupied by the Allies and divided into four separate zones, which would eventually lead to the creation of two states: West and East Germany.
- The USSR acquired territory in Finland and seized all of Estonia, Latvia and Lithuania.

IMPACT OF WAR ON CIVILIANS

For each of the following effects of the war, consider how it would impact people trying to return to daily life.

Effect	Impact on returning to daily life
War trials	
Casualties	
Destruction	
Population transfer	

SOURCE ANALYSIS

Examine the source below.

SOURCE 6

A photograph taken of a damaged street in Aachen, Germany, 1944.

10 What does the source suggest about the effects of war in Germany?
11 Why is this source useful to a historian studying the effects of war?
12 What limitations does this source have?

New political realities

Attacks by Axis powers brought both the USA and USSR into the Second World War, something both countries were keen to avoid.

Public opinion in the USA was primarily **isolationist**; the public did not want to see their country involving itself in European affairs. The USSR was desperate to avoid another conflict such as the First World War, which had been so destructive. However, once both nations were involved, the conflict was undoubtedly a global one, and after the war's end, both the USA and the USSR decided they should both be involved in diplomacy for the best chance of a lasting peace.

United Nations

The **United Nations** (UN) was formed after the war, and was initially made up of the Allied powers. It replaced the unsuccessful League of Nations and included some important changes to help make it more effective. For example, both the USA and USSR joined, a Security Council of fifteen member states was formed that had the ability to undertake peacekeeping missions, and the UN had the right to authorize the use of military force in certain situations.

Decolonization

British colonies

The war weakened Britain's ability to hold a large empire:

- Britain could no longer produce enough goods to be consumed and traded within its colonies, but instead had to import products from the USA.
- Britain was also heavily indebted to the USA as it had to buy so many raw materials and armaments during the war.
- Many colonies felt they deserved independence from Britain due to the contributions they had made during the war, and subsequently pro-independence movements grew.

Decolonization became an aim for the British government after the war as it could no longer afford to maintain its empire:

- India and Ceylon (now Sri Lanka) were granted independence in 1947.
- In 1948, Britain withdrew from the mandate of Palestine, which was then divided up to form a Jewish zone and a Palestinian Arab zone.
- Egypt became independent in 1952.

French colonies

Japan had taken over **French Indochina** during the war and France's Middle Eastern mandates either declared independence or were occupied by Britain. France attempted to reassert control in Indochina once Japan had been defeated; however, it was eventually defeated by communist guerrillas in 1954. France's north African colonies, such as Morocco and Tunisia, gained independence in the 1950s.

Italian colonies

Italy lost control of most of its colonies during the war and agreed the following losses at the Treaty of Peace, which was signed in 1947:

- Abyssinia, now known as Ethiopia, became independent once again.
- Italian Somaliland was placed under UN control and granted independence in 1960 as Somalia.
- Libya became independent in 1951.
- Albania regained independence in 1945.

The Cold War

The **Cold War** is the name given to the geopolitical tensions that arose after the Second World War.

The Soviets in eastern Europe

The Allied powers agreed at the Yalta Conference in February 1945 to restore democratically elected governments in the European states occupied by Allies. This included the many states of eastern Europe, which were Soviet-occupied after the war. The Soviets took no steps to carry out this agreement, however, claiming that eastern Europe was too unstable. While it is true that eastern Europe was unstable, it is also thought that the Soviets wanted to maintain control over the states it occupied as they provided a buffer zone between western Europe and the USSR. By 1948, various states in eastern Europe, such as Czechoslovakia, Hungary and Romania had become **Soviet satellites** with communist-led governments.

COMPARISON ACTIVITY

Compare this war with another war of your choice that you have studied. Draw up a table of similarities and differences of effects. Once you have created the list, highlight each point to identify whether it was a political, economic or social effect.

Similarities	Differences

WRITE AN INTRODUCTION

Using the information from the previous activity and the information in the preceding pages, write an introduction to the following practice exam question.

Compare and contrast the political and social effects of two 20th-century wars.

When writing an introduction, you should:

- demonstrate a clear understanding of the demands of the question
- state a clear thesis or line of argument
- explain the intended structure for the remainder of the essay.

Tensions were high at the end of the war, between the USA, Britain and France, and the Soviets. These tensions increased once the war was over and the common aim of fighting the Axis powers was gone. Soviet and US relations also struggled after the death of President **Franklin D. Roosevelt**, who was replaced with the more combative **Harry Truman**.

The Truman Doctrine, March 1947

Greece erupted into civil war in 1946 when the constitutional monarch was challenged by Greek communists. Britain, and later the USA, provided Greece with funds and weapons to help beat the communists. The US policy of containing communism within the USSR and its satellite states in Eastern Europe was named the Truman Doctrine.

US economic policy in Europe

The Allies agreed to dismantle German industry, to provide little assistance to the German population, and that Germany should provide reparations to the USSR. In 1947, the USA altered this policy by calling for the industrialization of Germany and its economic integration into Europe. This was done without consulting the USSR. The USA believed that communism thrived in economically desolated areas, therefore a strong industrialized Germany would help to prevent the spread of communist ideology.

The USA launched the Marshall Plan in 1948, which provided $13 billion for the economic recovery of Europe. Countries across Western Europe, along with Greece and Turkey, benefited from the grants and saw rapid economic recovery. The USSR and its satellites were offered funds but refused them, causing further tensions and an increasing economic divide between East and West Europe.

Berlin Blockade and Airlift, 1948

Berlin was located in the Soviet-occupied zone of Germany, but was itself split into four zones, occupied respectively by the USSR, USA, Britain and France. The USA, Britain and France merged their zones in 1948, angering the USSR. The Soviets protested by blockading access routes into West Berlin. All food and fuel shipments were stopped; all train tracks, roads and canals were blocked by the Soviets. Rather than giving up on West Berlin as the Soviet leader Stalin had hoped, the USA, Britain and France agreed to airlift supplies into Berlin in June 1948. The airlift lasted for eleven months and by its final months almost 9000 tons arrived in West Berlin daily.

NATO 1949

The North Atlantic Treaty Organization (NATO) was formed in April 1949. It was a military alliance between countries across Western Europe and the USA and Canada. Greece and Turkey joined NATO in 1952 and West Germany became a member in 1955. The USSR saw NATO as a direct threat and formed its own military alliance with its allies in 1955, known as the Warsaw Pact.

COMECON

The USSR formed the Council for Mutual Economic Assistance (COMECON) in 1949 as a response to the USA's Marshall Plan. COMECON aimed to integrate the USSR and its satellite states economically in a free-trade zone. It did not prove to be successful, but did further highlight the growing division between East and West Europe.

Conclusion

The Cold War was a highly significant long-term effect of the Second World War. The tensions that emerged between communism and capitalism after 1945 spread around the world and resulted in more than 40 years of political and military rivalry.

IMPACT OF WAR ON DIFFERENT COUNTRIES

Consider how different countries were affected by the war. In the table below, bullet point information to evidence how countries were affected.

Think about the following factors:

- civilian and military casualties
- women
- territory
- the economy
- physical destruction
- decolonization
- political changes.

Country	How was it affected by war?
Germany	
Britain	
France	
USA	
Italy	
USSR	

Make sure you read Chapter 4 to see the full effects of war on the USA.

PRIORITIZING EFFECTS

Considering the evidence you have placed in the table above, rank the countries in terms of how significant the effects of war were on them. Write the name of each country in the diamond shape below, with the country you think was most affected at the top and least affected at the bottom.

CHAPTER 3 Exam focus

Sample question and answer

Review the response to the essay question below. Consider its strengths and limitations as you read through.

To what extent was the use of technology the key factor in the outcome of one 20th-century war?

Technological advances on air, land and sea undoubtedly played an important role in the Allied victory in the Second World War in Europe, 1939–45. The Allies utilized weapons effectively and developed new, crucial instruments, such as sonar, which helped them navigate to victory. However, the Axis powers also developed advanced technology during the war, yet still lost. This could have been because they did not utilize technological developments as well as the Allied powers. Nevertheless, while technology was important to the war's outcome, the more crucial factor in the Allied victory was the mobilization of human resources.

A clear thesis, or line of argument, has been identified.

There were many land battles over the course of the Second World War, with the offensives in eastern Europe in the years 1941–5 proving crucial to the Allies' victory. The Germans made important gains during Operation Barbarossa through the clever coordinated use of aircraft, tanks and artillery units. It initially appeared that Germany's technological advantage would force a Soviet surrender. While this operation was devastating for the USSR, it failed to decisively defeat the Soviets. The sheer numbers of the Soviet civilian and armed population proved too much for the Germans in the end. For example, the Battle of Stalingrad involved 2.5 million Soviet soldiers compared to 300,000 Axis troops. The Germans were not able to eliminate the Soviets and this battle marked the first major Axis defeat of the Second World War in Europe. The Soviets then continued to make territorial gains across the USSR and eastern Europe until Germany was eventually invaded in 1944. The Soviet victory against the Germans at Stalingrad is widely regarded as one of the key turning points of the war, and it was a victory through human mobilization, not technological advancement.

This opening sentence identifies a clear theme, but the line of argument is not clear.

Some good examples are chosen to evidence points.

The student returns to their thesis at the end of the paragraph.

The war in the air showcased advances in aerial technology on both sides, yet did not prove crucial in determining the overall outcome of the conflict. Both the Allied and Axis powers used the tactic of bombing civilian targets with larger bomber aircraft developed just before and during the conflict in the hope that it would lower civilian morale, yet in both instances there is little evidence that this was the case. In fact, it seemed to increase civilian morale. The Allies developed bomber aircraft which were used in raids across Germany, Romania and Italy. The accuracy of these bombers improved over the course of the war and they were incredibly destructive, destroying towns, factories, oilfields and homes. The destructive nature of this technology did not prove to be critical in determining the outcome of war, however. Germany quickly rebuilt factories or moved output areas; for example, in Hamburg a bombing campaign destroyed 600 factories, yet industrial output had recovered within two months. More important than technology was human resolve and mobilization.

A good point is made, but it lacks development.

The final sentence of this paragraph returns to the student's thesis but doesn't justify why this argument is correct.

Perhaps the strongest argument for technology being the key factor comes when considering naval warfare. During the Battle of the Atlantic, the Germans deciphered British codes and used submarines, organized into wolf packs, to attack Allied military and merchant ships. This initial technological advancement on the side of the Germans gave them the upper hand in the battle and added to the numerous early successes which the Axis powers had in the war. However, the Allies deployed anti-submarine technology, such as sonar and depth charges, which helped to take the advantage away from the Germans. In 1941, the British developed the technology to break the German Enigma code, giving them a huge advantage. Eventually, the Allied efforts proved victorious as Germany could not maintain the production of submarines necessary to sustain its efforts in the Atlantic. Its technological capacities were maxed out, whereas the Allies, supported by the USA from 1942, could keep going. While this is a strong argument, it does not conclusively show that technology was essential in the overall outcome of the Second World War. The Allied naval victory was important; it ensured supplies could continue to be transported and boosted morale, yet it did not signal a turning point in the war in the same way that the land battles in the USSR did. Therefore, the argument still remains stronger that human mobilization, as opposed to technology, was the key factor.

A strong argument has been constructed in this paragraph, using a range of relevant examples.

In conclusion, technology played an important role in the war, and had the Axis powers all been similar in strength to Germany then it is quite possible that their technological might would have been too much for the Allies. However, when comparing the Allied and Axis powers and considering where the decisive moments in the outcome of the war were, it cannot be argued that technology was more important than human mobilization. It was the sheer number and will of the Soviet troops that brought about victory against the Axis powers, and that was the key turning point of the war. The aerial campaigns failed to have much of an impact and the naval campaigns, while won by technology, were also not crucial in shifting the tide of war in the same way that the Soviets' victory was.

The conclusion brings the main points of the essay together and the student's viewpoint is clear.

A well-written response that demonstrates a clear line of argument and an effective thematic structure. A range of evidence is used to support points and much of this is analysed well. There is little awareness of historical perspectives, which would improve the essay, and at times points are left undeveloped. The conclusion argues consistently with the evidence presented throughout the essay.

Exam practice

Now either attempt the above essay question or try one of the following questions, with reference to the Second World War in Europe and north Africa.

1 The territorial effects of war are more significant than the economic ones. Discuss with reference to one 20th-century war.

2 Examine the short-term causes of two 20th-century wars, each from a different region.

3 Evaluate the political repercussions of one 20th-century war.

4 Second World War in Asia and the Pacific 1941–5

The Second World War was in fact two world conflicts that shared a similar timeframe, and some of the same warring participants. The Asia–Pacific theatre of war involved many nations, but the most significant were Japan, China and the USA. It began as a regional conflict in 1937, but escalated into a global war by the end of 1941 with the Japanese attack on **Pearl Harbor**, as the Empire of Japan and the USA became locked in total war with each other. Ultimately, Japan was defeated and its empire collapsed; China became independent once again, as a civil war resumed for its future; and the USA gained great influence in the Asia–Pacific region.

The long-term causes of the Second World War in Asia and the Pacific

Revised

Japan's growing imperial ideology

The Second World War in the Asia–Pacific region was largely a result of aggressive Japanese imperialism, which began in the late nineteenth century during the **Meiji period**. There were several reasons for growing Japanese imperial designs:

- Japan had followed a policy of relative isolationism for centuries. Then, in the mid-1850s, the USA, closely followed by other imperialist powers, forced Japan to open for trade based on **unequal treaties** that severely undermined Japanese sovereignty. Many leading figures in Japan vowed at this time to catch up and overtake the West by studying Westerners, and then using what they learnt to overcome them.
- The Meiji government quickly began to learn from the American and European colonizers. They sent a mission around the world from 1871 to 1873 to learn from the West, called the **Iwakura Mission**. One of the things that the Japanese government learnt on this mission was the importance of colonies to many of the Western powers. They resolved to join the imperial powers.
- Japan industrialized rapidly in the late nineteenth century using Western techniques, and built a modern army and navy in the process. The military grew in power and began to dominate the nation's government.
- Japan was the first Asian nation to go through a full-scale industrial revolution and build a modern military. The Japanese leadership was aware of the military advantages that this gave them over the other Asian nations.
- The islands that constituted Japan suffered from a lack of raw materials needed for modern industrial development, so the Meiji oligarchs felt that they needed to acquire colonies to meet Japan's growing industrial needs.
- Japanese **national exceptionalism**, which promoted militarism and racial superiority, permeated society and this further encouraged an aggressive foreign policy.

Timeline of Japanese imperial expansion 1895–1919

Date	Event
1895	Japan defeated China in the First Sino-Japanese War and annexed Formosa (today's Taiwan)
1905	Japan defeated Russia in the Russo-Japanese War and gained Port Arthur and the South Manchurian Railway, which were both in China, but had been controlled by Russia
1910	Korea was annexed by Japan
1914	As one of the Allies in the First World War, Japan took the German naval base in China at Kiaochow (today's Jiaozhou)
1919	As a result of the post-First World War peace treaties, Japan was rewarded with the South Sea Mandate that gave it control of large numbers of islands in the Pacific Ocean, which had formerly been part of the German Empire

THE CHRONOLOGY OF LONG-TERM JAPANESE IMPERIALISM

Sort the following events into chronological order and create a timeline in the box below. Then, next to each event, explain why you think it was significant in helping to fuel Japan's ever-increasing imperial designs.

- Iwakura Mission.
- Japan defeated China in the First Sino-Japanese War and annexed Formosa.
- Japan was forced to accept the unequal treaties by the Western powers.
- Korea was annexed by Japan.
- Japan defeated Russia in the Russo-Japanese War and gained Port Arthur and the South Manchurian Railway.
- Japan industrialized rapidly.
- As a result of the post-First World War peace treaties, Japan was rewarded with the South Sea Mandate.
- As one of the Allies in the First World War, Japan took the German naval base in China at Kiaochow.

WHY DID THE JAPANESE EMPIRE GROW UNCHECKED IN THE SECOND HALF OF THE NINETEENTH AND EARLY TWENTIETH CENTURIES?

For each statement below, explain whether you agree or disagree with it, and why.

Statement	Agree or disagree?
As Japan won more wars and territory, its desire to acquire more territory only increased	
National exceptionalism is an ideology which can encourage imperialism	
Japanese economic and military advances played little part in encouraging their imperialism	

Increasing Japanese imperial designs and the Manchurian Crisis 1931–2

In September 1931, Japan staged a **false flag** event, termed the Mukden Incident. Japanese soldiers detonated a small bomb near the South Manchurian Railway line and blamed it on the Chinese army. Within the next few months Japan had seized the entire Chinese province of Manchuria, establishing the **puppet-state** of Manchukuo in 1932. There were several reasons why the Japanese military annexed this Chinese province, further extending Japan's empire:

- Japan had faced serious economic decline and social strife as a result of the worldwide economic crisis, known as the Great Depression, which was triggered by the 1929 Wall Street Crash in the USA.
- Manchuria was enormous, underpopulated and rich in resources. Japan had a rapidly growing population who could be resettled there.
- Manchuria was poorly defended and Japan already had a strong military presence in the region guarding the South Manchurian Railway. China at this point was divided and relatively weak compared to Japan, as a civil war was raging between the Nationalists and the **Chinese Communist Party (CCP)**, which distracted China from meeting the Japanese threat.
- Japan felt that in the troubles of the Great Depression the international community was unlikely to oppose its actions.

Japan were correct in this last assumption: China's protests to the League of Nations led to only a minor reprimand of Japan, as the idea of **collective security** was found wanting. The USA, not a member of the League and suffering greatly from the Great Depression, also stood by and did nothing of substance, as it followed a policy of isolationism. Japan withdrew from the League, and proceeded to colonize most of northern China by 1935.

Second Sino-Japanese War 1937–45

In July 1937, the Japanese military used Manchuria as a base and launched a full-scale invasion of China, ostensibly to gain natural resources and food. The Nationalists and the CCP formed the Second United Front and met the Japanese military in battle. However, the Japanese forces proved too strong and achieved many successes:

- In November 1937, Shanghai, China's largest city, fell.
- In December 1937, Nanjing, the capital of China, was captured. This city was now the scene of the **Rape of Nanjing**, which saw approximately 300,000 Chinese civilians intentionally killed after the city fell, and tens of thousands of Chinese women raped. These atrocities alarmed many countries.
- China appealed to the League of Nations again in 1937, but barely received a response. Britain and France were occupied with the growing Nazi threat in Europe and did not have the capacity to intervene in Asia.
- The Chinese Nationalist forces retreated to the city of Chongqing, which they made their capital. Here, they were being supplied through French Indochina. However, the Japanese forces successfully invaded these French-held territories in September 1940, cutting off the supply lines to Chongqing.
- By the end of 1940, most of eastern China had fallen. Japan set up a puppet government to rule the parts of China they had conquered, and consolidated their hold on the major eastern cities of China and along the railway lines that connected them.

Japan was now the **hegemonic power** of the Asia–Pacific region. This was a meteoric rise for a previously isolated set of islands that had been largely insignificant in geopolitics just half a century earlier. The only other big power left in the region now was the USA, which held several strategically important territories, most notably the Philippines and the Hawaiian Islands.

WHY WAS JAPAN ABLE TO ESTABLISH SUCH A VAST EMPIRE IN THE ASIA–PACIFIC REGION?

Read the extract below from historian Jonathan Fenby's account of why Japan was victorious over China in the First Sino-Japanese War. According to Fenby, why was Japan victorious? Highlight the key arguments that he makes in this extract.

SOURCE 1

Extract from Jonathan Fenby, *Modern China: The Fall and Rise of a Great Power, 1850 to the Present*, HarperCollins, New York, 2008, page 81.

In 1894, one of the great international conflict lines of modern times opened up between China and Japan. '999 out of every 1000 Chinese are sure big China can thrash little Japan,' wrote Robert Hall. On paper, China had just over a million men at arms to throw into the war – 325,000 of them Banner troops, about the same number of 'Green Standard' Han soldiers, plus 400,000 other men said to have undergone training. The real numbers fell some way below these totals, however, and some elite Manchu forces still prided themselves in their expertise with bows and arrows rather than guns. Japan's 270,000 troops were well trained and had modern arms. Tokyo had also broken China's military cable codes. Qing armies were split between regional and princely chiefs; Japan's were unified. On the other hand, Japanese commanders were given clear objectives and left to get on with the job in pincer attacks which flummoxed the Chinese. On the sea, this war provided the first test for the navy of thirty warships which Li had built up with purchases from Europe, despite the depredations of members of his family, who had pocketed the money allocated for explosives and packed shell casings with sand. Two days after the Japanese took Pyongyang, they won a six-hour naval battle at the mouth of the Yalu river on the Korean border. China lost four ships.

COMPLETE THE BODY PARAGRAPH

Below is a sample Paper 2 question.

Write a body paragraph on the long-term territorial causes of the Second World War in Asia and the Pacific, following from the opening sentence which has already been written.

Examine the causes of one 20th-century war.

The Second World War in Asia and the Pacific was caused by a number of long-term factors, one of the most significant being the aggressive territorial expansion of Japan, which threatened US interests in the Asia-Pacific region.

The short-term causes of the Second World War in Asia and the Pacific

Revised

The USA challenges Japan

The USA was increasingly concerned with Japan's growing empire and decided to respond with aggressive trade embargos aimed at weakening the Japanese military. The USA did not want to see further Japanese expansion that would endanger their territories throughout the region, such as the Philippines, which had US naval and army bases, as well as airfields. The USA took the following steps to challenge Japan:

- US President Franklin D. Roosevelt was limited by Neutrality Acts that prevented American intervention in wars unless it was itself directly attacked, but these were repealed in March 1941.
- They were replaced by the Lend–Lease programme that allowed the USA to openly sell military goods to nations that were at war with Germany, Italy or Japan.
- US oil exports to Japan were also banned. This was an especially damaging blow to Japan, as its military and industry were almost entirely dependent on US oil.

Japan plans to attack the USA

Given these tough US sanctions, Japan calculated that it would have only two years of oil reserves for its military operations left. Japan decided to try to take control of the oilfields in the Dutch East Indies (present-day Indonesia) to guarantee a permanent supply. This was a strategy that Japan knew the USA would resist, as the US-controlled Philippines were located on the route between Japan and the Dutch East Indies. Therefore, Japan prepared **pre-emptive strikes** on strategic US positions in the Pacific. The Japanese military calculated that if its attacks were on a large enough scale, the USA would not have the desire, or the capacity, to strike back. Japanese plans were as follows:

- Assault many of the major US-held territories in the region. These included the Hawaiian Islands, which held a major US naval base and multiple airfields at Pearl Harbor, where its Pacific fleet of warships was stationed. Guam and the Wake Islands, which held US airbases, were also to be attacked.
- Attack and conquer British territories, such as Hong Kong and Singapore.
- Launch these attacks simultaneously to prevent a quick US counterattack.
- Invade the Dutch East Indies and take the oilfields.
- Fortify their defences in the Dutch East Indies so that if the USA did decide to retaliate, which the Japanese military calculated would take about a year, as they had to rebuild their naval fleet, Japan would be ready.

Japan attacks, starting the Second World War in Asia and the Pacific

On 7 December 1941 (8 December in Asia), the Empire of Japan attacked the military installations of the USA, Britain and other nations throughout the Asia–Pacific region. The assault on Pearl Harbor was devastating as it:

- damaged four battleships and sank four others
- damaged or sank three cruisers, three destroyers and two other naval vessels
- destroyed 188 aircraft
- killed over 2400 people and injured 1200 others.

This was the culmination of Japanese foreign policy that began in the late nineteenth century. The USA did not back down as Japan had hoped, but in fact declared war on Japan a day after the attack on Pearl Harbor, starting the Second World War in Asia and the Pacific.

MULTICAUSAL EXPLANATIONS OF THE SECOND WORLD WAR IN ASIA AND THE PACIFIC

Use the information on the preceding pages to add examples to the right-hand column for each of the causal themes for the Second World War in Asia and the Pacific.

Causal theme	Examples to support this causal theme
Economic	
Political	
Ideological	
Territorial	
Other causes	

WHAT WERE THE MOST SIGNIFICANT CAUSES OF THE SECOND WORLD WAR IN ASIA AND THE PACIFIC?

Use the information on the preceding pages and your completed table above to decide on the most important causes of the Second World War in Asia and the Pacific. Write the causes in the box below. Place the more important causes higher up on the arrow. Include all of the causal themes from the table above: economic, political, ideological, territorial and any other causes you think are important. Add explanations next to the cause to explain why you placed it where you did in the box.

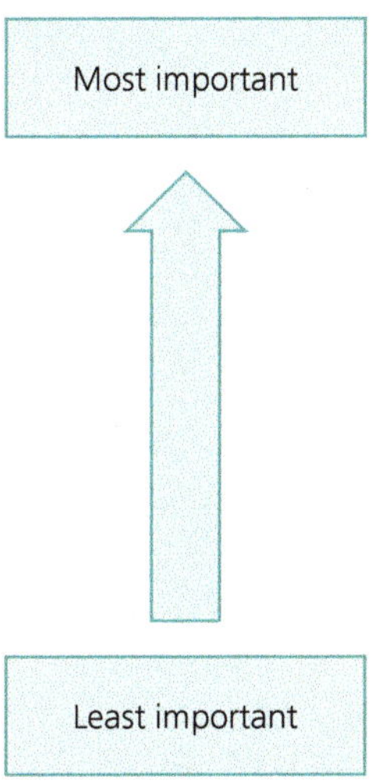

The course of the Second World War in Asia and the Pacific 1941–5

Revised

Japan in the ascendancy 1941

Japan attacked various targets in December 1941 and enjoyed huge military success. By May 1942, Japan occupied much of east Asia, bringing hundreds of millions of people under their rule. They called their empire the **Greater Asia Co-prosperity Sphere**. Puppet governments were created to rule over the conquered territories.

The table below contains details of the most significant Japanese victories:

Date	Territory	Significant details
Dec. 1941–May 1942	Philippines	• The largest US-held territory in Asia • The capture of the Philippines was one the biggest defeats in US history in terms of troop losses, with over 25,000 soldiers killed, 21,000 wounded and 100,000 captured • Japanese losses were 9000 dead and just over 13,000 wounded
8–23 Dec. 1941	Guam and Wake Island	• Guam was a junction for undersea cables linking the USA and the Philippines, so its capture by Japan disrupted US communications • Wake Island was of strategic importance, and its fall gave Japanese aircraft control over a large area of the Pacific Ocean
Dec. 1941–Feb. 1942	Malaya (present-day Malaysia) and Singapore	• Malaya was quickly overrun and, with the fall of Singapore, 80,000 British troops were captured by Japan, with 5000 killed • Japan lost fewer than 2000 men • British warships *HMS Prince of Wales* and *HMS Repulse* had been destroyed by Japanese aircraft, which showed that without protection from aircraft, traditional battleships were easy targets • Japan now controlled the Indian Ocean
Dec. 1941–May 1942	Burma (also known as Myanmar)	• British forces were pushed out of Burma by a rapid Japanese invasion, and they fled into eastern India • Japan now controlled Burmese oilfields and their vast areas of rice paddies
Dec. 1941–Feb. 1942	Dutch East Indies, New Guinea and Rabaul	• All of these islands fell in a couple of months following aerial attacks and ground invasions • Japan now gained access to the oilfields of the Dutch East Indies • In Rabaul, Japan built a naval and air base for over 100,000 troops

This map below shows Japanese military conquests from December 1941 to May 1942.

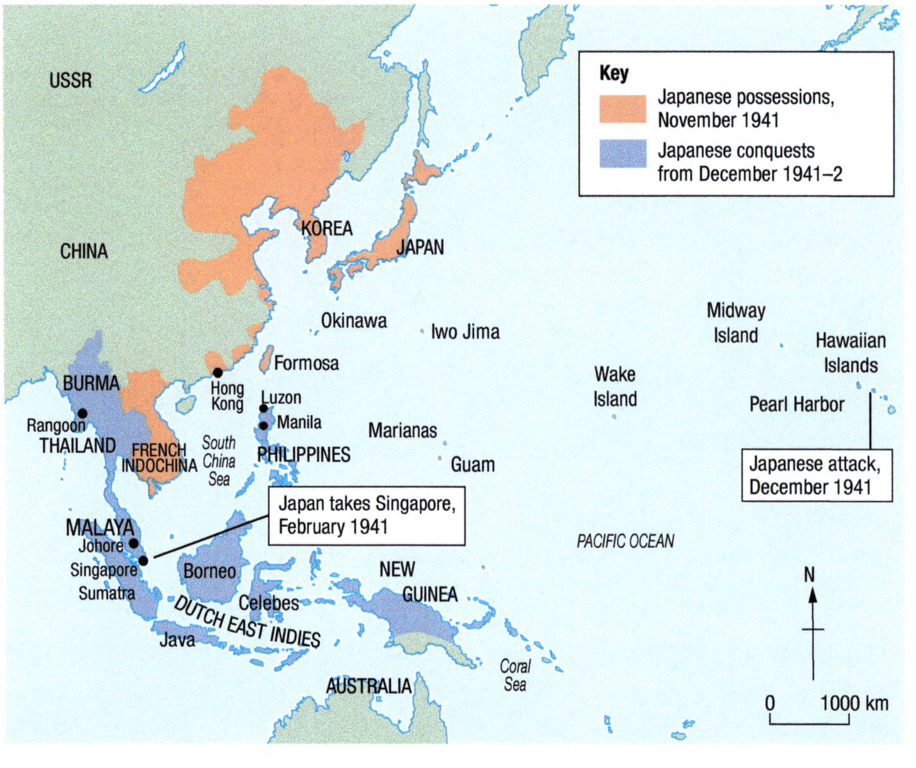

JAPAN IN THE ASCENDANCY 1941: WHY WERE ITS VICTORIES SIGNIFICANT?

Below on the left are the most significant territories conquered by Japan, and on the right are reasons why each victory was significant.

Match the territory to the explanation as to why the victory was significant.

Territory conquered by Japan	Why was this victory significant?
Philippines	Gave Japan access to oilfields and large areas of rice paddies to help feed its armies
Guam	This was the largest US-held colony in Asia, and its defeat was one of the largest in the country's history
Wake Island	Its capture by Japan disrupted US communications as it was a junction for undersea cables
Malaya	Gave Japanese aircraft control over a large area of the Pacific Ocean
Singapore	Resulted in Japanese control of the Indian Ocean, and the capturing of 80,000 British troops
Burma	It gave Japan access to Singapore
Dutch East Indies	Japan built a massive naval and air base on this territory for over 100,000 troops
Rabaul	Japan gained access to huge oilfields, which it needed to fuel transport, industry and the military

The USA fights back successfully and turns the course of the war 1942

In the second half of 1942, the USA turned the tide of the war against Japan in three major battles. By the end of these battles, the USA was in the ascendancy, thanks in large measure to its successful **code-breaking** efforts. Japan's capacity to hold on to the vast tracts of land it had gained was fatally undermined, and it would not be able to recover from these three major losses.

Battle of the Coral Sea, 4–8 May 1942

Japan wanted to capture Port Moresby, New Guinea, to gain control of the sea around northern Australia, allowing it to launch sustained attacks on Australian targets. However, Japan was defeated. The battle proceeded as follows:

- The USA had managed to decode the Japanese naval signals and was aware of their invasion plan, and that Japan had three aircraft carriers in their attack fleet. Crucially, they also knew where these carriers were in the seas.
- In preparation for the Japanese attack, the USA moved two of their carriers, and supporting ships, into the region.
- Japan was not aware of such a strong US presence in the region. Japan lost one carrier and two were badly damaged, which delayed their invasion of Port Moresby.
- Australian troops secured the port, preventing an invasion of Australia for the rest of the war.

Battle of Midway, 4–7 June 1942

The strategically important US base called Midway **Atoll** was about 2100 km (1300 miles) from Pearl Harbor. The **Imperial Japanese Navy (IJN)** planned to occupy Midway and lure the US fleet from Pearl Harbor, where it was now well protected by aircraft. The battle proceeded as follows:

- US code breakers had deciphered Japanese cyphers and were aware of the IJN's movements. US forces moved to intercept the IJN before it could establish its own aircraft at Midway.
- Aircraft from the four Japanese carriers attacked Midway Atoll and the US carrier *Yorktown*, but the Japanese military did not realize that there were two other US carriers in the region.
- Aircraft from all three US carriers and Midway Atoll's airfield inflicted huge damage on the IJN. Japan lost all four of its carriers, 240 aircraft, a cruiser and 3000 men.
- The USA's losses were lighter: one carrier, 150 aircraft, a destroyer and 300 men.

For many reasons, the Battle of Midway is seen by historians as a turning point in the war in the Pacific:

- It was the first major victory that the US navy achieved against the IJN.
- The battle left Japan with only six carriers in the Pacific and it lacked the industrial capacity and resources to rebuild the lost ships quickly enough.
- Japan's loss of highly trained military personnel with great expertise, such as pilots, mechanics and carrier crews, significantly hindered their war effort.
- The carrier losses prevented Japan from launching any major new attacks on US forces for months, which allowed the USA to begin its own offensive operations, notably at Guadalcanal two months after the Battle of Midway.

Battles at Guadalcanal, 7 August 1942 to February 1943

Guadalcanal was a strategically important island in the Solomon Islands. A series of hard-fought battles was held on and around the island in the air, on the land and at sea. The Battles at Guadalcanal are seen as a significant turning point in the war by historians for several reasons:

- This was the first time in the war that Japan was defeated on land, in the air and at sea.
- Japan lost three carriers, 38 ships, 88 aircraft and 31,000 troops. Japan did not have the industrial capacity to replace these losses quickly enough to challenge growing US power.
- The USA suffered losses, but it had the industrial capacity to rebuild, and actually was able to increase its pace of shipbuilding at this point in the war.
- The USA's capturing of Guadalcanal meant that Australia and New Zealand could be more easily supplied by US ships, preventing their invasion.

HOW DID THE USA AND ITS ALLIES TURN THE COURSE OF THE WAR IN 1942, AND WHY WERE THEIR VICTORIES OVER JAPAN SIGNIFICANT?

Complete the table below using the information on the page opposite and your own knowledge.

Battle	How did the USA and its allies defeat Japan?	Why was the outcome of this battle significant in determining the course of the war?
Battle of the Coral Sea		
Battle of Midway		
Battles at Guadalcanal		

WHY DID THE USA AND ITS ALLIES DEFEAT JAPAN IN THE KEY BATTLES OF 1942?

For each statement below, explain whether you agree or disagree with it, and why.

Statement	Agree or disagree?
Code breaking played a vital role in deciding the outcome of the key battles of 1942	
The Battle of Midway was more significant than the Battle of the Coral Sea	
Japan had the industrial capacity to replace the elements of their navy that they had lost, such as several carriers, so the IJN was not too concerned by its defeats in 1942	

The USA and its allies defeat Japan 1943–5

US naval and air superiority was confirmed by early 1943, and the USA was now faced with the difficult task of conquering the territories that Japan had occupied. Japanese troops were fiercely committed to fighting almost to the last man to defend the territory that they had won. The USA discovered this during the land battles for Guadalcanal. The USA had expected the isolated Japanese troops to surrender, but instead needed to land 60,000 troops and fight for half a year to take the island. As such, they developed a new strategy called island hopping to minimize US casualties.

Island hopping involved the US military avoiding direct attacks on major Japanese fortified islands, such as Rabaul. Instead, it would bypass them and capture less well-defended surrounding islands, on which they would build airfields. The US air force would then destroy any ships sent to resupply the fortified islands. The US military aimed to steadily move closer and closer to Japan, which would allow it to get bombers in range of the Japanese home islands, which would then be bombed into surrender. It was hoped that this would avoid the need to invade Japan.

The table below details the major US victories in the war in the Pacific between late 1943 and 1945.

Date	Territory	Significant details
20–23 Nov. 1943	Tarawa	• Tarawa Atoll housed an important airfield, and was attacked by the largest US fleet assembled, with 17 carriers, 12 battleships and 35,000 troops • The USA was opposed by 5000 Japanese and Korean people, of whom about half were construction workers. Only 17 Japanese soldiers surrendered and the rest died fighting. The USA lost 1700 men • The Japanese commitment to fight almost to the last man made the US military wonder what would happen when they reached the Japanese home islands. This hardened the prevailing attitude in the US military that Japan needed to be bombed into surrendering
31 Jan.–20 Feb. 1944	Marshall Islands and Truk	• The Marshall Islands were part of the Japanese home islands' outer defences, and the USA needed to take them in order to get to Saipan, which was an island within bombing range of Japan • The battle for Kwajalein Atoll saw 7780 Japanese deaths and 100 captured, and at Eniwetok Atoll 2677 died and 16 surrendered • Truk was a major Japanese naval and air base, which the USA decided it did not need to hold as part of its island-hopping strategy, but it did need to neutralize. The USA successfully did this, as they destroyed 15 Japanese warships and 270 aircraft
15 June–9 July 1944	Saipan	• In taking Saipan, the USA lost almost 3500 troops, but Japan lost 24,000 in the fighting and 5000 through suicide • In October 1944, 100 B-29 US bombers attacked Tokyo, Japan's capital, flying from Saipan. This was the first of many aerial raids
19 June–15 Aug. 1944	Philippines	• The USA decided to invade the Philippines as they supplied rubber for Japanese industry, and they were on the shipping route for oil tankers travelling from the Dutch East Indies • Japan lost 330,000 troops, and the USA and its allies 14,000
1 April–21 June 1945	Okinawa	• Okinawa, an island that is part of Japan, but south of the main islands, was within bombing range of most Japanese cities, so a key US target • As in other campaigns in the Pacific, most Japanese troops fought to the death, as they felt it was better to die with honour than surrender. 95,000 Japanese soldiers died, and 7000 US troops were lost • ***Kamikaze*** attacks destroyed around 30 vessels and damaged 370 others, killing a further 5000 US troops • US military command felt that if Japan defended its main populated islands with the same will to fight to the death as they had on the uninhabited Okinawa, then invading would cost huge US casualties

WHY DID THE US STRATEGY OF ISLAND HOPPING DEVELOP AS IT DID?

Below on the left are significant territories conquered by the USA, and on the right reasons why each territory was taken.

Match the territory to the explanation as to why the USA needed that land.

Territory conquered by the USA	Why was this territory needed by the USA?
Tarawa	This territory was part of the Japanese home islands' outer defences, and the USA needed to take them to get to Saipan
Marshall Islands	This atoll was home to an important airfield
Truk	This island was within bombing range of the Japanese home islands
Saipan	The USA wanted to neutralize the Japanese military presence on this island, but it did not need to conquer it as part of its island-hopping strategy
Philippines	This territory was within bombing range of most Japanese cities
Okinawa	These islands gave Japan access to raw materials, such as rubber, and they were on a key shipping route for oil tankers

WHY WAS ISLAND HOPPING AN EFFECTIVE STRATEGY FOR THE USA TO ADOPT?

Read the following statements about the strategy of island hopping, and decide if they are true or false:

Statement	True or false?
Allowed the US army to minimize its casualties	
Helped US bombers to get in range of the Japanese home islands as quickly as possible	
Led to increased US casualties	
Avoided direct US attacks on major Japanese fortified islands	
Did not contribute to the USA's ultimate victory in the war	
Was decided on due to the Japanese army's tenacity in defending its empire	
The eventual plan was to bomb the Japanese home islands into surrender	

Atomic bombs and the Japanese surrender, 6–9 August 1945

As a result of the **Manhattan Project**, the USA had nuclear bombs at its disposal. It decided to use them for several reasons:

- The Japanese government was refusing to make an unconditional surrender, so it was thought that a dramatic show of force might make it submit.
- Japanese troops had shown a willingness to fight to the death, including suicidal *kamikaze* attacks, to defend various Pacific islands. The belief in the US military was that they would defend their homeland with the same tenacity.
- An invasion of Japan would be terribly costly in terms of US lives.

Hiroshima, 6 August 1945

A US B-29 bomber dropped a 13-kiloton nuclear bomb on Hiroshima, which completely destroyed twelve square kilometres (five square miles) of the city. Around 80,000 people died instantly and 70,000 were injured. The death toll continued to rise in the following months and years due to **radiation sickness**, and estimates of the total dead range up to 166,000 people. Japan still refused to surrender unconditionally.

Nagasaki, 9 August 1945

The city of Kokura was originally chosen for the second atomic bomb, but cloud cover on 9 August made it unfeasible as a target, so Nagasaki was bombed. The 21-kiloton bomb killed between 40,000 and 75,000 people instantly, and thousands more in the months and years that followed. Japan surrendered later that day to the USA, with only one condition: **Hirohito** was to remain as emperor.

The practices of the Second World War in Asia and the Pacific and their impact on its outcome

Revised

War production

Superior US production was perhaps the crucial factor in the USA's ultimate success against Japan. US production was so great that Japan would not have been able to match it, even if it did have access to unlimited raw materials. Japan did produce large quantities of aircraft and ships, but not on the scale of the USA, and it lagged behind in terms of raw materials. This can be seen in the table below:

Production and raw materials between 1941 and 1945	Japan	USA
Aircraft (all types)	76,000	300,000
Aircraft carriers (all types)	16	163
All other warships	241	1,028
Trucks	165,000	2,400,000
Tanks	2,500	88,500
Atomic bombs	0	3
Coal (tonnes)	185,000,000	2,100,000,000
Iron ore (tonnes)	21,000,000	400,000,000
Petroleum (tonnes)	5,000,000	830,000,000

There are several reasons for this great disparity in terms of war production:

- The Japanese homelands lacked raw materials, and even when Japan gained access to them as they expanded their empire, these materials often had to be sent over huge distances on ships that were vulnerable to attack.
- The USA had been the world's most industrialized country for decades before 1941, and had access to vast amounts of raw materials, so did not need to rely on imports. For example, it was the world's largest producer of petroleum.
- The USA produced 32.3% of the world's manufactures in 1941, and Japan 3.5%.
- In Japan, the government did not fully utilize the labour at its disposal. For example, women were discouraged from work even though factories needed workers.
- The USA had begun organizing its population with the **Victory Programme** before Pearl Harbor. It employed millions of women to produce war goods. By 1945, it had over 66,000,000 men and women working in the war industry. As a result, US production was on an unprecedented scale as it increased its production each month throughout the war.

WHY WAS US SUPERIOR WAR PRODUCTION SUCH A SIGNIFICANT FACTOR IN DECIDING THE OUTCOME OF THE WAR?

Read the following source on the reasons for Japan's defeat in the Second World War, and then answer the questions below.

SOURCE 2

Extract from Bernard C. Nalty (editor), *War in the Pacific: Pearl Harbor to Tokyo Bay*, Salamander Books, London, 1991, page 291.

Japan's industrial infrastructure proved too fragile to sustain modern warfare. Stockpiles, especially of oil, could be replenished only through conquest, and the very act of conquering drew upon these reserves. Handicapped by industries that produced just 3.5 percent of the world's manufactures, compared to 32.2 percent for the United States, plagued by shortages of essential materials, the Japanese had no strategy, a shortcoming masked by tactical successes like the devastation … at Pearl Harbor and the conquest of Malaya. Instead of clearly defining a strategic objective and marshaling the resources needed to achieve it, Japan devoutly believed that the warrior spirit would prevail, that Americans lacked courage and resolve and would accept a negotiated settlement leaving the Japanese in control of Asia and the western Pacific.

1 List the reasons that this source gives for Japan's defeat in the Second World War.

2 According to this source, what was the most significant reason why Japan lost the war?

BODY PARAGRAPH

Use the information on the preceding pages to write a body paragraph in response to the following IB-style question.

Evaluate the importance of the mobilization of economic resources in deciding the outcome of one 20th-century war.

Technological developments

Code breaking

Code breaking was a vital aspect of the war in the Pacific, as both the Japanese and US armies relied on secret codes to send commands and reports. If a code was figured out by **cryptanalysts**, then the other side would know what the enemy was planning and could counter effectively. The USA used the **Native American** language of the **Navajo**, which the Japanese army could not understand. Conversely, the USA was successful at breaking Japanese codes, and this played an important role in their winning major battles. They broke two major codes that each had a significant impact in the outcome of the war:

- JN-25: the main Japanese code for its naval fleet was labelled JN-25 by the US military, and had been broken by US cryptanalysts in May 1942. This meant that the USA was aware of the move by the IJN to capture Midway. As a result, the USA was able to destroy four vital Japanese carriers and decisively turn the course of the war in its favour at the Battle of Midway.
- JN-40: this was a code used by Japanese merchant ships that supplied Japan and its military forces, and it was cracked in November 1942, which allowed the USA to use its submarines to hinder Japan's capacity to move supplies, weapons and troops. This meant that the resource-poor Japanese home islands were slowly being starved of supplies, making the war effort ever more challenging for them.

Aircraft carriers

Aircraft carriers were floating, armed airfields and were the most valuable and important warships of the Second World War in the Pacific Ocean. Aircraft launched from these carriers could travel hundreds of kilometres to attack targets. Japan managed to build sixteen **fleet carriers** during the war, while the USA managed to construct over 160, which was a key reason for the USA's ultimate victory. Examples of Japanese and US fleet carriers are listed in the table below:

Name	Nation	Defensive guns	Range	Number of aircraft
Akagi	Japan	26	19,000 km (11,875 miles)	60
Enterprise	USA	94	23,150 km (14,470 miles)	90

Submarines

Submarines used torpedoes to destroy enemy shipping and had a significant impact on the war. By 1945, US submarines had crippled the Japanese merchant fleet to the point that it could no longer provide the homelands with food or raw materials. US submarines were also responsible for destroying eight Japanese carriers. The USA managed to make more effective use of submarines than Japan for several reasons:

- US code breakers had decrypted Japanese codes, so they knew where Japanese targets were.
- Japan failed to break the major US codes, so they could not significantly affect the US navy's ability to conduct the war, although they did destroy two US carriers.
- The USA could produce more submarines. By 1944, it had over 150 submarines hunting Japanese merchant ships.

HOW SIGNIFICANT WERE TECHNOLOGICAL DEVELOPMENTS IN DECIDING THE OUTCOME OF THE WAR?

Read the following source on the role of submarines in the Second World War, and then answer the questions below.

SOURCE 3

Extract from Alan J. Levine, *The Pacific War: Japan Versus the Allies*, Praeger, Westport, CT, 1995, pages 86–7.

In 1944 the submarine war reached a climax. There were fierce battles against convoys. In February, Jack sank four out of five tankers on a single convoy in the South China Sea. In June and July, Tang achieved a record, exceeded once later in the war, of 10 ships sunk in a single patrol. From February to May, the submarines wreaked great destruction on convoys carrying troops to the Marianas and New Guinea. The submarines were numerous enough to carry on the war against the convoys while strongly supporting the fleet; they sank two of the three enemy carriers destroyed in the Battle of the Philippine Sea in June. Submarines also carried supplies to the Filipino guerrillas … Submarines increasingly operated from advanced bases, especially at Guam and the Admiralty Islands, while the American advance across the Pacific crowded Japan's shipping toward the coast of Asia. By the summer of 1944, they were shutting down many shipping routes.

3 List the reasons that you can infer from this source as to why submarine warfare was important in the US campaign against Japan.

4 Why do you think Japan was not able to successfully counter these submarine attacks by this point in the war?

WHAT WAS THE MOST SIGNIFICANT TECHNOLOGICAL DEVELOPMENT IN THE SECOND WORLD WAR IN ASIA AND THE PACIFIC?

Rank the following technological developments depending on which you think was most significant in deciding the outcome of the war:

- code breaking
- aircraft carriers
- submarines.

Number 1 is the most significant, 3 is the least significant. Explain your reasoning in the space provided.

1

2

3

The effects of the Second World War in Asia and the Pacific

Revised

Political impact of the war

Occupied Japan

On 2 September 1945, US troops started to land in Japan to oversee the peace process. The USA wrote a new constitution for Japan in 1946, which was to be put into effect in 1947 by a new US-approved Japanese government. Most accounts comment that the majority of Japanese citizens were happy with the constitution, and it is followed to this day. The constitution stipulated the following provisions:

- a parliamentary system of government
- democratic elections with the franchise extended to men and women
- freedom of religion, speech, press and political association
- discrimination on the basis of gender, race, social status or family origin outlawed
- the emperor was to be head of state, but with no practical power
- Japan was banned from going to war under Article 9, and from maintaining land, sea or air forces.

The first general election under the new constitution took place on 10 April 1946. It was peaceful, and voter turnout was 72.1%. It was a victory for the Liberal Party. The US occupation ended in 1952 as Japan was stable, and the country continues to function as a liberal democracy to this day.

China

There was a power vacuum in China when Japan was defeated, which the Nationalists and the CCP quickly worked to fill (see Chapter 5). Both sides tried to gain control of as much territory as possible, and the Chinese Civil War resumed. The Second World War in Asia and the Pacific did not give a decisive advantage to either side and the fate of China was to be decided from 1945 to 1949. Yet, there were several notable effects of the Second World War on the subsequent civil war, which gave advantages to the CCP, the side that went on to win the civil war:

- The Soviet Union had taken over Manchuria, and gave the CCP access to Japanese arms depots, such as one at Shenyang which contained over 100,000 guns and artillery pieces.
- The Soviets transferred 200,000 Chinese troops from the Manchukuo regime who had surrendered to the Soviets over to the CCP, and stopped Nationalist troops from entering some of the key cities in Manchuria.
- The Nationalists' initial reluctance to fight Japan was highlighted by CCP propaganda, and led to a loss of popular support for the Nationalists.
- The major Nationalist cities were taken by Japan, and the Nationalist had been forced to retreat to Chongqing to set up a new capital. Here, they had little support and relied on coercion.
- The CCP derived its strength from rural areas, which Japan was not concerned with occupying. The Communists maintained their loyal rural support throughout the war with Japan.

The Cold War

The defeat of Japan left a power vacuum in much of Asia. The two superpowers – the USA and the Soviet Union – competed for influence and tried to promote their political and economic systems in Asia to fill this power vacuum. A clear example of this was Korea, which was annexed by Japan in 1910, but nominally became independent in 1945. The Cold War crisis developed as follows:

- The United Nations (UN) divided the peninsula along the **38th Parallel** into northern and southern zones. The north was to be administered by the Soviet Union, and the south by the USA.
- The Soviets set up a communist government in the north, while the US oversaw the implementation of democratic institutions and capitalism in the south. Both governments claimed to be the legitimate ruler of the whole Korean peninsula.
- In 1950, after several border disputes, the north invaded the south, sparking a bitter civil war. China was involved, heavily supporting the northern war effort, and the UN supported the south, although it was effectively a US-led operation.

- The fighting ended in a stalemate in 1953 with millions of Koreans dead and the peninsula divided almost exactly as it had been before the conflict, with a demilitarized zone separating the two sides. The north was still communist and the south a democratic, capitalist state.

THE POLITICAL IMPACT OF THE WAR

Read the following source on the results of the Soviet Union's invasion of Manchuria, and then answer the questions below.

SOURCE 4

Extract from Jonathan Fenby, *Modern China: The Fall and Rise of a Great Power, 1850 to the Present*, HarperCollins, New York, 2008, pages 327–8.

Two days before Hirohito surrendered, the Communists [CCP] rejected an instruction from [Chinese President General Chiang Kai-Shek, leader of the Nationalists] for their forces not to advance into territory formerly held by the [Japanese] invaders. Instead, they sent in troops to link up with the Soviets, and brought back units that had been sheltering in Siberia. The new invaders handed them 100,000 guns from Japanese stores, and 200,000 Manchukuo troops were recruited.

5 What were the results of the Soviet Union's invasion of Manchuria?

____

____

____

6 How did this affect the Civil War in China between the CCP and the Nationalists, and the subsequent politics of the country?

____

____

____

SPIDER DIAGRAM ON THE POLITICAL IMPACT OF THE WAR

Using the information on the preceding page and your own knowledge, complete the spider diagram below, noting down the main political impacts of the war under the headings.

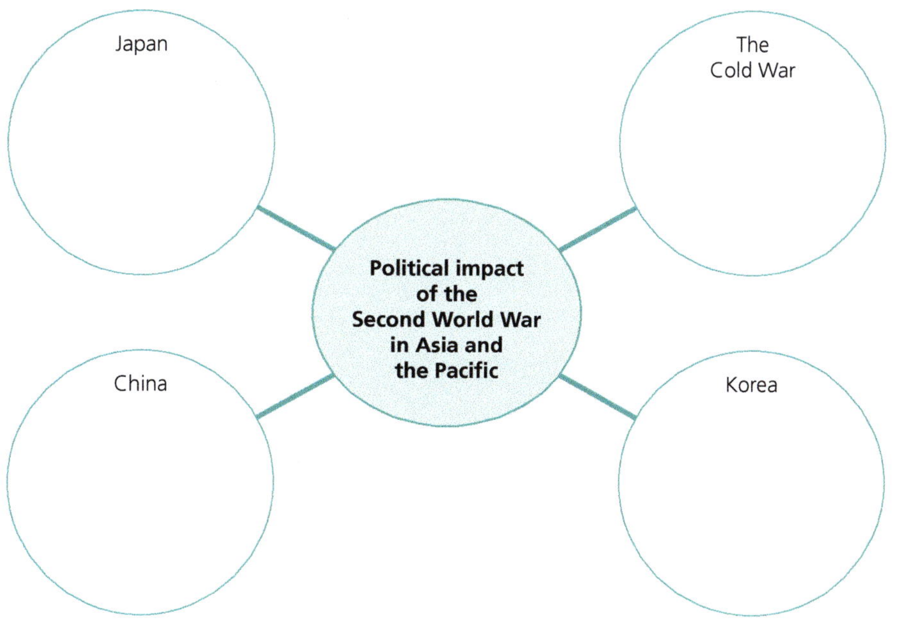

Geopolitical impact of the war

Decolonization

The **Atlantic Charter** was signed by the USA, Britain and their Allies during the Second World War. Japan had lost a vast empire, and the charter stated that all people now had the right to self-determination. It was quoted by people in Asia who wanted to see their nations free from colonial rule now that Japan had been defeated. The Allies found it difficult to grant self-determination and end their own imperial ambitions for several reasons:

- Colonies, such as Singapore, Hong Kong and the Dutch East Indies, were of economic value.
- Loss of empire equated to a loss of prestige and geopolitical influence.
- The Cold War (see page 112) that was developing between the Soviet Union and the USA in order to determine who was the dominant world power, meant that influencing the ideology of Asian states was important.

The desire of most imperial powers to keep control in Asia did not generally work. **Independence movements** were too strong in many nations, but some territories captured from Japan are still not independent today. These include New Caledonia, Guam and American Samoa. Yet most nations did gain independence, often after bitter wars and many years. This process of decolonization can be seen in the map below.

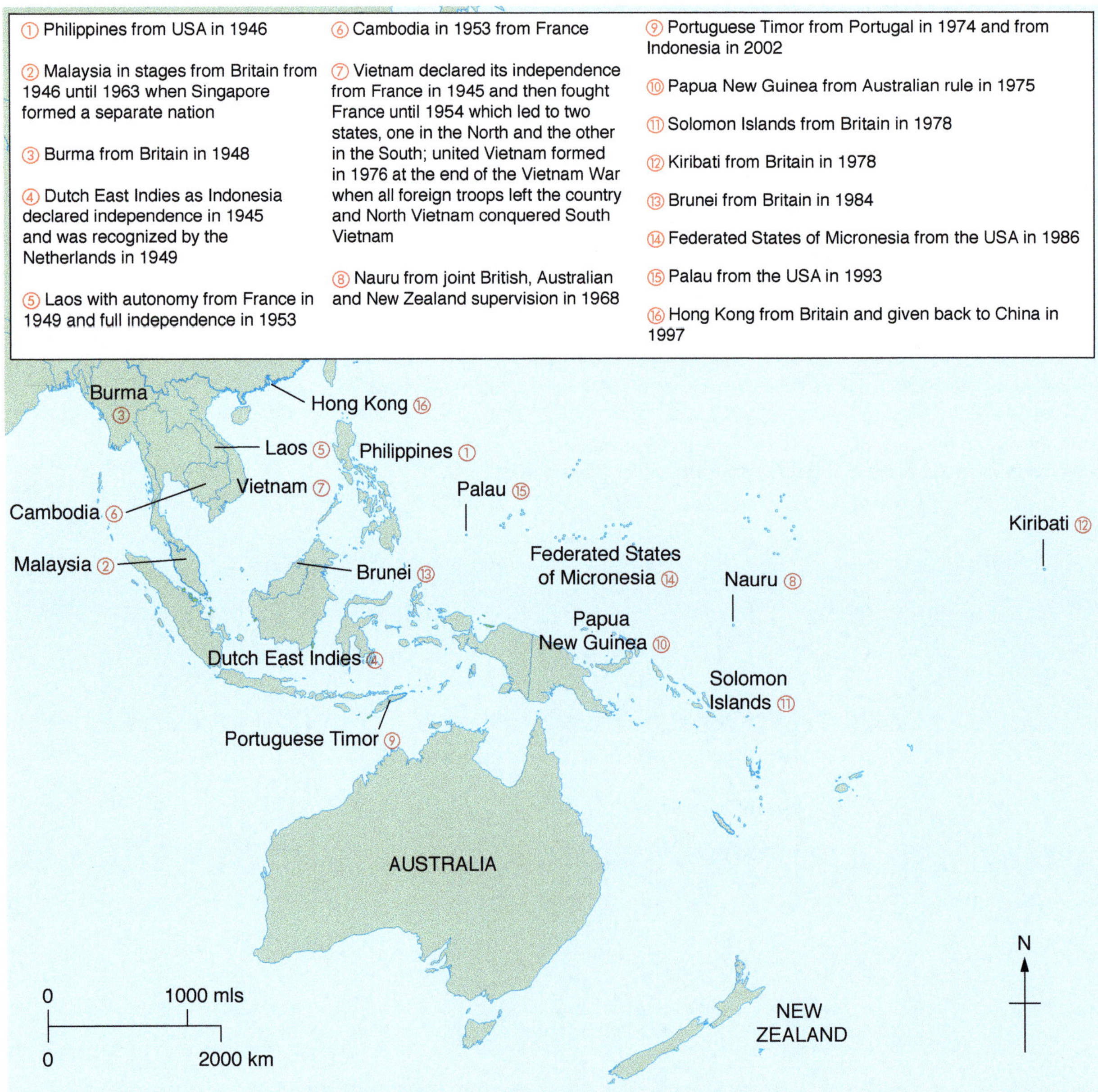

THE POLITICAL IMPACT OF THE WAR

Read the following source on decolonization and the attitude towards imperial powers in the Asia–Pacific region after the Second World War, and then answer the question below.

SOURCE 5

Extract from Robert Smith Thompson, *Empires on the Pacific: World War II and the Struggle for the Mastery of Asia*, Basic Books, New York, 2001, page 377.

Throughout East Asia, the old order had receded and a new order had taken its place. When the Japanese surrendered, the Union Jack rose again over Hong Kong and Mark Young, the pre-war governor now emaciated from his imprisonment, returned to Government House. But Man-Kan Lu, leader of the Legislative Council, made clear that henceforth the resident Chinese would receive just and equitable treatment.

On September 5, 1945, British reoccupation forces, headed by Lord Mountbatten, landed at Singapore, but they found a largely Chinese local population unwilling again to accept colonialism. Lee Kuan Yew, formerly a brilliant student at Cambridge University and later prime minister of independent Singapore, stated in a talk given in 1961 that 'My colleagues and I are of the generation of young men who went through the Second World War and the Japanese occupation and emerged determined that no one – neither the Japanese nor the British – had the right to push and kick us around.'

7 What does this source reveal to you about the political consequences of the Second World War?

____

____

____

ESSAY-WRITING SKILLS: PLANNING AN IB ESSAY

Read the IB-style question below on the effects of war and plan an answer in the box provided, staying focused on the political repercussions of the Second World War in Asia and the Pacific. You should give yourself five minutes to plan an essay to replicate exam conditions.

Discuss the political repercussions of one 20th-century war.

Thesis:

Paragraph 1 theme:

Paragraph 2 theme:

Paragraph 3 theme:

Paragraph 4 theme:

Socioeconomic impact of the war on Japan

The Japanese people suffered hugely and their infrastructure was left in ruins, as can be illustrated by the approximate statistics below.

Human loss and suffering

According to historian John Dower (1999):

- 1.74 million armed forces were dead and 4.5 million injured or ill.
- A million dead civilians.
- 30% of urban populations were homeless, with 9 million people homeless in total.
- 3.5 million members of the army and 3 million civilians were stranded overseas.
- Hundreds of thousands of orphans and homeless children, as well as widows and injured soldiers, were left in Japan in need of support and reintegration into society.

Infrastructural damage

According to historian John Dower (1999):

- 66 major cities had been heavily bombed.
- 40% of all urban areas had been destroyed.
- 80% of all ships, 33% of industrial machinery and 25% of railway equipment was destroyed.

Rebuilding of society

- The family-orientated culture of Japan had never had to deal with such societal dislocation, so orphans, homeless people, people who had been maimed and widows were often stigmatized and neglected by society and the government, sometimes for decades.
- The **repatriation** of 6.5 million Japanese people from overseas was incredibly difficult. Many were ill or injured, many were children and there was a severe shortage of housing.
- Approximately a million Koreans were repatriated to Korea in the years that followed the war. They had been used in Japan as forced labourers.

Economic recovery and political independence

- Japan suffered mass unemployment, price inflation and hunger for several years after the war. There were discussions of reparations, but these were dropped due to the need to rebuild Japan.
- The driver of economic recovery in Japan was the Korean War in 1950, which led to the US government placing billions of dollars' worth of orders from Japanese industry. Costs were low, and it would reduce the cost of shipping goods from the USA.
- As a result of demand stimulated by the Korean War there was a 300% increase in Japanese exports and a 70% increase in production.
- By 1952, Japan was economically and politically stable and it became independent again, as the US occupation ended in April of that year.

Socioeconomic impact of the war on other countries

China

- Around 1.3 million Chinese people died fighting against Japan, and 2 million were wounded.
- There were approximately 17 million civilian deaths.
- Towns and cities, such as Nanjing and Shanghai, were left devastated by the war.

US forces and other civilian dead

- 100,000 men in the US military were killed, and 250,000 were wounded.
- US infrastructure remained intact, and the USA remained the world's leading economy.
- In the US colony of the Philippines, an estimated 1 million civilians had died.
- In the Dutch East Indies, approximately 3.5 million civilians died; in Burma, approximately 250,000, and in French Indochina approximately 1 million.

SOCIOECONOMIC IMPACT OF THE WAR

Read the following source on Japanese recovery after the Second World War due to the Korean War, and answer the questions below.

SOURCE 6

Extract from Andrew Gordon, *A Modern History of Japan: From Tokugawa Times to the Present*, Oxford University Press, Oxford, 2003, page 241.

This tragedy across the straits [the Korean War] conferred great fortune on Japan. With the war came a surge of American military procurement orders placed with Japanese industries, which were located conveniently close to the front. In the years 1951–53, war procurements amounted to about two billion dollars, or roughly 60 per cent of all Japan's exports. Japanese leaders tastelessly celebrated what Prime Minister Yoshida called a 'gift of the gods' and businessmen dubbed 'blessed rain from heaven.' From 1949 to 1951 exports nearly tripled, and production rose nearly 70 per cent. Corporations began to show profits for the first time since the surrender, and they responded with a surge of investment in new plants and equipment. The **gross national product** began to increase at double-digit rates. Japan's recovery was underway.

With reforms in place and the economy on the mend, and with the Korean War placing great demands on American military resources, pressures in Washington [the US capital] mounted to end the occupation. The end came sooner than many had anticipated; in 1945, some top officials in the United States had spoken of the need to occupy Japan for two decades, or even a century. As it turned out, the era of formal occupation lasted just under seven years.

8 According to this source, what effects did the Korean War have on Japan? List them below.

9 Using this source, and the opposite page, why did the US occupation of Japan end in 1952, leaving Japan as an independent nation again?

STATEMENTS ON THE SOCIOECONOMIC IMPACT OF THE WAR

For each statement below, explain whether you agree or disagree with it, and why.

Statement	Agree or disagree?
The repatriation of 6.5 million Japanese people from overseas back into the home islands was a relatively easy process	
The decision of the USA not to demand reparations from Japan was a sensible one given Japan's weak economy post-Second World War	
The Korean War was the primary reason that Japan's economy was able to recover post-Second World War	

Impact of the war on women

Japan

The role of women in Japan's war effort changed during the war, as the government was initially reluctant to force women to work. The main developments were as follows:

- In 1941, the Japanese government forced all unmarried women between 16 and 25 into war production industries. One million women began work with the initiative.
- Due to the shortage of labour, women with families were encouraged to work starting in 1943.
- By 1945, the number of women working outside the home had risen to 14 million, constituting approximately 42% of all workers, with many working in agriculture.

An unfortunate role that women were forced to play by Japan was as '**comfort women**'. After the Rape of Nanjing in 1937 shocked the world, Japan developed the policy of comfort women to address the sexual needs of their soldiers. At the end of the war, the Japanese military destroyed documents related to '**comfort houses**' and the Japanese government denied their existence until 1993, so exact details are hard to deduce. However, historians agree on the following:

- They were military-operated brothels referred to as 'comfort houses' or 'comfort stations'.
- The women had been kidnapped and were forced to work as enslaved sex workers.
- Estimates are that in excess of 200,000 women were used in this way.
- About 80% were Korean, but Chinese and some European women were also enslaved.

USA

Women participated to a greater extent in the US war effort than in any other country, except the Soviet Union. Their main work was in war production, which enabled the USA to produce huge quantities of war goods, but they also joined the military in large numbers. The main developments were as follows:

- In 1941, over 14.5 million women worked outside the home. By 1945, this number had increased to over 19 million, which made up 36% of all workers in the USA.
- Women were heavily involved in new war-related industries, with 91% of new workers being women in 185 war-related factories in Detroit, Michigan.
- In terms of the shipbuilding industry, women played no role prior to 1941, but by 1943, ten per cent of all production was completed by women.
- In excess of 300,000 women joined the military, serving in the army, navy and marines in many capacities, excluding combat. The army created the Women's Army Corps (WAC), the navy created the Women Accepted for Volunteer Emergency Service (WAVES) and the air force set up the Women Air Force Service Pilots (WASPs).
- According to historian Allan M. Winkler, women joined for a myriad of reasons, which included a sense of patriotic duty, a desire to escape the monotony of domestic work, and the chance to earn money and gain a degree of independence.
- Even after the war, women remained in factories in large numbers, but continued to face discrimination in terms of pay, types of job roles on offer and not being allowed to serve in combat in the army.

War criminals

As part of the social healing and peacekeeping methods after the war, many types of courts formed across the Asia–Pacific region to administer justice. The most famous were those carried out by the **International Military Tribunal for the Far East**, also known as the '**Tokyo Trials**'. As a result of these trials:

- 25 persons were delineated as Class A war criminals, and 5700 as Class B or Class C.
- 920 were executed, 475 received life sentences and 2944 received some prison time.
- The majority were Japanese, but included were 178 people of Taiwanese ethnic origin and 148 Koreans.
- Various war crimes were exposed, such as mass killings, human experimentations, torture, the use of chemical and biological weapons, as well as cannibalism.

THE EFFECTS OF THE SECOND WORLD WAR IN ASIA AND THE PACIFIC

Read the definitions below based on the IB prescribed content and add relevant examples for each area from the preceding pages and your own knowledge for the effects of this war.

Prescribed content	Definition	Examples from the Second World War in Asia and the Pacific
Peacemaking	The attempts to uphold peace after a war. Major aims include trying to prevent further loss of life and conflict, trying to rebuild a nation by ensuring civilians are protected, and rebuilding infrastructure. However, peace terms are often decided by the victors alone who have other motives, such as revenge and gain for their nation. These motives may result in unsustainable peace terms	
Territorial changes	Changes to who governs areas of land. This can involve the creation of new countries and empires, and the end to others. The implications for the populations of these areas are often significant	
Political repercussions	Repercussions of war for political systems. War can often lead to significant upheavals to the governing classes of countries, and result in regime changes and new ideologies taking precedence. Sometimes these include greater rights for people, other times the complete opposite occurs	
Economic impact	Warfare can impact on the economy in areas such as gross domestic product and employment levels. It can also leave countries facing huge war debts in the form of reparations. The reconstruction of an economy after a war can be a tricky, protracted process	
Social impact	Warfare can impact on society in areas such as culture, religion, familial relations, relations between different groups in society, lifestyle changes, wealth and living conditions	
Demographic impact	Demographic studies attempt to measure quantifiable characteristics of a given population. War may impact the number of people left alive, the average age in a country, the ethnic makeup of a country and the gender balance, to name a few of the most common indicators	
Changes in the role and status of women	War may have a big impact on the role and status of women as the demands of war may require greater numbers of women to enter the workforce or join the army. This can lead to the enfranchisement and empowerment of women	

CHAPTER 4 Exam focus

Sample question and answer

Consider the response to the essay question below. Read it and the examiner's comments around it.

Examine the role of technology in determining the outcome of one 20th-century war.

The outcome of the Second World War in Asia and the Pacific (1941–5) was defeat for Japan at the hands of the USA and its allies. What role did the technology available play in deciding this outcome? It will be argued that modern military technology played a vital role in deciding the outcome of this conflict. A combination of successful US code-breaking efforts, which gave the USA a great advantage in knowing the IJN's movements in the Pacific, and superior production of modern aircraft carriers and submarines proved decisive in defeating Japan. First, this essay will discuss code-breaking efforts, then aircraft carriers and finally submarines. In all three areas of technology, the USA performed better than Japan, and therefore this goes a long way to explaining its ultimate victory.

> This is a focused introduction that outlines the structure of the rest of the essay, and states the main arguments that the essay will be making.

The USA's successful code-breaking efforts, in comparison with Japan's failed attempts to break major US codes, was a key reason for the ultimate defeat of Japan. This was a vital technological aspect of the war in the Pacific, as both the Japanese and US armies relied on codes to send commands and reports. If a code was figured out by cryptanalysts, then the other side would know what the enemy was planning and could counter effectively. The USA used the Native American language of the Navajo, which Japan failed to break. Conversely, the USA was successful at breaking Japanese codes, and this played a big role in them winning major battles. For example, they successfully broke Japanese code JN-25 in May 1942, and this meant that the USA was aware of the move by the IJN to capture Midway. Therefore, US forces moved to intercept the IJN before it could establish its own aircraft at Midway, and caught the Japanese military by surprise as they were unaware of such a large US presence in the region. As a result, at the Battle of Midway, the USA was able to inflict huge damage on the IJN. Japan lost all four of their carriers, 240 aircraft, a cruiser and 3000 men. The USA's losses were lighter: one carrier, 150 aircraft, a destroyer and 300 men. Many historians agree that this battle decisively turned the course of the war in the USA's favour, and that US victory largely rested on their successful code-breaking efforts.

> This is a focused first line to a paragraph that sets out the argument that will be made in the paragraph, and is clearly focused on the question.

> There are strong examples used as evidence in these lines that show how code breaking allowed the USA to inflict heavy losses on the Japanese army.

Another key technology, which played a decisive role in determining the outcome of the Second World War in Asia and the Pacific, was aircraft carriers. They were essentially floating, armed airfields and were the most valuable and important warships of the war. Aircraft launched from these carriers could travel hundreds of kilometres to attack targets. Both sides had access to this modern technology of war, but the USA's ability to build far more of these carriers and replace any losses at a greater rate than Japan gave them a vital advantage. From 1941 to 1945, Japan managed to build sixteen fleet carriers, while the USA managed more than ten times that number, constructing 163 in total. Indeed, Japan was unable to recover after they lost four carriers at the Battle of Midway in 1942. As historian Bernard C. Nalty persuasively argues: 'Japan's industrial infrastructure proved too fragile to sustain modern warfare. Stockpiles, especially of oil, could be replenished only through conquest, and the very act of conquering drew upon these reserves.' Oil, essential in constructing and maintaining a large fleet of modern

> This is a strong evaluation of a historian's perspective. This engagement with the opinion of an expert adds another layer of analysis.

aircraft carriers, was difficult for Japan to come by; conversely, the USA was the world's largest producer of petroleum. Here, once again, technology played a vital role in deciding the outcome of the war, as the USA was able to send a far greater number of aircraft carriers into war than Japan.

Another key form of modern military technology that had a significant impact in deciding the outcome of the war was submarines, which used torpedoes to destroy enemy shipping. By 1945, US submarines had decimated the Japanese merchant fleet to the point that it could no longer provide the homelands with food or raw materials. US submarines were also responsible for destroying eight Japanese carriers. The USA managed to make more effective use of submarines than Japan for two major reasons. First, the US code breakers had figured out the Japanese codes, so they knew where Japanese targets were, whereas Japan failed to break the major US codes. Second, similarly to the aircraft carriers, the USA could produce more submarines. By 1944, the USA had over 150 submarines hunting Japanese merchant ships. According to historian Alan J. Levine, 'by the summer of 1944, they [submarines] were shutting down many [Japanese] shipping routes [to their home islands]'. This was important in deciding the outcome of the war, as the starvation of the Japanese home islands made their surrender more likely.

There is an analytical link between factors here, which shows how code-breaking successes led to more effective use of submarines by the USA.

To conclude, the successful use of modern technology was a major reason why the USA and its allies won the Second World War in Asia and the Pacific. The USA's breaking of Japanese military codes gave them a huge advantage in knowing where the IJN was, and its plans for battles. In contrast, Japan failed to crack major US codes. As such, the US forces could prepare effectively with their intelligence and win major battles, such as Midway. However, that alone did not account for the USA's victory, since it needed a modern, technologically advanced military to defeat Japan in battle. Here, the aircraft carriers and submarines were vital pieces, and the USA had them in far greater numbers than Japan, giving it an insurmountable advantage in this conflict. As such, modern military technology, and access to it, played a huge role in the defeat of Japan.

This is a good conclusion because it is consistent with the rest of the essay, and draws out the main arguments made in the essay. It stays clearly focused on the question, and remains analytically nuanced.

A well-written response that stays focused on the question, and develops a reasoned line of argument that is well supported by evidence. The structure is clear, and a variety of technology in relation to this war is considered and its contribution to the outcome examined. The conclusion is consistent with the rest of the essay.

Exam practice

Now either have a go at the above essay question or try one of the following questions, with reference to the Second World War in Asia and the Pacific.

1 'Territorial ambition was the primary cause of war.' With reference to one 20th-century war, to what extent do you agree with this statement?

2 Discuss the role of economic resources in deciding the outcome of two 20th-century wars.

3 Examine the political repercussions of two 20th-century wars.

5 Chinese Civil War 1927–37 and 1945–9

The Chinese Civil War, in two main phases from 1927 to 1937 and from 1945 to 1949, saw the Chinese Communist Party (CCP) fight against the Nationalist Party, also known as the **Guomindang (GMD)**, for control of China. The Second Sino-Japanese War was ostensibly put on hold while both sides formed a fragile alliance against Japan in the years 1937–45, with fighting resuming once the Second World War had ended. Ultimately, the CCP was victorious, leading to the establishment of a communist regime led by **Mao Zedong** and the flight of the Nationalists to Taiwan.

The long-term causes of the Chinese Civil War

Revised

Economic and social conditions, c.1900–37

Chinese society had profound socioeconomic inequalities in both rural and urban areas, which created conditions that were conducive for revolution.

Rural poverty

Approximately 85% of the population of China in the 1930s consisted of agricultural labourers who lived in poverty, often just one bad harvest away from starvation.

- Farming techniques were very basic, as were living conditions, with most homes having no running water or electricity.
- Most agricultural labourers did not own their land but rented it, usually at extortionate rates. In Hunan province, for example, rents usually equated to 70% of the value of crops produced, and thus landlords were very unpopular.

Urban poverty

China's urban population was very small at the start of the twentieth century; however, industry was developing along the east coast, leading to increased urbanization. China's industrial sector began to grow in the 1920s and 1930s due to an increase in foreign investment and the development of new manufacturing techniques. This led to population growth in eastern cities such as Shanghai, which had over 1.5 million residents by the 1920s. By the 1930s, approximately 4.5% of the population lived in towns of over 100,000 inhabitants. China's industrial centres had the following features:

- Living conditions for urban workers were poor. Sanitation was terrible, wages were low and social security was non-existent.
- Death as a result of hunger or disease was not uncommon. In 1920s Shanghai, 20,000 dead bodies were collected from the streets every year by municipal sanitation teams.
- The CCP helped to develop trade unions in this period, leading to strike action in the 1920s and an increase in union membership. The Central Shanghai General Union had 821,000 members by March 1927, compared to just 43,000 in June 1925.
- The number of unionized members as a percentage of the whole workforce was relatively small, and thus their impact was limited. Trade unions also struggled to unite the many artisanal workers and failed to reach many of the workers who were concentrated in the newer and larger steel and textile factories.

Political fragmentation 1912–27

The timeline on page 123 outlines the fragmentation and instability that characterized Chinese politics in the lead-up to the Chinese Civil War in 1927.

Date	Event
1912	The Imperial Qing dynasty collapsed after a military revolt inspired by the reformist Nationalist Party. China held its first democratic election and the Nationalist Party won
1912–16	General Yuan Shikai established himself as a military dictator, preventing the democratic will of the people. He attempted to have himself crowned emperor
1916	General Yuan Shikai died, leaving a power vacuum. Political power fragmented as regional warlords established power as independent dictators across China
1921	The CCP was established in China
1923–5	The First United Front was formed, as the CCP and the Nationalist Party agreed to work together to eliminate the warlords and unify China. Despite huge ideological differences, both sides agreed to the alliance as the Nationalist Party needed foreign aid from the USSR, and the CCP needed access to the much larger support base that the Nationalists had built up. The Nationalist Party, assisted by military advisers from the USSR, set up the Whampoa Military Academy near Canton (present-day Guangzhou) to prepare an army to take control of China
1926	The United Front launched the North Expedition. This was a military campaign that aimed to defeat the warlords and reunite China. The campaign was mostly successful
1927	The Nationalist Party emerged as the ruling party in China. However, the alliance between the Nationalists and the CCP broke down, leading to the first clash between them

WHY WAS THERE SUCH WIDESPREAD LONG-TERM DISCONTENT IN CHINA, AND HOW COULD IT BE USED BY THOSE SEEKING TO TAKE POWER?

For each statement below, explain whether you agree or disagree with it, and why, using the information from the opposite page and your own knowledge.

Statement	Agree or disagree?
Terrible living conditions in both rural and urban China were a significant cause of discontent among Chinese citizens	
Economics was the most significant cause of discontent in China among workers and agricultural labourers in the first quarter of the twentieth century	
The conditions in China in the first couple of decades of the twentieth century were perfect for a Marxist revolution	
The key to winning power in China was to gain the support of agricultural labourers	

MULTICAUSAL EXPLANATIONS

Use the information on the page opposite, this page and the next page, and your own knowledge, to add examples to the right-hand column for each of the long-term causal themes for the Chinese Civil War.

Causal theme	Examples to support this causal theme
Economic	
Political	
Ideological	
Territorial	
Other causes	

Ideological differences

The ideologies of the Nationalists and the CCP were fundamentally incompatible. This meant that their alliance was only going to be a temporary measure to defeat the warlords.

The ideology of the Nationalist Party and its appeal

The Nationalist Party envisioned a China which was unified, modern and free from foreign control. Its ideology was based on the 'Three Principles of the People' which had been codified by **Sun Yat-sen**: nationalism, democracy and the people's livelihood (or welfare). The Nationalists also effectively promoted capitalism, as they valued private property. These ideas were popular with many Chinese people, for the following reasons:

- Nationalism appealed to the Chinese people who felt fed up that their land and resources were being exploited by foreign powers. Foreign powers had the right to set their own taxes and trade tariffs and live by their own laws in areas known as foreign concessions. In Shanghai, the International Settlement effectively operated as an independent city outside Chinese rule with three-quarters of a million people, including 30,000 non-Chinese people.
- Democracy was a popular ideal, particularly among the growing middle classes whose potential political power had been denied during previous decades.
- The people's livelihood policy aimed to introduce social reforms, such as land redistribution and state support. This ideal was popular among agricultural labourers; however, the Nationalists failed to build a significant support base among them, and had wealthy urban, middle-class party support.

The ideology of the CCP and its appeal

The CCP and the Nationalist Party shared some ideological beliefs. For example, the CCP also wished to see China free from foreign influence. However, the CCP wanted society to be restructured along Marxist principles, borne out of a revolution of oppressed classes. However, Mao was concerned to make **Marxism** fit China's context and so he argued that the agents of the revolution would be agricultural labourers, and encouraged nationalism to overthrow foreign imperialist powers. The CCP were popular for the following reasons:

- Similarly to the Nationalists, the CCP appealed to nationalist impulses of the Chinese people and their desire to be free from foreign imperialist powers.
- The Communists actively set out to win the support of agricultural labourers, and they prioritized them over any other class. They attacked landlords; this gained them huge support.
- In keeping with Marx's ideas on equality, the CCP promoted equality between men and women, which won them many female supporters.

Early clashes between the Nationalists and the CCP 1927–35

The First United Front held until Shanghai was captured in 1927. However, it was an uneasy alliance. The CCP had been spreading its message among agricultural labourers as the Northern Expedition advanced, which led to fears in the Nationalist camp that their alliance might make the CCP too strong. The Nationalists struck first with the White Terror, thereby ending the First United Front. The next decade saw intermittent warfare between the two sides. The Chinese Civil War had begun, and developed as follows:

- In April 1927, the White Terror in Shanghai saw a criminal organization called the Green Gang launch a series of anti-communist attacks ordered by Chiang Kai-shek, killing an estimated 5000 Communists. The Nationalist Party did nothing to stop the violence. This attack devastated the CCP's base in Shanghai, where it had been founded.
- Between August and December 1927, the Communists launched two main counterattacks. The Autumn Harvest Uprising led by Mao saw Communist forces attempt guerrilla warfare against the Nationalists, but they were ill-disciplined and ill-organized and easily crushed. The CCP's second attack in Canton in December was also defeated, with thousands of deaths.
- Very much in retreat, the Communist leadership regrouped in Jiangxi, setting up the **Jiangxi Soviet**. This rural base became the CCP's main stronghold from 1928 to 1934, and here it courted agricultural labourers with land reform policies to gain their loyalty.
- From 1930 to 1934, the Nationalists launched a series of assaults on the CCP bases in Jiangxi, which aimed to encircle them and cut off their supply lines. The first four encirclement campaigns were not successful, as the CCP effectively used guerrilla tactics to defend its rural locations. But these defensive strategies could not break the encirclement completely. The Communists' supplies were being exhausted, and they were in a desperate situation.

THE IDEOLOGIES OF THE CCP AND THE NATIONALISTS, AND THEIR RESPECTIVE APPEALS

Read the page opposite and complete the Venn diagram, noting the differences in the ideologies of the CCP and the Nationalists, and the areas where they overlap. Then, in the box outside the Venn diagram annotate the ideologies explaining to which areas of Chinese society these ideologies appealed. Include: agricultural labourers, working class, landowners, middle class, women.

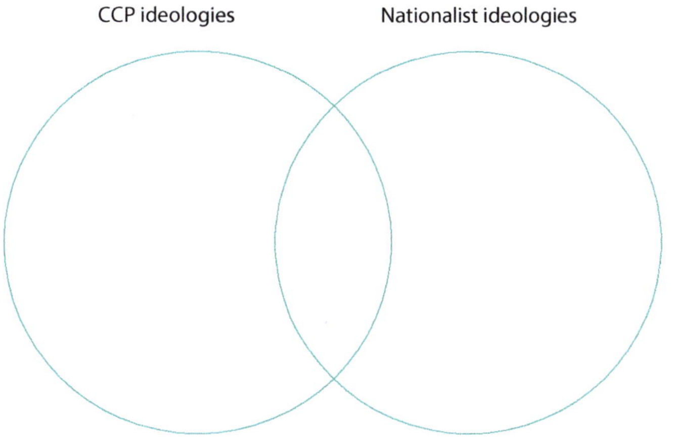

WHO WON THE CLASHES BETWEEN THE NATIONALISTS AND THE CCP, 1927–35, AND WHY WERE THEY SIGNIFICANT?

Complete the table below using the page opposite, the next page and your own knowledge. For each event note what each side gained, and which side you think was victorious, and then explain why you think this event was significant.

Event	What did each side gain from this event? Which side, if any, do you think was victorious?	Why was this event significant?
The White Terror		
The Autumn Harvest Uprising		
The five encirclement campaigns		
The Long March		

- In 1934, the fifth campaign succeeded in taking the CCP's rural stronghold in Jiangxi, forcing the CCP to evacuate after a failed attempt to meet the Nationalists head on.
- In October 1934, 90,000 CCP members embarked on the **Long March** away from the Jiangxi province. Pursued by the Nationalists, the march took the Communists through eleven provinces, over 9000 km (5500 miles), across 24 rivers and eighteen mountain ranges. The exhausting conditions, combined with a number of battles against the Nationalists, meant that only approximately 8000 Communists survived. They marched for just over a year, arriving in Yanan in October 1935, where they set up a new base.

The Nationalists in government 1928–37

Successes of the Nanjing decade

The Nationalist government during the period known as the **Nanjing Decade** was unpopular with large sections of the Chinese population, but it did achieve some successes:

- The Nationalists strengthened the central power of the Chinese state by forming alliances with warlords, such as Yan Xishan and Zhang Xueliang.
- The number of foreign concessions was reduced from 33 to 13.
- There was strong economic growth with gross domestic product at nine per cent per annum.
- Nearly 5000 km (3000 miles) of railways were laid, and the first commercial airline in China was opened.
- The government had support from commercial elites and the landowning classes.

Failures of the Nanjing decade

Politically, the regime was authoritarian, with Chiang Kai-shek as the dictator. Methods of control included arrest without trial, torture and execution. This went against the ideological principle of democracy, which alienated many of the well-educated elites.

With the Long March allowing Communist survival, Chiang had failed to eliminate the CCP. The CCP arrived in Yanan after the Long March and built up a strong base among agricultural labourers due to its popular land reform policies, as it redistributed land from landlords to agricultural labourers.

Socially, the Nationalists failed to alleviate suffering among agricultural labourers, as the regime maintained the existing social hierarchy, which favoured landlords. The 'Three Principles of the People' had promised social reforms, but Chiang failed to deliver. This enabled the CCP to garner support among agricultural labourers, who made up over 80% of the population.

Militarily, the Nationalists and Chiang appeared weak when responding to Japan's invasion of Manchuria in 1931. Japan established the puppet-state of Manchukuo in 1932, and in 1933 its troops had entered lands north of Beijing and Inner Mongolia. Chiang first appealed to the League of Nations, which did nothing of substance to stop Japan. With no significant international assistance, Chiang adopted a strategy of trading space for time. The Treaty of Tanggu in May 1933 saw the Nationalists acknowledge the independence of Manchukuo. Many Chinese people perceived this as weak, as they were fearful of Japanese occupation and wanted protection from their government.

Concessions to the Japanese government were in stark contrast to Chiang's aggressive policy towards the CCP, evidenced by the encirclement campaigns of 1930–4. Chiang pursued the Communists ruthlessly, because he believed that: 'the Japanese are a disease of the skin, whereas the Communists are a disease of the heart'. This greatly undermined his respect in the eyes of the Chinese people, as he was prioritizing attacking fellow Chinese people over a foreign invader.

In 1935, opposition to Chiang's policy towards Japan led to the 9 December Movement, during which students protested against Chiang's policy. All of this tension culminated in the Xi'an incident of 1936, where Chiang was detained by a warlord, Zhang Xueliang, and only released on the promise of a revived United Front alliance with the CCP to fight Japan.

HOW DID LONG-TERM CAUSES INTERACT TO CAUSE THE CHINESE CIVIL WAR?

Read the example below that links long-term socioeconomic discontent with the ideological appeal of the CCP, which posed a huge threat to the Nationalists. Try to do the same for two other causes, completing the empty arrows and boxes using examples and ideas from the opposite pages and your own knowledge.

Long-term cause	Interrelationship between causes	Long-term cause
Approximately 85% of the population of China in the 1930s were agricultural labourers who lived in poverty. Most agricultural labourers did not own their land but rented it, usually at extortionate rates. In Hunan province, for example, rents usually equated to 70% of the value of crops produced, and thus landlords were unpopular	The CCP appealed to these impoverished agricultural labourers and promised them land, which threatened the Nationalists	This is because the Nationalists promoted capitalism and had wealthy, middle-class support. Significantly, many of their supporters owned property. Therefore, the CCP's ideology of land redistribution was a direct attack on the Nationalists' principles. Given their fundamentally incompatible ideologies, war became a more likely eventuality.

PRIORITIZATION OF CAUSES

Create your own argument by organizing the causes of the Chinese Civil War (listed in the boxes on the right) into the pyramid to show their relative importance. You can put more than one cause in the different sections if you feel that helps your argument. Explain your reasoning around the pyramid.

- Ideological
- Economic
- Political
- Territorial
- Other causes

CCP survival and growth strategies 1935–45

In Yanan after the Long March, the survival of the CCP was in grave doubt and the prospect of victory over the Nationalists slim. Yet it adopted skilful strategies to grow greatly in strength. The Communists:

- confiscated land from landlords and redistributed it to agricultural labourers through committees
- abolished unpopular traditional customs, such as arranged marriage and foot-binding, which prevented women from working
- allowed no abuse of people by Red Army soldiers in order to build good relations
- used terror and coercion against landlords and wealthy agricultural labourers, encouraging poorer agricultural labourers to attack and often kill landlords, thereby allowing the CCP to assert its authority more easily
- campaigned against Japan through propaganda, training guerrilla soldiers in the Anti-Japanese University, and then launching attacks on Japan in Manchuria starting in 1931
- were willing to ally with the Nationalists in the United Front against Japan, which contrasted with Chiang's approach and helped to attract new recruits due to their staunchly anti-Japanese approach, raising CCP membership from 40,000 in 1937 to 700,000 in 1941.

The short-term causes of the Chinese Civil War

Revised

The Second Sino-Japanese War 1937–45

The Second Sino-Japanese War officially began in July 1937. The Nationalists and the CCP focused on their common enemy, Japan. However, tensions between these two parties remained high throughout the war. When Japan was defeated in 1945, war between the two sides for control of China was inevitable. By the time Japan was defeated in 1945, the CCP had been strengthened, and the Nationalists also enjoyed increased military power by means of aid from the USA. However, the Nationalists lost the battle for the popular support of the Chinese people due to their initial reluctance to fight Japan and their failure to prevent the Japanese occupation.

The Nationalists during the Second Sino-Japanese War

Japan's advance into China was rapid and brutal. Shanghai had fallen by October 1937 and the capital Nanjing fell in December. During the Rape of Nanjing as many as 300,000 Chinese civilians were murdered, and thousands raped and tortured.

In October 1938, Chiang moved China's capital to Chongqing in what he saw as a strategic withdrawal, but this was unpopular with many civilians who felt that the Nationalists were abandoning them by withdrawing beyond the reach of Japan's military. This weakened support for the Nationalists.

By September 1944, Japan occupied all of southern and eastern China, leaving the Nationalists isolated in Chongqing and increasingly unpopular among the Chinese population. In total, the Nationalists lost half a million troops to the war effort.

The Japanese military subjected the Nationalists in Chongqing to relentless aerial bombardment. It was hard for the Nationalists to maintain supplies after Burma fell to Japan in 1942, so food was scarce. This led to inflation, and starvation was common in Chongqing.

The USA militarily assisted the Nationalists, and airlifted vital supplies over the Himalayas.

The CCP during the Second Sino-Japanese War

CCP-controlled territory in the north grew in size from its base at Yanan. The CCP's land reforms won it support. The Japanese forces in the north only really worried about controlling the cities and railway lines, leaving the countryside to the CCP. The Communists utilized:

- guerrilla warfare to combat Japanese troops and disrupt their supply lines, such as the Hundred Regiments Campaign in July and August 1940, during which Japanese railways to coalmines in Jingxing were destroyed
- propaganda to generate support, such as in January 1941 when the Nationalists killed 3000 of the Communist Fourth Route Army for entering an area south of the Yangtze River; CCP propaganda vilified Chiang for attacking fellow Chinese people instead of Japanese troops
- increasing membership, from 22,000 members in 1936 to 1,200,000 in 1945, and an increase in the size of the Red Army from 22,000 in 1936 to 910,000 in 1945.

USING HISTORIANS' INTERPRETATIONS TO HELP WITH THE PRIORITIZATION OF CAUSES

There are many interpretations that exist as to why the Chinese Civil War occurred. Engaging with the perspectives of historians in your essay can help you to develop your own line of argument, as you can argue whether you agree or disagree with their interpretations of events.

Read the three extracts below and then complete the activity beneath.

SOURCE 1

Extract from Rana Mitter, *China's War With Japan*, Allen Lane, London, 2013, page 23.

Chiang received an education which was highly traditional in many ways, and learned the values of the Confucian system of thought, including ideas of propriety, righteousness and shame. In addition he would be China's first leader to have experience of the outside world: a youthful visit to the newly formed Soviet Russia shaped a lifetime of visceral hatred for communism.

SOURCE 2

Extract from Charles Holcombe, *A History of East Asia: From the Origin of Civilization to the Twenty-first Century*, Cambridge University Press, Cambridge, 2011, page 313.

The American hope was to prevent full-scale civil war and promote democracy in China, and for that purpose, in late 1945, President Truman appointed one of America's most distinguished military leaders and statesmen, General George C. Marshall, as a special envoy to China. General Marshall remained in China for a little over a year. [...] But General Marshall expressed concern that efforts at reaching a peace settlement were being frustrated by extremists on both sides. In fact, the bitter antagonisms between the Chinese Nationalists and Communists ultimately proved too deep to sustain the uneasy truce.

SOURCE 3

Extract from Jonathan D. Spence, *The Search for Modern China*, W.W. Norton, New York, 2013, pages 258–9.

The alliance of the Communists and the Nationalists was born of a shared desperation and a shared hope. ... Despite competing long-range goals and clashing personalities, Communists and Nationalists could agree at least on the need to attempt reunification of the country through a mixture of military force and social reform. ... The speed of victory over warlord forces only highlighted the depth of disagreement over social policy, and 1927 became a year of disaster for the Communists as they tried to outmaneuver their Nationalist allies and change the direction of the new state, only to see their movement all but crushed in the attempt.

Add examples from the preceding pages to support the three interpretations of the causes of the Chinese Civil War. In the second column add examples to support this interpretation. In the third column explain the extent to which you find this interpretation persuasive.

Interpretation	Examples to support this interpretation	Explain the extent to which you find this interpretation persuasive
Rana Mitter		
Charles Holcombe		
Jonathan D. Spence		

Japanese surrender and the start of the Chinese Civil War, August 1945

Japan formally surrendered to the Allies, including the USA, the USSR and the Nationalist Chinese government, on 2 September 1945. The CCP and Nationalists worked rapidly to take the previously Japanese-held territories. They would gain not only land, but also weapons from surrendering Japanese soldiers. The civil war resumed.

The course of the Chinese Civil War

Revised

Communist victory in the Chinese Civil War was achieved through a combination of Nationalist weakness and CCP strength. The CCP effectively mobilized both human and economic resources and formed a military strategy that was superior to that of the Nationalists.

The civil war in 1945

Initial Nationalist advantages

The Nationalists began the war with significant advantages over the Communists. Therefore, eventual victory for the Communists was far from assured. The Nationalists had:

- a three-to-one troop advantage over the Red Army
- superior weaponry, including airpower and support from the USA for naval and air transport; the CCP had no air force or navy
- a larger territory from which to gather troops and resources; by August 1945, the GMD controlled seventeen major cities.

Initial Communist advantages

While the Communists were perhaps the weaker side when Japan surrendered, they too had a number of potential advantages at the outbreak of war. They:

- were dominant in rural, northern China, including nineteen bases and a population of 95.5 million
- were popular in areas under their control through land distribution to agricultural labourers at the expense of feudal landlords
- seized weapons from surrendering Japanese troops and received support from the communist Soviet Union, which occupied adjoining areas.

In early autumn 1945, the Communists developed an effective new strategy called **mobile defence**, in response to the Nationalist domination of key cities in northern China. Mao had learnt an important lesson: a conventional military strategy would lead to swift defeat. Mobile defence used guerrilla tactics of sabotage and ambush to weaken the enemy. The aim was to disrupt supply lines and inflict casualties, but not the enlargement of territorial control, at least in the short term. Support of the local rural population, which the CCP had, was vital for this type of strategy. The aim was to wear down the enemy slowly.

The race to control Manchuria

In October 1945, the CCP attempted to seize all of Manchuria. As a result, the Soviets:

- gave the CCP access to Japanese arms depots, such as one at Shenyang which contained over 100,000 guns and artillery pieces
- transferred 200,000 Chinese troops from the Manchukuo regime who had surrendered to the Soviets to the CCP, and stopped Nationalists from entering some of the key cities in Manchuria.

The Soviets, however, instructed the CCP in November 1945 to:

- leave major cities
- dismantle industrial machinery throughout Manchuria and ship it to the USSR.

This may have resulted from the Soviet belief that the CCP was soon to be defeated, as evidenced by the November 1945 battle at Shanhaiguan Pass, which was a major defeat for the Red Army, and pressure on the Soviet Union from former allies in European issues.

While the CCP was clearly weakened and not supported by the Soviet Union as hoped, the GMD was also under pressure from the USA. US General Wedemeyer criticized Chiang's strategies, stating that he needed to secure Nationalist areas instead of overstretching his army in the north against the CCP.

COMPARING AND CONTRASTING THE INITIAL STRENGTHS AND WEAKNESSES OF THE TWO ARMIES IN 1945 WHEN WAR BROKE OUT

The initial strengths and weaknesses of forces at the outbreak of war can play a big role in deciding the eventual outcome of the conflict.

Use the information on the page opposite and your own knowledge to complete the following table, noting down the key features of the two armies in 1945 across the categories in the left-hand column. Then make an argument as to which side was in the stronger position for each area, in the right-hand column.

Key feature	The Nationalist army in 1945	The Red Army in 1945	Which side was stronger in this category, and why?
Human resources			
Technology			
Tactics			
Foreign support			
Territory held			
Ideology			
Support of the Chinese people			

The civil war in 1946: inconclusive results

In the early part of 1946, the Nationalists continued to exert control over southern and eastern China while making further gains in urban areas of northern China and Manchuria. The main strength of the CCP was its control of the northern countryside.

The truce in Manchuria, June to October 1946, and the resumption of hostilities

In May 1946, Soviet troops withdrew from Manchuria and the CCP occupied the major cities that they vacated. However, the Nationalists took these cities in weeks and the CCP was forced to retreat. By June it seemed as though the CCP would have to abandon its last Manchurian stronghold, the city of Harbin. Yet, in June 1946 a ceasefire was agreed in Manchuria, arranged by the USA. This came at a very fortunate time for the CCP as it allowed it to strengthen its army.

Chiang later came to regret this truce, and said it was a key part of his eventual defeat. However, the USA pressured him to accept and he felt that his overstretched forces would benefit from a temporary cessation of the fighting. He believed at the time that a brief truce would not prevent his ultimate triumph.

The four-month-long truce allowed the CCP to improve Harbin's defences. The CCP also received vital supplies from the Soviets. Historians Jung Chang and Jon Halliday have shown that over 2000 wagonloads of ex-Japanese military supplies arrived from Korea on railways that the Soviets had helped to repair. The supplies included heavy artillery, machine guns and rifles. As a result of these measures, when the Nationalists resumed their attacks on Harbin, the CCP successfully defended the city.

The truce also allowed the CCP military commander, Lin Biao, to reorganize the Red Army, transforming it from a series of small guerrilla detachments to larger, professional units that could engage in conventional warfare. This transformed Red Army performed well in a surprise attack on the Nationalists camped near the Sungari River in the winter of 1946–7. Although the Red Army failed to take the railway junction at Siping, it inflicted huge casualties on the Nationalists and captured large amounts of their weaponry. By the end of the year, the situation in Manchuria was uncertain; the Nationalists controlled most of the cities and the CCP controlled most of the countryside.

The civil war in 1947

Nationalists on the offensive; CCP strengthens

The Nationalists targeted key cities in 1947, but neglected rural China, strengthening the CCP. In 1947, the Nationalists:

- seized the CCP base in Yanan in March 1947
- launched the **Strongpoint Offensive** in May 1947 that captured cities in Shandon, Shanxi and Shaanxi provinces.

The CCP, however, continued to control the countryside, which allowed mobile defence operations to continue. More cities captured and garrisoned by the Nationalists meant more exposed, vulnerable supply lines through the Communist-held countryside.

The tactics of the CCP shifted in November 1947 to large-scale attacks on urban areas. The Communists were now in a stronger position as they had been able to stockpile weapons in the 1946 truce, and because the Nationalists were now weaker. The Nationalists had to spread their troops thinly in order to defend all of the major cities they were now in control of, and supplies and reinforcements were disrupted by CCP sabotage missions. The CCP successfully captured its first major city – Shijiazhuang in Hebei province – in November 1947, followed by the key Manchurian city of Siping in the winter.

HOW DID THE CHINESE CIVIL WAR DEVELOP FROM 1945 TO 1947, AND WHICH SIDE WAS IN A STRONGER POSITION BY THE END OF 1947?

By the end of 1946, the Chinese Civil War had reached a stalemate, yet by the end of 1947 the CCP appeared to be in the ascendancy. From the fighting in these years we can learn a lot about what factors were going to be significant in determining the overall winner of the conflict.

Using the preceding pages, complete the table below, noting the main successes of each army in the years 1945–7, and then make an argument as to which side had the better of the fighting in each year, and why.

Year	Nationalist successes	Communist successes	Which side had the better of the fighting in that year, and why?
1945			
1946			
1947			

WHAT WERE THE DECISIVE FACTORS DETERMINING THE OUTCOME OF THE CHINESE CIVIL WAR IN THE YEARS 1945–7?

For each statement below, explain whether you agree or disagree with it, and why.

Statement	Agree or disagree?
The ceasefire instigated by the USA in June 1946 benefited the CCP more than the Nationalists	
The failure of the Nationalists to deal with the CCP in rural areas of China, and their insistence on focusing on the cities, were vital reasons for their eventual defeat	
Foreign intervention was the most significant factor in determining the course of the conflict from 1945 to 1947, more significant than the CCP's use of mobile defence	
The CCP was in a stronger position in the Chinese Civil War by the end of 1947 because it had won the hearts and minds of Chinese agricultural labourers	

The Chinese Civil War in 1948–9: CCP victory

The CCP campaigns of 1948–9 resulted in victory. The Communists transitioned from their guerrilla mobile defence strategy to a brand of conventional war, as they attacked the urban areas held by the Nationalists. By January 1949, the war was effectively over.

The Communist Manchuria Campaign of October to November 1948 involved the CCP launching assaults on major cities in Manchuria, resulting in the region being firmly under CCP control by November 1948. The capture of Changchun on 26 October was the result of a brutal siege which resulted in 250,000 deaths, mainly from starvation.

From November 1948 to January 1949, the Huai-hai Campaign was launched. The CCP assaulted cities in China's central provinces, focusing on the city of Xuchou. The city was encircled, with all neighbouring villages destroyed in a 30-km (19-mile) radius, before a winter siege was put in place by the Red Army. Nationalist troops, short on food and supplies, began to desert in large numbers, allowing the CCP to capture the city.

The Pingjin Campaign, which ran simultaneously to the Huai-hai Campaign, focused on control in central China. From November 1948 to January 1949, Red Army forces launched artillery attacks on the cities of Xinbaoan, Zhangjiakou and Taiyuan, successfully capturing each. The campaign culminated with the Nationalist commander, Fu Zuoyi, surrendering Beijing on 16 January 1949.

The CCP, having gained control of northern and central China, focused on securing territory south of the Yangzi River and it faced only weak resistance. Nanjing city was taken in April 1949, Shanghai and Wuhan were taken in May, Xian and Changsha were taken in August, and Chongqing and Xiamen were taken in November. Chiang and the remaining Nationalist forces fled to Taiwan and Mao proclaimed the establishment of the Communist People's Republic of China (PRC) in Beijing in October 1949.

The practices of the Chinese Civil War and their impact on its outcome

Revised

Influence of foreign powers

Both the CCP and the Nationalists had limited domestic capabilities to manufacture armaments, so they relied heavily on foreign supplies. While the Nationalists began the war with greater access to modern weaponry, the CCP was more effective at sustaining crucial foreign aid throughout the war.

Foreign support for the Nationalists

The Nationalists were supported by the USA. The USA gave $798 million in military supplies from 1945 to 1949, plus over $1 billion in other types of aid in the same period. Historian Freda Utley has indicated that only $360 million of this amount was used to buy effective military supplies; the rest was wasted or went into the pockets of Chiang and other GMD officials and supporters. The US foreign minister, Secretary of State Dean Acheson, stated in August 1949 that he believed the Nationalists should have won the war, but misuse of equipment and corruption prevented victory.

The USA imposed an embargo on weapon sales between 1946 and July 1947 in order to get the CCP and GMD to attend peace talks. This may have weakened the GMD when it still had a chance of winning the war. Once the embargo was ended, supplies did not come very quickly, with some arriving only in early 1949 when the war was effectively over.

WHY WAS THE CCP SUCCESSFUL IN ITS CAMPAIGNS OF 1948–9?

For each campaign below, explain why the CCP was victorious, using the information on the preceding pages and your own knowledge. Try to consider both the strengths of the CCP and the shortcomings of the Nationalists.

Manchuria Campaign

Huai-hai Campaign

Pingjin Campaign

HOW BENEFICIAL WAS FOREIGN SUPPORT FOR THE NATIONALISTS?

Using the preceding pages and your own knowledge, note the benefits and drawbacks for the Nationalists in terms of the foreign aid that they received during the Chinese Civil War. Then answer the question in the bottom box.

Benefits	Drawbacks

Overall, did the benefits of foreign aid outweigh the drawbacks for the Nationalists?

Foreign support for the Communists

In the early months of the war, the Soviet Union gave the CCP access to huge stockpiles of Japanese weapons in northern China and Manchuria. The Soviets oversaw the transfer of 900 Japanese aircraft, 700 tanks and almost 4000 artillery pieces, and nearly 12,000 machine guns. The Soviets also trained CCP commanders at Russian military training schools.

As the war progressed, captured Nationalist weapons constituted the majority of CCP armaments. These were obtained through raids on arms depots or from deserters. It was a joke going around the Red Army that, 'Chiang was our best supplier of American weapons'. The CCP lacked airpower and armoured vehicles compared to the Nationalists. However, the adoption of mobile defence tactics and avoidance of conventional battles negated this potential problem.

Mobilization of human and economic resources

The Nationalists began the war with a larger army, yet this was not a decisive factor in the outcome of the war, as they failed to win the conflict in 1945–6 despite having a numerical advantage. CCP military strategies, such as mobile defence tactics, nullified the benefit of greater numbers of troops. Also, in a civil war, the ability to gain the support of the civilian population is vital in order to raise and supply troops, and the CCP were far more effective at doing this.

The Nationalists: human resources

In August 1945, the Nationalists' army, which stood at 2.7 million troops, was approximately three times the size of the Red Army. By June 1946, the Nationalist forces had risen to 4.3 million and the CCP had 1.27 million. The Nationalists still had a three-to-one advantage.

The Nationalists relied on conscripts for a significant amount of their army. Recruitment gangs were ordered into the countryside to collect troops using brutal techniques. This did not create a loyal force, as malnourished and reluctant agricultural labourers were tied together with ropes to prevent them from escaping, and forced into battle. Nationalist troops were not as disciplined as the Communist soldiers and mistreated the civilian population. There were many accounts of looting and rape.

The Nationalists: economic resources

The Nationalists, without access to much of the countryside, were hit hard by food shortages. As their strongholds were the cities, they relied on railways to get food to the urban areas, but the CCP often cut the lines and prevented supplies reaching the Nationalists. As a result, there were perennial shortages in Nationalist-held areas. What limited food there was became incredibly expensive, as inflation was rampant in Nationalist cities. In 1940, 100 yuan would have bought one pig, by 1946 only one egg. It was common for Nationalist soldiers to simply be given mugs of congee to eat. The Nationalists relied on foreign loans and printed vast amounts of paper money, which, along with food shortages, caused this rapid inflationary increase.

The Nationalists failed to win the hearts and minds of most of the civilian population. They used propaganda to target business and commercial elites with the message of the dangers of socioeconomic revolution that a Communist victory would bring. However, there was much disenchantment with the Nationalists due to increasing hardships in the cities. Many Nationalist officials hoarded food to sell for higher prices, and there was a resultant perception of corruption among Nationalist officials, which further served to turn the populace against them.

HOW BENEFICIAL WAS FOREIGN SUPPORT FOR THE CCP?

Using the preceding pages and your own knowledge, note the benefits and drawbacks for the CCP in terms of the foreign aid that it received during the war. Then answer the question in the bottom box.

Benefits	Drawbacks

Overall, did the benefits of foreign aid outweigh the drawbacks for the CCP?

HOW SUCCESSFUL WERE THE NATIONALISTS AT MOBILIZING HUMAN AND ECONOMIC RESOURCES?

Using the preceding pages and your own knowledge, note the successes and failures of the Nationalists at mobilizing human and economic resources in the second column. Then make an overall judgement as to how successful they were, in the right-hand column, explaining your reasoning.

Human resources	Successes:	Overall judgement:
	Failures:	
Economic resources	Successes:	Overall judgement:
	Failures:	

The CCP: human resources

The significance of the Nationalists' troop advantage in the first two years of the war was not decisive, as they failed to win the war in these years when they outnumbered the CCP. This was because the mobile defence tactics of the CCP neutralized this numerical advantage. The CCP also used conscripts. For example, historians Chang and Halliday estimate that in the 1948 Pingjin Campaign they had 1.5 million conscripts of agricultural labourers. However, a key difference was that the CCP treated its troops better than the Nationalists did theirs.

The CCP troops were disciplined and respectful, on Mao's insistence. As historian Chang wrote: 'Another good thing that captured the goodwill of the locals was the discipline of the Communist soldiers. Not only was there no looting or rape, but many went out of their way to demonstrate exemplary behaviour. This was in sharp contrast to the Guomindang troops.' From 1947 onwards, as the CCP began to take more territory, numerical superiority began to swing in favour of the CCP, as was evident in the massive Huai-hai and Pingjin Campaigns in November 1948 to January 1949.

The CCP: economic resources

The CCP was successful at gaining the support of the civilian population. Communist socioeconomic reform policies, such as land redistribution, gained the CCP huge levels of support among agricultural labourers. Thousands of landlords were put on trial and executed, and their land was redistributed. As a result, the CCP had access to vast networks of untrained militias from these agricultural labourers. In August 1945, this force was estimated to be 2.2 million strong. While they were ill-equipped, the militias were generally loyal supporters of Mao's ideas.

Red Army ranks were swelled by Nationalist defectors and prisoners as the war progressed. The CCP promised them good treatment and food, which encouraged Nationalists to switch sides, especially as the Nationalists were often short of food supplies. In 1948, following CCP victories in Shandong, many ex-Nationalists were assimilated into the Red Army and this allowed the CCP to successfully attack Xuzhou before Chiang could reinforce the defences.

The CCP controlled the countryside, which gave it access to a vast amount of food to feed its armies. Food was requisitioned from every household in CCP-held areas. These supplies enabled the Communists to pursue the strategy of mobile defence, which was essential in their overall victory, as their forces could live off the land around their bases.

The effects of the Chinese Civil War

Revised

Political impact of the war

The Chinese Civil War resulted in sweeping political change within China as a communist dictatorship took shape under Mao's leadership. While authoritarianism had deep roots in China, Mao's brand of communism represented a significant break from the past. The war also had huge political effects across the world, as the establishment of a communist regime intensified Cold War rivalries.

Communist dictatorship in China

A single-party CCP dictatorship was set up with Chairman Mao as the dictator. Small CCP committees were created all across China to discuss local issues. By the 1950s, there were over 1 million of these local CCP committees. All other political organizations were outlawed and in October 1950 a campaign to crush all counter-revolutionaries was launched. The definition of a counter-revolutionary remained vague, encouraging the settling of local grievances. This resulted in an atmosphere of terror, fear and compliance.

A surveillance society was encouraged, with Order Keeping Committees established in workplaces and schools to watch the behaviour of people. In Shandong province alone, approximately 28,000 people were executed as a result of this policy. The 1951 Three-Antis Campaign and the 1952 Five-Antis Campaign continued the terror. They targeted those believed to be guilty of financial misdeeds and were effectively aimed at property owners and private businessmen, who were class enemies according to the CCP. The neologism 'classicide' has been used to name these killings. They resulted in the deaths of 90–95% of the 15 million individuals that had constituted the landlord class in China.

THE RELATIVE SIGNIFICANCE OF DIFFERENT VARIABLES IN EXPLAINING THE OUTCOME OF THE CHINESE CIVIL WAR

Using the preceding pages and your own knowledge, explain the impact that each of the following had on the outcome of the Chinese Civil War, and then decide on the significance of each.

Variable	Explain the impact that this had on the outcome of the Chinese Civil War	How significant was the impact of this on the outcome of the Chinese Civil War?
Human resources		
Economic resources		
Foreign involvement		
Tactics		
Technological developments		
Ideology		

The reunification of China

At the war's end in 1949, China was more unified than it had been for decades. The CCP wanted to establish control over Guangdong, Xinjiang and Tibet, outlying regions that had distinct ethnic and religious identities. Mao launched a series of Reunification Campaigns to achieve this. Guangdong and Xinjiang were assimilated into Mao's China with relative ease. In Guangdong, the government surrendered to the CCP just two weeks after the PRC was declared in Beijing. In Xinjiang, the CCP was able to use diplomacy to persuade the leadership of the outlying region to surrender in return for political positions in the new CCP-controlled government.

Red Army troops were sent to Tibet in 1950 to assimilate the region into mainland China, and it took about six months for them to establish control. Tibet was renamed Xizang, the teaching of Tibetan language and history was forbidden in schools, and the public practice of Tibet's form of Buddhism, *lama*, was outlawed. The Tibetans fought back in a national uprising in 1959, but this was crushed with an estimated 87,000 killed. Tibet was forcibly incorporated into Mao's China.

Communist and Nationalist rivalry

In Taiwan, Chiang Kai-shek and his Nationalist followers claimed that their government, the Republic of China (ROC), was the rightful government of mainland China. This was a threat to the legitimacy of Mao's Communist PRC. Due to the Cold War climate, most Western nations and the United Nations (UN) recognized the Taiwanese government as the legitimate government of China until the 1970s.

Tensions sometimes boiled over into clashes over the islands in the Taiwan Strait. The ROC set up military fortifications on the islands of Matsu and Quemoy, and the PRC retaliated in August 1954 by shelling the islands and declaring that Taiwan should be liberated from Nationalist rule. This was known as the First Taiwan Strait Crisis. The USA, in particular, saw it as vital that Taiwan did not become communist, so it sent troops to Taiwan after passing the Formosa Resolution in 1955. However, the tensions de-escalated as the PRC stopped the shelling in May 1955, so these US troops were not involved in combat. In 1958, the Second Taiwan Strait Crisis occurred, which again saw limited military action. The results of this crisis were similar to the first crisis.

Intensification of the Cold War rivalry

For many in the USA, the victory of the CCP in the Chinese Civil War further emphasized the danger of the global spread of communism. Harry Truman was nicknamed 'the man who lost China', and many Americans felt that their government should have done more to prevent this eventuality. As a result, the USA became even more determined to challenge the international communist threat.

When the Korean War broke out in 1950 between communists in the north and non-communists in the south, the USA forced the UN to provide military assistance to the south. The great majority of the troops sent to aid the south were from the USA. The result of this conflict was the division of Korea along the 38th Parallel in 1953. A communist dictatorship was set up in the north, and the south has now become a liberal democracy with a capitalist-style economy, but has had periods of authoritarian rule since 1953.

US President Dwight Eisenhower, who was Truman's successor, saw himself as a 'Cold War Warrior', and was determined to challenge communism. He passed the Formosa Resolution in 1955, which allowed US troops to defend Taiwan in the First Taiwan Strait Crisis. He also increased military and economic assistance to the non-communist regime in Vietnam to fight Ho Chi Minh's communists. The eventual full-scale US military intervention in Vietnam was the most unfortunate example of how the perceived 'loss' of China to the CCP would haunt US politicians and result in a more interventionist and militaristic foreign policy.

THE POLITICAL IMPACT OF THE CHINESE CIVIL WAR

Using the information on the preceding pages and your own knowledge, complete the spider diagram below, noting the main political impacts of the Chinese Civil War.

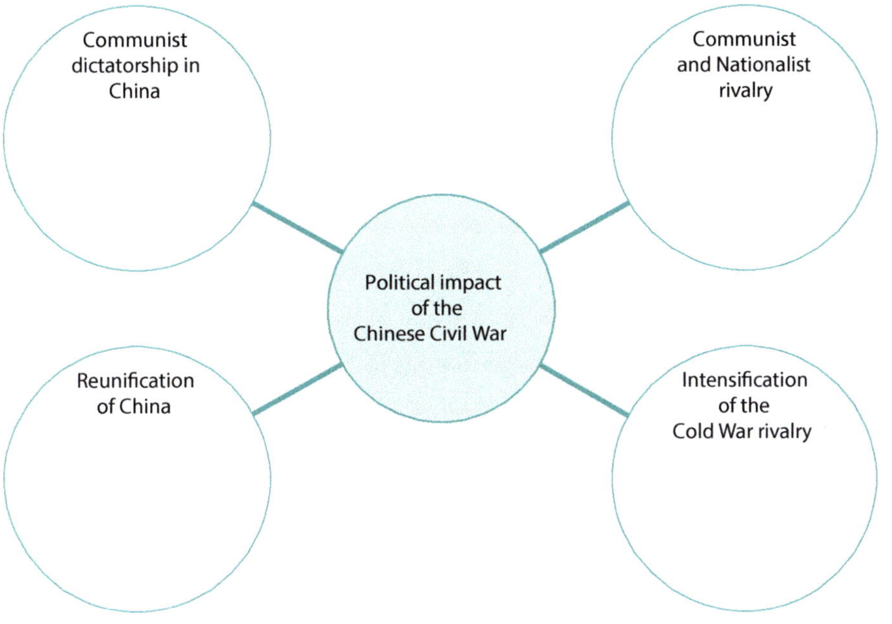

ESSAY-WRITING SKILLS: PLANNING AN IB ESSAY

Read the IB-style question below on the effects of war, and plan an answer in the box provided, staying focused on the political repercussions of the Chinese Civil War. You should give yourself five minutes to plan an essay to replicate exam conditions.

Evaluate the political repercussions of one 20th-century war.

Thesis:

Paragraph 1 theme:

Paragraph 2 theme:

Paragraph 3 theme:

Paragraph 4 theme:

Social impact of the war

The Chinese Civil War caused vast social change in terms of casualties, the socioeconomic structure in China and opportunities for women. Mao's government implemented communist reforms that would prove to be revolutionary for Chinese society.

Casualties

Approximately 4–6 million deaths occurred between 1945 and 1949, including deaths due to combat, famine and destruction caused by the war. In the three major campaigns of 1948–9 alone, the Nationalists suffered 1.5 million deaths, and the CCP a quarter of a million. This is far less than died during the Second Sino-Japanese War, which resulted in 3 million combat casualties and 18 million civilian deaths as a result of famine and conflict.

Social structure

During the Civil War there were significant changes to the structure of Chinese society in Communist-held areas. Landlords were removed from power and persecuted by local agricultural labourers. These changes affected territory in which 160 million people lived, and a probable estimate is that 16 million landlords were persecuted on some level during the Civil War. At least 1 million landlords were killed between 1945 and 1949. Between 1945 and 1949, millions of agricultural labourers found that they had become landowners for the first time. This process continued in the early years of Mao's rule as the 1950 Agrarian Reform Law gave land to agricultural labourers, and set up 'People's Courts' to put landlords on trial. In this way, the old feudal system in rural China was destroyed.

In 1953, Mao deviated from this path of private ownership and introduced collectivization, which brought agriculture under the control of the state. Regions were split into 25,000 huge communes, each containing about 5000 families. All decisions, such as crop yield targets, the prices at which to sell crops and the type of crops to be grown, were centrally decided.

Between 1958 and 1962, Mao oversaw the **Great Leap Forward**, which aimed to transform China from an agrarian economy into a socialist one via collectivization and industrialization. This was a brutal process that caused the Great Chinese Famine, which had a death toll estimated to range anywhere from 18 million to 55 million.

In 1966, Mao launched the infamous **Cultural Revolution**. Mao called on China's young people to remove 'impure' elements in Chinese society. China's young people formed into paramilitary groups called Red Guards and attacked non-communist elements, older people and intellectuals. Approximately 1.5 million people died in these purges and millions more were imprisoned, tortured, left without property or publicly humiliated.

Religion – both Western and traditional Chinese varieties – was attacked, and attempts were made to destroy it. During the Cultural Revolution it was labelled as one of the 'Four Olds' to be eradicated. Places of worship, such as churches, were destroyed and religious figures were ridiculed and attacked. Traditional Chinese ancestor worship was condemned. Only culture that promoted Communist values was allowed, and all traditional Chinese and Western culture was outlawed. This included traditional songs, dances, festivals and drama.

A national system of primary education was constructed and drastically increased the literacy rate, from 20% in 1949 to 70% in 1976. A phonetic form of Mandarin called *pinyin* was introduced, which made the language easier to acquire. These successes in the primary years did not continue higher up the education system. In 1982, only a quarter of the working population had attended school beyond the age of twelve, and only one per cent held degrees.

Impact of the war on women

The traditional role of women

Traditionally, China was a patriarchal society, with women enjoying few rights. They had to follow the 'Three Obediences', where they had to be obedient to their fathers, to their husbands and to their sons. They were also subject to arranged marriages and foot-binding, which prevented women from working. They had a clearly defined role as mothers and homemakers.

USING HISTORIANS' INTERPRETATIONS TO EVALUATE THE EFFECTS OF THE CHINESE CIVIL WAR

There are many interpretations that exist about what the main effects of the Chinese Civil War were. Engaging with these perspectives of historians in your essay can help you to develop your own line of argument, as you can argue whether you agree, or disagree, with their interpretation of events.

Read the three extracts below and then complete the activity beneath.

SOURCE 4

Extract from Michael Lynch, *Mao*, Routledge, London, 2004, page 230.

The People's Republic of China under Mao exhibited the oppressive tendencies that were discernible in all the major absolutist regimes of the twentieth century. There are obvious parallels between Mao's China, Nazi Germany and Soviet Russia. Each of these regimes witnessed deliberately ordered mass 'cleansing' and extermination.

SOURCE 5

Extract from Immanuel Hsu, *The Rise of Modern China*, Routledge, London, 1990, page 703.

In retrospect, the Cultural Revolution ushered in a decade of turmoil and civil strife that drove the country to utter chaos and the brink of bankruptcy. The party had been decimated and many of its leaders purged or dismissed. Poignantly, the Cultural Revolution turned out to be anti-cultural, anti-intellectual, and anti-scientific, for knowledge was considered the source of reactionary thought and action.

SOURCE 6

Extract from Frank Dikötter, *Mao's Great Famine*, Bloomsbury, London, 2010, page 299.

Mass killings are not usually associated with Mao and the Great Leap Forward, and China continues to benefit from a more favourable comparison with Cambodia or the Soviet Union. But as fresh and abundant archival evidence shows, coercion, terror and systematic violence were the foundation of the Great Leap, and between 1958 and 1962, by a rough approximation, some 6 to 8 per cent of those who died were tortured to death or summarily killed – amounting to at least 3 million victims.

Add examples from the preceding pages to support the three interpretations of the effects of the Chinese Civil War. In the second column add examples to support this interpretation, then in the third column explain the extent to which you find this interpretation persuasive.

Interpretation	Examples to support this interpretation	Explain the extent to which you find this interpretation persuasive
Michael Lynch		
Immanuel Hsu		
Frank Dikötter		

Women in Nationalist zones during the Chinese Civil War

In 1930, the Nationalist government in Nanjing passed the Civil Code, which stipulated that arranged marriages had to have the consent of the woman, that women could now initiate divorce proceedings and that daughters would get equal inheritance rights to sons. In 1931, a labour law stated that women should be paid the same as men for the same work. By 1935, there were over 6000 colleges and universities that admitted women. However, for the vast majority of women these legal changes brought little change to their lives, especially in rural communities. The Japanese invasions also meant that there was little legal oversight to uphold these laws.

Women in Communist zones during the Chinese Civil War

In Communist areas during the war, there was a theoretical acceptance of equality with men due to the Marxist underpinnings of their movement. Mao declared that 'women hold up half the sky'. There were also some practical advances, as women were encouraged to be part of CCP committees, foot-binding was prohibited and arranged marriages were discouraged. Women had new opportunities to be manual labourers, and were encouraged to take part in rural economic life, especially as more men were conscripted into the Red Army. There were notable examples of women fulfilling military roles. For instance, the Special Company of the Second Independent Division of the Chinese Red Army was a female-only unit.

Women in the Communist PRC

The Marriage Law of 1950 granted much greater rights for women:

- Arranged marriages were abolished and women could seek divorce with the same rights as men.
- Women had the same inheritance rights as men.
- A husband could not file for divorce if his wife was pregnant, or within one year of the child's birth.
- Concubinage and child-marriage were abolished.

In the communes in rural China, women were expected to work on the same terms as men and, as a result, nurseries were created to care for children. Eventually, there were too many women wanting divorces and so CCP officials started to refuse permission.

Economic impact of the war

China had experienced over a century of intermittent conflict, which created deep-seated economic problems. The destruction caused by the Chinese Civil War added to these difficulties. Furthermore, Mao brought in far-reaching left-wing economic reforms, which were often disastrous.

The Chinese Civil War adversely impacted the Chinese economy in many ways. Industrial production was weakened due to the destruction caused in urban areas, and the Soviet removal of much of Manchuria's industrial infrastructure. In rural China, a large fraction of male agricultural labourers who usually farmed the land were conscripted into the armies on both sides and so crop yields fell. Also, the CCP's attacks on landlords further disrupted the agricultural economy. Because of food shortages, inflation was rampant.

After 1949, the CCP's agricultural policies were economically disastrous. The collectivization of agriculture led to great inefficiencies, due to excessive centralization, and stagnation, due to a lack of incentive to innovate. More damaging still was the following of Trofim Lysenko's pseudoscientific ideas, which were based on the faulty genetic beliefs of the Russian biologist Ivan Michurin. Symbolic of the mistakes of the CCP was the Great Sparrow Campaign of 1958, which encouraged people to kill sparrows as they ate grain. However, by exterminating them, the food chain was disrupted and pests increased in number, which in fact reduced crop yields even further.

As a result of Mao's Great Leap Forward, from 1958 to 1960, grain production dropped from 200 million tonnes to 143 million, and meat production from 4 million tonnes to 1 million. This caused what is now termed the Three Bitter Years from 1959 to 1961, which saw somewhere in the range of 18 million to 55 million people die in the Great Chinese Famine.

THE EFFECTS OF THE CHINESE CIVIL WAR

Read the definitions below and add relevant examples for each area from the preceding pages and your own knowledge of the effects of this war.

Prescribed content	Definition	Examples from Chinese Civil War
Territorial changes	Changes to who governs areas of land. This can involve the creation of new countries and empires, and the end to others. The implications for the populations of these areas are often significant	
Political repercussions	Repercussions of war for political systems. War can often lead to significant upheavals to the governing classes of countries, and result in regime changes and new ideologies taking precedence. Sometimes these include greater rights for people, other times the complete opposite occurs	
Economic impact	Warfare can impact on the economy in areas such as gross domestic product and employment levels. It can also leave countries facing huge war debts in the form of reparations. The reconstruction of an economy after a war can be a tricky, protracted process	
Social impact	Warfare can impact on society in areas such as culture, religion, familial relations, relations between different groups in society, lifestyle changes, wealth and living conditions	
Demographic impact	Demographic studies attempt to measure quantifiable characteristics of a given population. War may impact the number of people left alive, the average age in a country, the ethnic makeup of a country and the gender balance, to name a few of the most common indicators	
Changes in the role and status of women	War may have a big impact on the role and status of women as the demands of war may require greater numbers of women to enter the workforce or join the army. This can lead to the enfranchisement and empowerment of women	

CHAPTER 5 Exam focus

Sample question and answer

Consider the response to the essay question below. Read it and the examiner's comments.

To what extent was one country affected economically by the result of one 20th-century war?

The Chinese Civil War was to a great extent a disaster for most people in China, both during the conflict and after its conclusion. During the war, the economy suffered from destruction, but also from foreign intervention. At the war's conclusion, the new government's economic policies benefited some, at least temporarily, but were ultimately a disaster that led to the death of millions. To a great extent, the results of the Chinese Civil War had a negative effect on the Chinese people.

> This is a focused introduction that indicates what the essay will discuss.

> The argument is made clear.

The Chinese Civil War caused great economic destruction. China's industrial production, already weak by contemporary standards, was damaged further due to the fighting in urban areas. Additionally, the economy of northern China was negatively affected by the removal of industrial machinery in Manchuria in 1946, valued at $858 million at the time. More economic disruption occurred as the Nationalists and the Chinese Communist Party (CCP) conscripted agricultural labourers into their armies. This meant fewer farmers and that meant less food was grown. This in turn led to food shortages, famine and a huge increase in the cost of food for civilians in the cities.

> Examples of the effect of the war on China's economy are clearly stated at the beginnings of the second and third paragraphs.

More importantly, rural areas had their economy altered during the war. Rural areas were dominated by the CCP and their economic systems intentionally collapsed. Farmland was seized from owners and turned over to the agricultural labourers who worked the land. Although this benefited agricultural labourers, it meant a complete breakdown of the rural economy as at least 1 million former landlords were killed and millions were attacked in various ways. The reorganization of the rural economy meant that millions went hungry in the cities and there was tremendous price inflation. One hundred yuan in 1940 would have purchased a pig, but by 1946, only one egg. The war devastated the Chinese economy, with the reorganization of the rural economy having the most negative effect.

> Using terms like 'more importantly' indicates analysis.

The Chinese Civil War ended in 1949 with a CCP victory. Starting in 1949 with the Agrarian Reform Law, all farmland throughout China was turned over to agricultural labourers and former landlords were put on trial, leading to the death of millions. This was similar to what occurred in CCP-occupied areas during the Civil War but was now conducted on a much greater scale. The rural economy continued to be disrupted as the new landowners lacked tools and money to buy seeds, in many cases. Although agricultural labourers temporarily gained ownership, the government soon ordered them to merge their holdings to form larger agricultural units called collectives, through the process of collectivization in 1953. Government officials, knowing little about agriculture, set impressive goals for grain production, for example, that were not realistic, leading to problems of supply and resources.

The Great Leap Forward was an economic programme started in 1958 and lasting until 1962 in which the CCP ordered mass industrialization, especially in the countryside. This disrupted agriculture further as millions of agricultural labourers were now forced into industrial jobs and agricultural land was turned into areas for mining, factories or other

> Concrete data, such as dates and names of laws, indicate depth of knowledge and evidence to support the argument.

industrial activities. By 1962, tens of millions of people were starving through lack of food and the state was on the verge of collapse. The Great Leap Forward was one of the great human disasters of the twentieth century and is the best example of the negative economic consequences of the results of warfare possible.

Economically, it could be argued that there were some benefits to the Chinese Civil War. Women, for the first time in China's long history, were made equal citizens of the state, at least by law. Starting in 1950, women were economically equal. Instead of having to stay home and care for children, leaving them economically weak, childcare services were offered in factories. As they were now able to earn money outside the home, they had more freedom, including the right to divorce and to education. Agricultural labourers, one could argue, also benefited economically. The old feudal system of agriculture ensured that poor agricultural labourers remained poor as they could never have enough money, regardless of how hard they laboured, to purchase farmland and therefore economic independence. As the result of Communist policies, they were, technically, landowners for the first time. After the collectivization of farmland, they remained, at least in law, equal to all other citizens, with rights and responsibilities. Both women and agricultural labourers gained economically as the result of the Communist victory at the end of the war in 1949.

Counter-opinions to the argument are acknowledged and evaluated.

Overall, the Chinese Civil War was an economic disaster for most Chinese people. During and after the war, the reorganization of the rural economy was the most significant economic disaster, and led to starvation and economic collapse in the countryside. After the war, CCP policies led to the deaths of tens of millions through starvation, although women and agricultural labourers were, in theory, economically liberated. To a great extent, the Chinese Civil War affected the people of China economically in a tremendously disastrous way.

This is a good conclusion because it is consistent with the rest of the essay, and draws out the main 'to what extent' arguments made in the essay. It summarizes the argument and comes to a definite conclusion.

A well-written response that focuses on the question. It develops a reasoned and nuanced line of argument in response to the 'to what extent' prompt. In addition, the structure is clear. The conclusion is consistent with the rest of the essay.

Exam practice

Now either attempt the above essay question or try one of the following questions, with reference to the Chinese Civil War.

1 Examine the role of ideology in causing two 20th-century wars, each chosen from a different region.

2 Evaluate the role of foreign intervention in deciding the outcome of two 20th-century wars.

3 Compare and contrast the impact of two 20th-century wars on the role and status of women.

6 Nicaraguan Revolution 1976–9

The Nicaraguan Revolution resulted from people's unhappiness with Nicaragua's ruling family, the Somozas, and their complete control of the country for over 40 years. This unhappiness, combined with economic troubles and natural disasters, sowed the seeds for a guerrilla campaign which would see the end of the Somoza regime.

The long-term causes of the Nicaraguan Revolution

Revised

The USA considered building a canal through Nicaragua (the canal was eventually built through Panama instead) and deployed troops to the country in 1909 to help stabilize it after a series of revolts. The USA established the **National Guard** in Nicaragua in 1927 to maintain order. The first leader of the National Guard was **Anastasio Somoza García**. Somoza Senior, as he was known, orchestrated the overthrow of the government in 1936 and became president in 1937.

The Somoza dynasty

Somoza effectively ruled as a military dictator, using the National Guard to maintain order and ensure he won all political elections. He formed close ties with the USA by declaring war on Japan after the bombing of Pearl Harbor in 1942 and always siding with the USA on issues debated in the United Nations. Somoza allowed the USA to use Nicaragua as the staging area for the **Bay of Pigs** attack on Cuba in 1961.

Somoza changed laws within Nicaragua as necessary in order to maintain control. For example, in 1955 the constitution changed to allow him to run for president again. He ensured that power would remain within his family after his death by grooming his sons to hold important positions of power. The elder son, **Luis Somoza Debayle**, was to become president after his father and the second son, **Anastasio Somoza Debayle**, was to command the National Guard.

Somoza was assassinated in 1956 and immediately replaced by his son Luis Somoza. Luis shifted the family's power from direct rule to indirect rule by making **René Schick** president in 1963. Schick died in 1966, followed by Luis Somoza in 1967, leading to the younger brother, Somoza Debayle, becoming president.

Early opposition to the Somoza dynasty

The Somoza dynasty faced little opposition from the country's largely rural population. Any opposition that did exist was dealt with moderately: usually imprisonment followed by a pardon or possible exile. The majority of the Nicaraguan people were highly unengaged with politics, spending their time working long hours on agricultural estates that were owned by either the Somoza family or other rich landowners.

Opposition did exist, however, mostly from the educated elite within Nicaragua.

Chamorro

La Prensa, the country's largest newspaper, was owned and operated by **Pedro Joaquín Chamorro Cardenal** ('Chamorro'), arguably the Somoza family's biggest political opponent.

Chamorro attempted a rebellion in 1954, leading to his being imprisoned for a year. This was followed by another stint in prison after Somoza Senior was assassinated (even though Chamorro played no role in the assassination), after which Chamorro fled to Costa Rica in 1957. He returned to Nicaragua in 1959 and staged another failed rebellion, leading to another year in prison. In 1969, he focused his efforts on inciting opposition through his newspaper.

WHY CAN DICTATORSHIPS CAUSE RESISTANCE?

Using the information about the Somoza dynasty on the previous page, and your own thoughts about political governments, fill in the table below considering what the benefits and limitations are for a country having a dictator in charge. Underneath the table explain your initial thoughts on why people in Nicaragua would not have liked the Somoza dynasty.

Benefits of a dictatorship	Limitations of a dictatorship

____

____

____

____

HOW DID SOMOZA MAINTAIN CONTROL?

For each of the following, explain how it would have helped Somoza to maintain control in Nicaragua.

- National Guard

  ____

  ____

- USA

  ____

  ____

- Cold War

  ____

  ____

- Family

  ____

  ____

Frente Sandinista de Liberación Nacional

The **Frente Sandinista de Liberación Nacional (FSLN)** (also known as **Sandinistas**) was set up in 1961, having been inspired by **Fidel Castro**'s recent success in the Cuban Revolution. While the organization's aims were unclear, all members agreed on the need to remove the Somoza family from power and that mobilizing agricultural labourers would be the best way to achieve this.

In 1962, 60 members travelled from Honduras to Nicaragua in an attempt to seize a small area of land from which to expand control. This was unsuccessful, however, as the National Guard quickly killed around twenty Sandinistas and captured almost all the rest.

In December 1966, a small group of Sandinistas once again arrived in Nicaragua in an attempt to engage the National Guard in battle. Within a year the Sandinistas either had been killed or had fled.

In 1969, FSLN published its overall goals, which included wanting to improve health and education, land redistribution, and an improvement in the status of women and minorities. Another attempt at revolution failed, but did inspire Catholic young people in Managua, the capital, who subsequently formed an underground movement.

The FSLN's failed revolutions did not generate support among agricultural labourers, but the organization learnt that support for a revolution was most likely to come from urban, more affluent young people who had the desire to see political reform.

Marxism

Marxism, also commonly referred to as communism, is a theory which identifies progress in history as coming about through class conflict and revolution, with the ultimate goal being the establishment of a society without government, private property or hierarchy. Many of the FSLN members were inspired by the recent Cuban Revolution, which saw Fidel Castro overthrow a regime propped up by the USA. Castro formed close ties with the USSR and announced that Cuba was a communist state.

Economics

The Somoza family controlled the economy, using government institutions to buy the best farmland in the country. Any unregistered land was seized by the family. The Somoza family would then use government money to build infrastructure on the land to maximize its productivity. The Somozas created an economic empire consisting of sugar mills, cattle plantations, coffee plantations, alcohol distilleries and much more.

Alongside this, Somoza Senior held the role of director of the Pacific Railroad Company, received financial gifts from US companies and prohibited the importation of goods from other companies.

After Somoza Senior's death, his son expanded the family's economic control even further. By the mid-1970s, the family owned 346 companies and roughly 75,000 km^2 (29,000 sq. miles) of land.

In stark contrast to this was that the vast majority of the Nicaraguan population were agricultural labourers, many of whom worked on the land owned by the Somozas. The World Health Organization reported that Nicaragua had the second highest incidence of disease in the Americas.

While the Nicaraguan economy saw a sharp rise in gross national product during the 1960s, the conditions of the rural population did not improve, highlighting the gap between the rich and the poor.

COMPLETE THE TABLE

Use your understanding of the material on the preceding pages to complete the table below. Summarize why each group/individual would want to overthrow the Somoza regime and rank how strongly you believe they opposed the Somoza regime. 1 = a little opposed; 5 = strongly opposed.

	Summary explanation	Rank (1–5)
Rural population		
Chamorro		
FSLN		

COMPLETE THE BODY PARAGRAPH

Below is a sample Paper 2 question.

Write a body paragraph on the long-term economic causes of the Nicaraguan Revolution, following from the opening sentence which has already been written.

Examine the causes of one 20th-century war.

The revolution in Nicaragua was caused by a number of long-term factors, including economic dissatisfaction.

The short-term causes of the Nicaraguan Revolution

Revised

Managua earthquake 1972

Opposition to the Somozas increased after an earthquake hit the Nicaraguan capital in December 1972, completely devastating the landscape and causing large numbers of deaths and widespread homelessness.

The USA supplied hundreds of millions of dollars in aid to the country, but the decision on how to spend this lay with the Somoza family, who prioritized rebuilding the homes of the wealthy. On top of this, high import taxes were placed on construction materials, making it difficult for the essential rebuilding efforts needed to take place.

The earthquake and the subsequent actions of Somoza made it very apparent to the urban population in Nicaragua that a change was needed to ensure the country's economic survival:

- The **Superior Council of Private Initiative (COSIP)** was an organization that included many of the capital's business owners. In 1974, COSIP organized a large gathering where it issued a public statement accusing Somoza of corruption.
- Chamorro, sensing a changing political climate, organized the **Unión Democrática de Liberación (UDEL)**, which was a coalition of seven political parties and labour unions.
- Christmas Party Raid: the Sandinistas stormed a dinner at the US ambassador's residence and took the Nicaraguan foreign minister and Somoza's brother-in-law hostage. The government eventually agreed to meet the Sandinistas' demands in return for the hostages' release. These demands included $1 million in cash, a flight to Cuba and the release of fourteen imprisoned Sandinista rebels. After the Sandinistas boarded their flight to Cuba, the National Guard launched a crackdown on FSLN activity, which effectively splintered the organization into various factions, shown in the table below.

Proletarian Faction	• Led by Jaime Wheelock • Believed in the need to educate people on Marxist principles • Opposed working with other political parties or the Catholic Church
Prolonged Popular War	• Strongly Marxist • Believed that a guerrilla war against the National Guard was needed
Terceristas	• Largest faction • Believed in the need to build alliances with other groups, including business owners and the Catholic Church
Northern Front	• Members of the Prolonged Popular War who fled Nicaragua for Honduras became known as the **Northern Front**
Southern Front	• Sandinista guerrillas based in Costa Rica became known as the Southern Front • Led by moderate, non-Marxist, **Edén Pastora**

National Guard Actions 1975–6

The National Guard, under the orders of Somoza, conducted anti-guerrilla operations against the Prolonged Popular War faction of the FSLN, who had begun a guerrilla campaign in the northern countryside of Nicaragua. The National Guard also carried out broader crackdown efforts, such as destroying farms and villages and torturing and killing agricultural labourers for information.

The actions of the National Guard did effectively drive out the Sandinistas, with many going into hiding in neighbouring Costa Rica. However, the actions also led to criticisms, mainly from the Catholic Church.

PRIORITIZING CAUSES OF THE REVOLUTION

Below are nine long-term and short-term causes of the revolution.

Complete the diamond-nine diagram beneath, placing the most significant cause at the top of the diamond and the least significant at the bottom.

Causes:

- The Somoza family ruled as a military dictatorship through the National Guard.
- The Somoza family controlled the economy in Nicaragua.
- The vast majority of the Nicaraguan people were agricultural labourers who did not benefit from Somoza's rule.
- Early opposition to the Somoza dynasty was not dealt with harshly; for example, Chamorro was given short prison sentences and able to continue to criticize the government once he had left prison.
- A large earthquake hit the Nicaraguan capital, Managua, in 1972, devastating the urban landscape.
- Somoza's response to the Managuan earthquake prioritized the needs of the rich.
- COSIP openly criticized the government and Somoza's corruption in the wake of the earthquake, creating an open climate of opposition.
- FSLN opposition increased in activity after the earthquake and successfully negotiated a ransom for the kidnapping of Nicaraguan politicians.
- National Guard oppression to opposition groups, particularly the FSLN, was extreme and drew criticism.

COMPLETE THE BODY PARAGRAPH

Using the activity above, write a body paragraph explaining why the cause you placed at the top of the diamond was more significant in causing the revolution than the cause you placed at the bottom of the diamond. Use the sentence starters to help you.

The most significant cause of the Nicaraguan Revolution was ...

This played a more important role in the outbreak of the revolution than ...

because ...

The course of the Nicaraguan Revolution

Revised

By 1977, it was clear to many in Nicaragua that Somoza needed to be replaced. Overthrowing the Somoza dynasty would be difficult: the family controlled the National Guard, received support from the USA and controlled the economy. However, through increased Sandinista efforts, shifting US allegiances and unpopular government actions this was achieved. By the end of 1979, the Somoza dynasty ended and the Sandinistas were firmly in control.

1977: Coalitions and committees

Opposition to Somoza was encouraged by the new US president, **Jimmy Carter**, who announced that US support to Nicaragua should no longer be considered automatic.

Sandinista actions

In early 1977:

- The *Terceristas*, FSLN's largest faction, began to make contact with business leaders and landowners in the hope of persuading them to join its cause.
- The faction realized that in order to gain support from the people within the country and sympathy from the USA, the organization needed to include non-Marxist aims.
- The organization created a plan which called for a multiparty political system, a mixed economy (both private and public businesses) and the ending of all international alliances with great powers.
- From this an anti-Somoza coalition was born, which included professionals as well as rebels.

In October 1977:

- The *Terceristas* organized a series of attacks against the National Guard, in the hope of inciting a rebellion. The attacks were a failure, with most of those involved being killed or captured and no national rebellion taking place, but others were inspired to join the anti-Somoza movement.
- Twelve members of the recently formed anti-Somoza coalition, known as ***Los Doce*** ('the Twelve'), began drafting a new political structure for Nicaragua. In order to achieve the overthrowing of Somoza, *Los Doce* agreed that:
  - the USA and neighbouring nations needed to be convinced that Nicaragua would not become a Marxist state
  - international efforts should concentrate on Somoza's corruption, the single-party state system and human rights violations
  - Sandinistas would form part of any future government.

Committee of National Dialogue

The **Committee of National Dialogue** was formed in 1977 by Archbishop **Miguel Obando y Bravo**, after concerns that the Sandinistas' actions may lead to a full-scale civil war. The Committee, led by COSIP's president, **Alfonso Robelo Callejas**, concluded that the Somoza family should no longer be in power. The Committee agreed that free elections should be held in 1980 and that a slow transition of power should take place which would ensure that the country did not descend into civil war.

The coalition outlined these ideas to Somoza, who did not reject the proposals, but also refused to agree to anything until local elections had taken place in 1978.

HOW DID THE REVOLUTION ESCALATE?

Below are key groups or individuals who helped to escalate the revolution in 1977.

Match these to their definitions.

Group/individual	Definition
The *Terceristas*	Twelve members of the anti-Somoza coalition
Los Doce	Organized in response to growing concerns about the unpopularity of Somoza with the aim of smoothly removing him from power
COSIP	FSLN's largest faction
The Coalition of National Dialogue	President of COSIP and leader of the Coalition of National Dialogue
Miguel Obando y Bravo	An organization consisting of most of Managua's business owners
Alfonso Robelo Callejas	The archbishop who founded the Coalition of National Dialogue

HOW SUCCESSFUL WAS THE REVOLUTION IN 1977?

Review the successes of the revolution by the end of 1977. In the left-hand column, summarize the successes that the revolution had achieved against Somoza. In the right-hand column, explain the failures or limitations that the revolution still faced.

Successes	Failures/limitations

1978: Somoza loses support

Assassination of Chamorro

On 10 January 1978, Chamorro was shot multiple times by three gunmen as he was on his way to work. The government quickly arrested and charged three men for the murder; however, it is unclear who (if anyone) ordered the killing.

The event had several important consequences for the revolution:

- Up to 50,000 people were involved in violent protests on the streets.
- Trade unions, including COSIP, went on strike for several weeks.
- The Committee of National Dialogue stopped calling for a slow transition of power and started calling for Somoza's immediate removal.
- In February, there were several rebellions by various sectors of society, including Native Americans and young people. The Sandinistas began organizing groups which could respond to disturbances quickly and help to escalate them.

Appeasing the USA

US President Jimmy Carter announced in 1977 that US support to Nicaragua should no longer be considered automatic. The US ambassador to Nicaragua went on to advise Somoza that he should step down at the end of 1980 once his term as president was over. Somoza agreed to this, knowing that Carter might well not be president by then. On 27 February, Somoza announced to the public that he would step down in 1980, hoping this would quell the unrest in the country. People were not satisfied with this as it gave Somoza plenty of time to find a replacement that he could control.

Central America's involvement

- Costa Rica: the new Costa Rican president allowed the Sandinistas to build rebel camps in the country, and to transport weapons and supplies.
- Venezuela: the Venezuelan president was a friend of Chamorro's and, after his assassination, opposed Somoza. He met with President Carter in March 1978 and expressed his belief that Somoza should be removed.
- Panama: Torrijos, Panama's leader, also met President Carter and expressed his concerns. Torrijos, himself a dictator, wanted to replace Somoza as America's main ally in Central America.

Once Somoza became aware that neighbouring countries wanted him removed from power, he made concessions to appease the USA, including a reformed electoral system and the release of many political prisoners.

The freeing of political prisoners allowed *Los Doce* to reform and it, along with other political parties, created the **Frente Amplio de Oposición (FAO)**. Robelo, the former president of COSIP, became the leader of FAO. FAO announced a sixteen-point plan for Somoza's removal. This included bringing about an end to Somoza's control over the National Guard and the creation of a united government.

SOURCE ANALYSIS

Read the source below. Use the source and the information on the previous page to answer the following questions:

1 Who did Chamorro's death impact and how?
2 Why was Chamorro's death a significant event in the revolution?

SOURCE 1

Extract from Patricia Taylor Edmisten, *Nicaragua Divided: La Prensa and the Chamorro Legacy*, University of West Florida Press, Pensacola, FL, 1990, page 7.

It was as if the assassination was the last straw for the people. The upper class, hoping for a peaceful change, had been waiting for pressure from Washington that would have persuaded Somoza to step down. These wealthy people, who might have disagreed with many of Pedro Joaquín's [Chamorro's] ideas, still had a deep respect for him. They viewed his murder as a terrifying omen that their country was now beyond the brink, and if it was to reclaim any dignity and autonomy, they would have to join the cause to bring down ... Somoza. These people, too, had experienced economic losses due to his incursions into their own business fields. He had interests in many Nicaraguan concerns, and his power was such that he pressured people to do business with him or suffer the consequences. Additionally, the upper class believed that if [Somoza] stayed in power and a more democratic president were not found, the Communists would surely gain control.

With Chamorro's assassination, the small middle class lost all hope. He had fought for them. He believed that their enterprises were crucial to the economic health of the nation. He praised their hard work and saw the dignity in their struggle to provide for their families.

The poor also loved Pedro Joaquín. He had visited them in their ***barrios*** and had inspired them to fight for their rights.

SOMOZA'S DECISION-MAKING

Somoza made various decisions in the early part of 1978.

For each decision in the table below, explain why you think Somoza made it and the possible impact it had on the revolution.

Somoza's decision	Why he made it	Impact on the revolution?
Ordered the arrest of three men quickly after Chamorro's murder		
Agreed to US President Carter's advice to step down at the end of 1980		
Reformed the electoral system		
Freed various political prisoners		

1978–79: The end of the Somoza regime

Seizure of the National Palace

In August 1978, the National Palace was stormed by 25 Sandinistas while the Nicaraguan Congress was in session. The Sandinistas quickly took control of the building and held those inside as captives. The Sandinistas demanded $10 million, that 83 political prisoners be released and that a series of statements be read on the radio.

The government mostly met these demands, leading to the Sandinistas releasing the hostages, except for a small number, which included a cousin of Somoza.

National unrest

- Immediately after the hostage situation at the National Palace had ended, the FAO announced a general strike, leading the government to arrest its leaders.
- Sandinistas attacked National Guard positions around Nicaragua, leading to far harsher reprisals by the government. Sixty-three rebels were killed along with hundreds of civilians, leaving the majority of Sandinistas dead or in exile.

International mediation

The **Organization of American States (OAS)** met to discuss the growing crisis in Nicaragua. The USA asked member countries to stop giving assistance to the Sandinistas during the period of negotiations and recommended to Somoza that he resign.

OAS discussions began to focus on how Somoza should step down and what should happen to Nicaragua after this. The FAO became central in the discussions, in which they presented a modified version of their sixteen-point plan. This version still called for Somoza's removal but did not insist on the abolition of the National Guard and did allow for there to be council representatives from Somoza's National Liberation Party. Somoza rejected these terms and insisted that he would remain in power until his term ended in 1980.

The OAS responded by insisting that a plebiscite (vote) be held in Nicaragua to see whether the public wanted Somoza to remain in power or not. Somoza refused to do this and the USA responded by cutting off all aid to Nicaragua.

Four months of OAS negotiations had not resolved the situation, causing the FAO and other organizations to lose faith in the USA's ability to solve the crisis.

Sandinista guerrilla campaign

The Sandinistas in exile regrouped and, by December 1978, had organized the **National Directorate** to coordinate activity among the various factions. The Sandinistas received a growing supply of weapons and ammunition from Cuba, helping the organization to grow in strength.

In April 1979, the Sandinista faction known as the Northern Front launched an attack on the city of Estelí. National Guard troops fought the Sandinistas on the streets, causing destruction and prompting international outrage at the level of violence. Attacks continued across the country throughout the months of April and June.

Junta of National Reconstruction

Leaders from the FAO, *Los Doce* and the Sandinistas met in the Costa Rican capital and agreed to form a provisional government which would lead post-Somoza Nicaragua. This would be called the **Junta of National Reconstruction**. Members included Robelo (leader of the FAO), **Violeta Barrios de Chamorro** (Chamorro's widow), **Sergio Ramírez** (member of *Los Doce* and the Sandinistas) and **Daniel Ortega** (member of the National Directorate and brother of a member of *Los Doce*). The new government announced itself to Nicaragua via radio on 17 June.

Final US attempts to remove Somoza

- The USA sent an ultimatum to Somoza on 18 June 1979, demanding that he resign and allow for the creation of a truly representative government. For this, Somoza would be allowed residency in the USA.
- Somoza responded the next day, agreeing that he would resign but only if the OAS would ensure a stable transition of power and only if the entire Somoza family were able to live permanently in the USA.

- On 23 June, the OAS passed a resolution that called for a ceasefire and an arms embargo, and for Somoza to be replaced with an interim government. However, this resolution was too late as violence between the Sandinistas and the National Guard was increasing.

Increasing insurrection

By the middle of June, the National Guard had abandoned León, Nicaragua's second largest city, and other towns were falling into the hands of rebels, some Sandinista but some not. Businesses and labour unions announced strikes and many civilians began to flee. The National Guard, with 10,000 troops, still significantly outnumbered the rebels.

CHRONOLOGY ACTIVITY

Sort the events in the table below into chronological order. In the right-hand column, give each event a number between 1 and 8 depending on when it occurred in relation to the other events.

Event	Order
Chamorro was assassinated	
The OAS met to discuss the growing crisis in Nicaragua	
The Committee of National Dialogue was formed	
The Frente Amplio de Oposición (FAO) was created and announced a sixteen-point plan for Somoza's removal	
The US president and Venezuelan president met to discuss how to ensure Somoza's removal	
25 Sandinistas stormed the National Palace	
Somoza announced reforms to the Nicaraguan electoral system	
Sandinistas launched attacks on the National Guard, leading to the death of 63 rebels	

COMPLETE THE BODY PARAGRAPH

Using the information on the course of the revolution so far, complete the body paragraph in response to the following question.

Evaluate the influence of foreign powers in the Nicaraguan Revolution.

Foreign powers played a highly influential role in the Nicaraguan Revolution. Various nations were involved in some way, such as ...

Of particular significance was ...

who influenced the revolution by ...

This was significant because ...

The Sandinista Southern Front

The Sandinistas' largest faction was based in the south of Nicaragua and was engaged in bloody battles near the border of Costa Rica, which resulted in the deaths of more than 400 Sandinista guerrillas. The extent of the violence encouraged the moderate Sandinista, Pastora, to request help from the USA in forcing the National Guard to back down. President Carter refused, however, hoping for a stalemate between the two sides and a smooth transition of government.

Somoza departs and Urcuyo assumes power

Date	Events
12 July	Somoza selected **Francisco Urcuyo Maliaño** ('Urcuyo'), the lower house speaker of the Nicaraguan Congress, as the temporary transitional president for whenever Somoza left the country
15 July	The USA approved the provisional government, pleased that the cabinet had been formed of members from a range of opposition groups Somoza subsequently agreed to name a replacement for his half-brother as the head of the National Guard
17 July	Somoza announced his resignation and Urcuyo asked for all factions to meet with him to create a new government, going against plans already laid out for a provisional government (Junta) The US ambassador met Urcuyo and instructed him to carry forward the plans already laid out by the Junta; Urcuyo refused The US ambassador then informed Urcuyo that he needed to resign and be replaced by Archbishop Obando. Again Urcuyo refused
18 July	The National Guard, unaware of the ongoing political negotiations, was rapidly running low on equipment and morale, allowing the Sandinistas to make gains across Nicaragua For fear of the country becoming a Marxist state under Sandinista control, the Costa Rican president flew the Junta members to León in Nicaragua to establish a transitional government
19 July	Urcuyo finally accepted that he was not able to maintain control in Nicaragua and fled the country
20 July	The remaining fighting members of the National Guard quickly fled or surrendered The Junta arrived in Managua to assume control

Victory achieved

By the end of 1979, the Sandinistas had established control in Nicaragua by manipulating the Junta. However, it would be simplistic to conclude that this was the result of their military campaign. The fall of Somoza was more the result of opposition groups fearing a Marxist state under Sandinista control and thus doing what they could to ensure that Somoza did step down, but in a smooth and non-violent manner. These opposition groups succeeded in forcing Somoza to resign, but failed in their objective of ensuring a smooth transfer of power.

HOW DID DIFFERENT FACTORS INFLUENCE THE OUTCOME OF THE REVOLUTION?

Using all the information about the course of the Nicaraguan Revolution on the preceding pages, complete the mind map to explain the role of different factors in the revolution.

The mind map uses the language of the IB guide, which is likely to appear in essay questions. You may have more to say in certain sections than others.

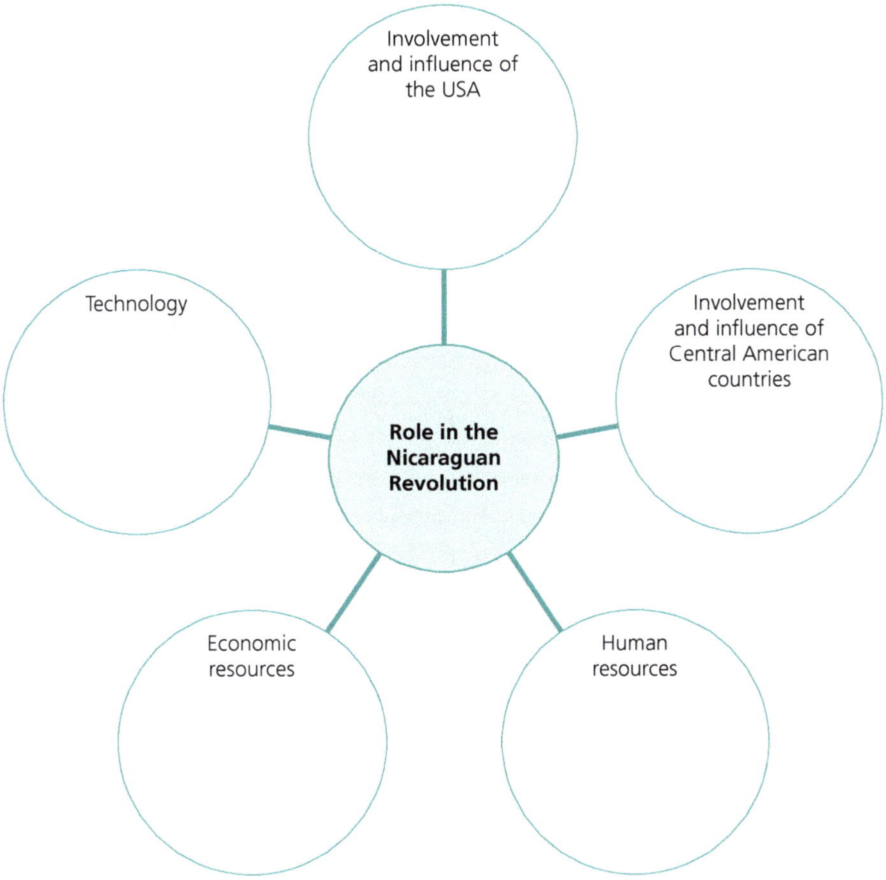

SIGNIFICANCE OF FACTORS

Using the information you have written in the mind map above, rank the different factors in order of their significance in overthrowing the Somoza regime. Write each factor as it is written in the mind map next to the appropriate number (1 = most significant; 5 = least significant).

1 ______________________________

____

2 ______________________________

____

3 ______________________________

____

4 ______________________________

____

5 ______________________________

____

The effects of the Nicaraguan Revolution

Revised

Political effects of the revolution

Governance

The agreements that had been made in Costa Rica before the fall of Somoza were largely ignored, as was the Junta for National Reconstruction. The Sandinistas dominated government:

- Government buildings and private homes owned by Somoza were taken over by the Sandinistas.
- The **Sandinista Popular Army** was created.
- Defence committees were created which encouraged Sandinista activities across the country.

These actions, along with the Sandinistas' refusal to arrange elections, prompted the resignation of Violeta Chamorro and Robelo in April 1980. Elections were eventually held in 1984, by which time the Sandinistas had garnered popular support throughout the country, leading to a victory with 67% of the popular vote. Daniel Ortega was elected president and remained in this position until 1990, when a coalition led by Violeta Chamorro replaced him. Chamorro became the first elected female leader in the Americas.

Human rights violations

There is strong evidence that human rights violations took place under the Sandinista regime, some of which were documented by the Nicaraguan Permanent Commission for Human Rights before the Sandinista government closed it shortly after establishing power.

- Family members of National Guardsmen were imprisoned.
- Hundreds of people disappeared after arrest and were never seen again.
- Mass graves were later found, suggesting that hundreds of civilians had been executed by the Sandinistas.
- Freedom of speech was limited as the government took control of the press.

Foreign relations

Nicaragua forged a close relationship with Cuba, which sent teachers, doctors, military advisers and more to assist the Sandinistas.

Nicaraguan relations with the USA changed after the revolution, with Nicaragua prioritizing relations with Cuba over the USA and its allies, such as Panama.

Many Sandinistas were outspoken against the USA, blaming it for Somoza's rule and demanding compensation. The USA did grant aid to Nicaragua in 1979 in the form of a loan; however, once it became clear that the Sandinistas were not prioritizing free elections, the USA ended its financial support and relations deteriorated further.

Contras

Various rebel groups who opposed the Sandinista regime were known collectively as the **Contras**. The groups included agricultural labourers who disliked the nationalization of farmland, former National Guardsmen, business owners and others.

The Contras waged war on the Sandinista government, a conflict which lasted from 1979 to 1990. The Contras received financial and military support from the USA in their early years, while the Sandinistas were assisted by the Soviet Union and Cuba. Official US support for the Contras did not last, however, as it emerged that the rebels were carrying out atrocities on civilian populations, such as rape and torture.

It later emerged, much to the embarrassment of the administration of US President **Ronald Reagan**, who followed President Carter, that the USA had continued to secretly supply the Contras with aid through Iran. This violated not only the US Congress's law banning assistance to the Contras, but also an arms embargo that had been imposed on Iran.

By the late 1980s, both the Contras and Sandinistas were exhausted; thousands had died or been uprooted from their homes. After the election of Chamorro in 1990, Contra groups disbanded and the fighting ended.

SUCCESSES AND FAILURES OF PEACEMAKING

Review the plans for Nicaragua after Somoza in the previous section and compare these with the information on the opposite page. Complete the table, considering the successes and failures of the peacemaking process.

Successes of peacemaking	Failures of peacemaking

WRITE AN INTRODUCTION

An effective introduction prepares the reader for the argument that answers the demands of the question. Therefore, it should be brief, perhaps about three to four sentences. The introduction is not the proper place for long, detailed descriptions. An effective introduction:

- grabs the reader's attention
- addresses the demands of the question by stating your argument or thesis
- identifies your argument's main points
- transitions into the first main point of the argument.

Using the information from the previous activity and your own knowledge, write an introduction to the following Paper 2-type question.

With reference to one 20th-century war, discuss the successes and failures of peacemaking.

Economic effects of the revolution

The Sandinista-dominated government followed Marxist ideology when creating its economic policy. For example, all banks, insurance companies and mining companies were nationalized. The government took charge of foreign exports and all Somoza property was seized.

Many business owners fled the country soon after the Somoza regime had fallen, with more doing so once the Sandinistas admitted that they wanted to turn Nicaragua into a Marxist state. By the end of 1980, 40% of the nation's economy was under Sandinista control.

Agricultural reform

Somoza had owned 25% of the nation's farmland, all of which was seized by the Sandinista government and the large farms were turned into state businesses. For many farmers, life remained the same, only the name of those they worked for changed.

In the mid-1980s, the government began to distribute land to small groups of agricultural labourers or individuals, allowing farmers the opportunity to work on their own land. This was largely in response to the Contras.

Social effects of the revolution

Deaths

- It is estimated that somewhere between 9000 and 50,000 civilians were killed during the revolution.
- Roughly 3000 Sandinistas were killed
- Around 10,000 National Guard members were killed.
- Somoza was eventually killed by a pro-Sandinista group in 1980 while in Paraguay.

Church

- Archbishop Obando, as a strong opponent of Somoza, accepted Sandinista actions during the revolution; however, by the early 1980s he opposed the Sandinista government, believing that their support of **Liberation Theology** clashed with the teachings of the Catholic Church.
- Liberation Theology did gain the support of some Catholics who also felt that the structure of the Catholic Church was backwards and believed that all ordinary people had the right to conduct their own religious ceremonies, without the need for an ordained priest.
- Archbishop Obando banned any priest from affiliating with the Sandinista government and became a prominent opponent, speaking out about a range of issues including human rights violations.

Literacy

A national literacy crusade was started by the Sandinista government, which aimed to rid the country of illiteracy. Students and teachers from elsewhere in Latin America assisted these efforts and the government printed large quantities of books by Sandinista-approved authors. In March 1980, around 50% of the population was illiterate, but by August this percentage had dropped to thirteen per cent.

Women

Under the Somoza regime, women had few rights and were expected to be subservient to men. Most women were poorly educated and illiterate, and lacked access to healthcare.

The Sandinistas promoted equality between men and women, allowing women to leave their traditional roles and improve their outlook in life.

- The Junta announced gender equality as law and introduced new laws to grant women more rights, including maternity leave and the right to divorce.
- Women took up jobs in education and healthcare.
- By 1987, over 30% of the management positions in the government were held by women.
- Over a third of industrial workers were women.

The improvement of women's lives after the revolution was considerable; however, it did not lead to women being completely equal to their male counterparts. Income inequality still existed and many of the equality laws introduced were not followed or enforced in practice.

HOW DID THE REVOLUTION IMPACT THE NICARAGUAN PEOPLE?

For each of the groups of people listed in the table, identify the positive and negative impacts that the revolution had, from the information on the previous page. You may leave some boxes empty.

	Positive impact	Negative impact
Catholics		
Rural population		
Women		

COMPARE AND CONTRAST

IB exams often have questions which require you to compare and contrast two wars.

Choose one other war that you have studied and complete the exercise below, comparing the impact that each war had on women.

	Role of women	Status of women
Comparison (similarities)		
Contrast (differences)		

CHAPTER 6 Exam focus

Sample question and answer

Below are two body paragraphs, each written by a different student in response to the following IB Paper 2-style question.

'Support from foreign powers can be crucial to winning civil wars.' With reference to one civil war, to what extent do you agree with this statement?

Body paragraph A

Support from foreign powers did prove to be very important in the successful overthrowing of the Somoza regime. The USA, once supportive of Somoza, withdrew its support under the presidency of Carter. Without the support of a superpower like the USA, Somoza struggled to withstand the growing pressure in Nicaragua to step down. Other foreign countries also assisted the rebels, which was important in bringing about victory against Somoza. For example, Costa Rica allowed Sandinistas to use it as a base from which to launch attacks into Nicaragua. Eventually the rebels became too strong and Somoza did not feel able to remain as leader.

What are the strengths of this paragraph?

What are its limitations? How might you improve it?

Body paragraph B

Foreign powers proved to be influential, although not crucial, in the Nicaraguan Revolution. The efforts which brought about an end to the Somoza regime were carried out by those within Nicaragua; however, the lack of resistance from neighbouring countries, along with the diplomatic pressures from the USA, did probably speed up Somoza's fall. The leaders of Costa Rica, Venezuela and Panama all publicly voiced their opinion that Somoza should step down in 1978. Costa Rica even allowed Sandinistas to base themselves in the country to keep safe from the National Guard. These actions alone were not enough to overthrow a dictator like Somoza, but combined with the growing efforts of the rebel forces, they sent an important message to Somoza that he lacked international political support. Similarly, the USA went from being a supporter of his regime to strongly advising

> that he resign. In fact, US policy in 1978 changed to focusing on what Nicaragua should look like post-Somoza, suggesting that in Carter's mind, Somoza must go. The USA never sent troops nor did it actively support the rebel forces, who ultimately created a climate in Nicaragua where Somoza had little choice but to resign; however, it did apply important political pressure which sped up the outcome of the revolution.

What are the strengths of this paragraph?

What are its limitations? How might you improve it?

Which response do you think is better, and why?

Exam practice

Now either attempt the above essay question or try one of the following questions, with reference to the Nicaraguan Revolution.

1 Civil wars are caused by ideological conflict. Discuss with reference to one 20th-century civil war.

2 Evaluate the view that the mobilization of human resources is more important than the mobilization of economic resources in winning a civil war.

3 Examine the political and economic impact of war on two states, each from a different region.

Glossary

38th Parallel Line of latitude used by the United Nations to divide the Korean peninsula after the Second World War.

Anarcho-syndicalist An anarchic belief in which proponents desire the central authority of the state to be replaced by the operation of control by trade unions.

Anschluss The name given to the annexation of Austria by Germany in 1938.

Anti-Comintern Pact Signed between Germany and Japan in 1936 against the USSR.

Arms race A competition between nations for military superiority.

Army of Africa Spanish and Spanish Moroccan troops stationed in Spanish Morocco.

ASDIC An early form of sonar technology, used by the Allies in the Second World War to detect German submarines.

Asturias Mining region in north-west Spain, the scene of a workers' revolt in 1934.

Atlantic Charter A declaration of goals of Allied nations in the Second World War.

Atoll An island formed from a coral reef.

Austro-Hungarian Empire Dual monarchy formed by the union of the Austrian Empire and the Kingdom of Hungary in 1867. It dissolved in 1918, at the end of the First World War.

Barrio Spanish word for a crowded, low-income city district.

Battle of Cambrai First World War British military offensive and German counterattack in northern France, 1917.

Battle of Jutland The only major naval battle of the First World War, fought between Britain and Germany off the North Sea coast of Denmark in 1916.

Battle of Passchendaele First World War battle fought between the Allies and Germany in Belgium, 1917. Officially known as the Third Battle of Ypres.

Battle of Tannenberg First World War battle fought between Germany and Russia in August 1914, resulting in a resounding German victory.

Battle of the Somme One of the deadliest battles of the First World War, fought between the armies of Britain and France on one side and Germany on the other in 1916.

Battle of Verdun The longest-lasting battle on the Western Front in the First World War, fought between the French and German armies in 1916.

Bay of Pigs The site of a failed CIA-backed attempt by Cuban émigrés to retake Cuba from Castro.

Black Hand Secret military organization in the Serbian government that worked to unite all South Slavs into one state.

Blitzkrieg German for 'lightning war'; a military strategy involving coordinated sudden attacks by air and on the ground.

Bolshevik Party The Russian Communist Party. It seized power in a revolution in October 1917.

Bolshevik Revolution The successful communist revolution in Russia in October 1917 led by the Bolshevik Party.

Brusilov Offensive Russian military offensive against Austria-Hungary in 1916, the largest Russian assault of the First World War.

Caucasus Campaign The series of conflicts fought primarily between Russia and the Ottoman Empire, part of the Middle Eastern theatre of the First World War.

Central Powers First World War alliance of Germany, Austria-Hungary, Bulgaria and the Ottoman Empire.

Chinese Communist Party (CCP) The Communist Party of China, established in 1921.

Code breaking The practice of deciphering encrypted messages, used during wartime to intercept and interpret enemy communications.

Cold War A decades-long period of tension between the USSR and the USA, and their respective allies, lasting from shortly after the end of the Second World War until the collapse of the USSR in 1991. Although the two major powers did not engage in direct conflict, they were involved in a number of proxy wars, such as the Korean War and the Vietnam War.

Collective security The concept that a war against one member of the League of Nations is a war against all member states.

Comfort houses Military-operated brothels in Japanese-occupied territories during the Second World War, staffed by women, many of whom had been abducted and forced into sexual slavery. Also known as comfort stations.

Comfort women Women forced into sexual slavery in Japanese-occupied territories by the Japanese Imperial Army.

Committee of National Dialogue Committee established by Archbishop Miguel Obando y Bravo in Nicaragua in 1977, which, fearing civil war, attempted to facilitate a transition from the Somoza regime to a democratic process of free elections.

Conscription Compulsory enrolment of civilians into an army.

Contras Various counter-revolutionary groups who fought against the Sandinistas in the 1980s. Contra is an abbreviation of the Spanish word for counter-revolution: *contrarrevolución*.

Convoy system The practice of ships sailing in large groups protected by naval destroyers rather than sailing individually.

Cryptanalyst An individual tasked with analysing and interpreting encrypted messages or codes.

Cultural Revolution A mass movement begun by Mao's supporters to purge the CCP and PRC society of those opposed to Mao's version of communism.

Decolonization Process of granting independence to colonies of primarily European states.

Demilitarized zone An area in which military activity is forbidden, as agreed by a treaty or agreement between conflicting nations. Examples include the demilitarized zone between North and South Korea at the end of the Korean War in 1953, and in the Rhineland on the western border of Germany, following the First World War.

Depth charge An explosive device fired from a battleship which is designed to detonate at a certain depth.

Falange Party Fascist political party established in Spain in February 1933 by José Antonio Primo de Rivera, the son of Miguel Primo de Rivera.

False flag An operation in which a country inflicts an attack on itself but blames an adversary, thereby creating a motivation for military action.

Fascism A term derived from the Fascist Party of Italy. It refers to a governing philosophy that glorifies the state, war and sacrificing oneself for the state while de-emphasizing individual rights and freedoms. This term is often used to refer to non-democratic, militaristic governments.

Final Solution The Nazi policy of exterminating European Jewish people in concentration camps, implemented during the Second World War.

Five Year Plans Economic programmes of the USSR which initially focused on mass industrialization.

Fleet carrier A type of aircraft carrier designed to operate on the front line, as part of a navy's main fleet.

French Indochina A French colony consisting of today's Laos, Cambodia and Vietnam.

Frente Amplio de Oposición (FAO) The Broad Opposition Front, formed by *Los Doce* and members of other political parties in Nicaragua to attempt to facilitate the replacement of Somoza by a united government.

Frente Sandinista de Liberación Nacional (FSLN) The Sandinista National Liberation Front, a revolutionary political party formed in Nicaragua in 1961 to oppose the Somoza regime. It seized power as a result of the Nicaraguan Revolution of 1979 and effectively ruled the country until 1990.

Gallipoli Peninsula The southernmost part of European Turkey, the site of a failed and costly offensive by the Allied forces against the Ottoman Empire in the First World War.

German Condor Legion German military unit sent by Hitler to support Franco's Nationalists in the Spanish Civil War, most famous for its involvement in the bombing of Guernica.

Golden years Phrase used to describe the period between 1924 and 1929 in Weimar Germany, reflecting the recovery of the economy following the First World War and the hyperinflation crisis of the preceding years.

Great Depression Economic depression which began in 1929 and adversely affected the world economy throughout much of the 1930s.

Great Leap Forward The second Five Year Plan in China, which involved the creation of communes and high industrial targets. It is largely regarded as a disaster for the country.

Greater Asia Co-prosperity Sphere Japanese-created and -led organization of puppet governments established in Japanese-occupied Asian nations that encouraged Asians to oppose European and US rule and to support Japan during the Second World War.

Gross national product All economic activity of a nation, which includes production, exports and imports.

Guerra celere Spanish phrase meaning rapid war, used to describe a sudden military offensive supported by aerial bombardment; similar to the German term *blitzkrieg*.

Guomindang (GMD) The Chinese Nationalist Party. It can also be transliterated to Kuomintang (KMT).

Hegemonic power The dominant state or group in a particular region, or globally.

High-frequency direction finding System employing at least two machines used by the Allies in the Second World War to detect the exact location of German submarines by focusing on German radio signals.

Hyperinflation When the value of a currency falls rapidly and leads to extremely high monetary inflation.

Imperial Japanese Navy (IJN) Japan's wartime naval forces.

Independence movement Campaign by the people of a particular country or region to gain independence from a ruling state or colonizer.

International Brigades Military units composed of volunteers from a range of countries.

International Military Tribunal for the Far East Trials of Japanese political and military leaders for war crimes following the Second World War.

Isolationism Foreign policy that involves the isolation of a particular nation from the affairs of others, for political, cultural or economic reasons.

Iwakura Mission A major Japanese diplomatic delegation to the USA and Europe, following centuries of isolationism. It lasted from 1871 to 1873.

Jiangxi Soviet An area under Chinese Communist Party control, 1927–34. The area was repeatedly attacked by Chiang during the Encirclement Campaigns.

July Crisis A month of diplomatic deliberations and military gesturing by the European powers in July 1914, following the assassination of Archduke Franz Ferdinand, which ultimately led to the outbreak of the First World War.

Junta of National Reconstruction Provisional Nicaraguan government established in opposition to the Somoza regime in June 1979, comprising individuals from across the political spectrum. The Junta officially assumed control after Somoza's resignation, but power was essentially held by the Sandinistas alone.

Kamikaze Suicide attacks, often using aircraft packed with explosives.

Latifundia Large, privately owned agricultural estates, on which workers are often subject to exploitative terms of employment.

League of Nations International organization established after the First World War to resolve conflicts between nations in order to prevent war.

Lebensraum Meaning 'living space', part of the Nazi ideology that sought more territory for Germany.

Left-wing Liberal, socialist or communist.

Lend–Lease US programme begun in March 1941 that lent over $50 billion ($650 billion in today's terms) worth of war supplies to Allied nations.

Liberation Theology Central American Catholic clergy movement, inspiring parishioners to work for change in this life, rather than waiting for their reward in heaven.

Long March Major retreat by Chinese Communists across China, 1934–5.

Los Doce Meaning 'the Twelve', a group of twelve figures from the Nicaraguan establishment who declared their support for the Sandinistas against the Somoza regime.

Ludendorff Offensive First World War military offensive launched by Germany on the Western Front in March 1918 in a failed attempt to capture a decisive victory before capitulating to the superior resources of the Allies.

Maginot Line A complex system of fortresses and other defences established by France on the French–German border.

Mandate Territory of the German or Ottoman Empire that was administered primarily by Britain, France or Japan under supervision of the League of Nations.

Manhattan Project Research project that led to the development of the atomic bombs that were to be dropped on Hiroshima and Nagasaki in August 1945.

Marxism Marxism is also often referred to as communism. It is an economic and sociopolitical theory which identifies progress in history as coming about through class conflict and revolution, with the ultimate goal being the establishment of a society without government, private property or hierarchy. It is named after the originator of the theory, Karl Marx (1818–83).

Meiji period Period of Japanese history (1868–1912) characterized by rapid modernization and imperial ambitions, after centuries of relative isolationism.

Mesopotamian Campaign Military campaign fought between British Empire forces and the Ottoman Empire in the Middle East as part of the First World War.

Milicianas Women who participated in front-line combat as part of Republican militias during the Spanish Civil War.

Militiamen Members of a militia.

Mobile defence A military strategy that uses the guerrilla tactics of sabotage and ambush to weaken the enemy by disrupting supply lines and inflicting casualties. It does not prioritize the enlargement of territorial control.

Nanjing Decade The period of Nationalist rule in China between 1928 and 1937. During this period the Nationalist Party's headquarters were in the city of Nanjing.

National Directorate Governing group of the Sandinistas which included members from all factions.

National exceptionalism The belief that one's nation has a unique and superior status to others.

National Guard Nicaraguan organization encompassing military and police functions, established by the occupying US forces in 1927. It was led by Anastasio Somoza García, who overthrew the government in 1936 and subsequently used the National Guard to maintain power.

Native Americans Indigenous inhabitants of the Americas.

Navajo Native American people, whose language was used as the basis of a code by the US military during the Second World War.

Non-Intervention Agreement An agreement signed by several countries pledging not to intervene in the Spanish Civil War.

Northern Front Sandinista faction which fled into Honduras following a crackdown on Sandinista action in 1974.

Organization of American States (OAS) Organization of governments of North and South America that works to resolve crises that affect the region.

Ottoman Empire The former Turkish empire that incorporated territory in Europe, Africa and the Middle East, lasting from the thirteenth century to 1918.

Pearl Harbor US naval base in Hawaii. It was attacked by Japan in December 1941, bringing the USA into the Second World War.

Plebiscite A vote by all of a nation's voters on a particular issue.

Popular Front Left-wing coalition that governed Spain from February 1936 until the outbreak of the Spanish Civil War in July 1936.

Power vacuum An absence of identifiable political authority, prone to exploitation by extreme political factions or undemocratic institutions.

Pre-emptive strike A military offensive prompted by a perceived threat or anticipated attack that has not yet materialized.

Puppet-state Government that operates at the will of and for the benefit of another government.

Radar Technology that uses radio waves to determine the distance, speed, direction and altitude of objects, such as aircraft, ships and surfaced submarines.

Radiation sickness A series of illnesses, including cancer, that result from exposure to radiation released in a nuclear explosion.

Rape of Nanjing Massacre committed by Japanese troops occupying the city of Nanjing, which was then the capital of China, between December 1937 and January 1938. Approximately 300,000 Chinese civilians were killed, and tens of thousands of women were raped.

Reconnaissance The gathering of military information.

Reparation payments Payments made by a defeated nation to a victorious one to compensate for war expenses and damage.

Repatriation The process of returning people to their own country.

Revisionist power A state that attempts to overthrow the existing order.

Right-wing Politically conservative or reactionary.

Russian Civil War A war between 1917 and 1922 that saw various groups fighting to control Russia. These groups included Bolsheviks, who overthrew the recognized government in October 1917 in order to establish a Marxist state, as well as international forces from Japan, Britain, France, and the USA, former prisoners of war from the Austro-Hungarian Empire, pro-democracy and pro-monarchy groups led by Russians, and independence movements and forces from ethnic groups that worked to free themselves from Russia. The Bolsheviks, soon to be called the Communist Party, prevailed.

Sandinista Popular Army Army established in 1979 to replace the National Guard in Sandinista-governed Nicaragua.

Sandinistas Members of the Sandinista National Liberation Front (FSLN).

Schlieffen Plan The German military plan by which they hoped to win the First World War by avoiding a substantial war on two fronts.

Second Battle of Ypres First World War battle fought in the Belgian town of Ypres between April and May 1915, during which German troops used poison gas for the first time.

Second Spanish Republic Republic formed following the dissolution of the Spanish monarchy in 1931. It was governed by alternating left- and right-wing coalitions until the outbreak of the Spanish Civil War in 1936.

Separatist Favouring a degree of political independence or autonomy for a particular region.

Soviet satellites Nations allied to and dominated by the USSR.

Spanish Morocco The significant proportion of Morocco that was controlled by Spain as a colony from 1906.

Spanish Socialist Party (PSOE) Political party which featured in both of the left-wing coalitions of the Second Spanish Republic, but was internally divided into opposing factions.

Stalemate State of affairs in which neither of two competing sides can progress or win.

***Status quo* power** A state that attempts to maintain the existing order.

Strategic bombing The bombing of targets such as factories, transportation networks and even civilians, in an attempt to gain strategic advantage.

Strongpoint Offensive Nationalist offensive in the Chinese Civil War, launched in May 1947. The Nationalists made symbolic, but strategically insignificant, gains.

Superior Council of Private Initiative (COSIP) Nicaraguan group of businessmen opposed to Somozan domination of the economic system in the mid-1970s.

Terceristas The largest faction of the fragmented FSLN; believed in the need to form alliances with other groups, such as the Catholic Church and business.

Tokyo Trials Alternative name for the International Military Tribunal for the Far East, the trials of Japanese leaders for war crimes following the Second World War.

Treaty of Brest-Litovsk Treaty signed in March 1918 between Russia's new Bolshevik government and the Central Powers, ending Russia's involvement in the First World War.

Treaty of Versailles Treaty signed between Germany and the Allies in June 1919, at the end of the First World War. Its terms were considered by many to be very harsh on Germany.

Trench systems Networks of trenches dug into the ground by opposing armies to secure their positions, and from which offensives can be launched.

Triple Alliance The alliance between Germany, Austria-Hungary and Italy, established in 1882.

Triple Entente The alliance between France, Britain and Russia, established in 1907.

Unequal treaties Treaties imposed on inferior powers by superior ones following military conflicts or aggression.

Unión Democrática de Liberación (UDEL) An anti-Somoza coalition of seven political parties and labour unions, led by Chamorro.

United Nations International organization whose member states work to resolve crises.

Victory Programme US government initiative to increase the size of its armed forces in mid-1941, although it was not at war with any country.

War of attrition A strategy in which the main goal is to achieve victory by wearing down the enemy's strength and will to fight, through the infliction of mass casualties and the limitation of their essential resources.

Warsaw Ghetto Section of Warsaw, Poland, where Jewish people were required to live.

Weimar Republic The German government between 1918 and 1934, named after the town of Weimar.

Weltpolitik Name given to Germany's imperialist foreign policy during the reign of Kaiser Wilhelm II in the decades preceding the First World War.

Key figures

Alcalá-Zamora, Niceto (1877–1949) President of the Second Spanish Republic, 1931–6.

Alfonso XIII (1886–1941) Spanish monarch who reigned from his birth in 1886 until the dissolution of the monarchy in 1931.

Broz, Josip (Tito) (1892–1980) Communist leader of Yugoslavia, 1943–80.

Carter, James 'Jimmy' (1924–) President of the USA, 1977–81.

Castro, Fidel (1926–2016) Revolutionary leader of Cuba, 1959–2008.

Chamorro Cardenal, Pedro Joaquín (1924–78) Editor of *La Prensa* newspaper and the most significant political opponent of the Somoza regime. He was assassinated in 1978.

Chamorro, Violeta Barrios de (1929–) Member of the Nicaraguan Junta of National Reconstruction formed in June 1979, which took power after Somoza's resignation. Chamorro resigned in April 1980 when it became apparent that power effectively lay solely with the Sandinistas. Between 1990 and 1997, she served as president of Nicaragua.

Churchill, Winston (1874–1965) Prime minister of the UK, 1940–5 and 1951–5.

Franco, Francisco (1892–1975) Spanish general who led the Nationalists to victory in the Spanish Civil War, before establishing himself as a military dictator. He ruled Spain from 1939 until his death in 1975.

Hirohito (1901–89) Emperor of Japan, 1926–89.

Hitler, Adolf (1889–1945) Leader of Germany, 1933–45.

Ibárruri, Dolores (1895–1989) Prominent member of the Spanish Communist Party during the Spanish Civil War, famed for her speeches and leadership of organizations trying to help victims of the war. In exile after the war, she became the General Secretary of the Central Committee of the Communist Party of Spain, a position she held between 1942 and 1960.

Largo Caballero, Francisco (1869–1946) Republican prime minister of Spain during the Spanish Civil War, 1936–7.

Mao Zedong (1893–1976) Leader of the People's Republic of China, 1949–76.

Mola, Emilio (1887–1937) Spanish general who led the Nationalist uprising in 1936 that directly led to the Spanish Civil War.

Mussolini, Benito (1883–1945) Leader of the Italian Fascist Party and ruler of Italy, 1922–43.

Negrín, Juan (1892–1956) Republican prime minister of Spain during the Spanish Civil War, 1937–9.

Obando y Bravo, Miguel (1926–2018) Archbishop of Managua, 1970–2005. He was a vocal opponent of the Somoza regime and later of the Sandinista government.

Odena, Lina (1911–36) Famous *miliciana*, who died by suicide rather than be captured by the Nationalists during the Spanish Civil War.

Ortega, Daniel (1945–) Sandinista leader of Nicaragua, formerly as coordinator of the Junta of National Reconstruction (1979–85) and latterly as president (1985–90, 2007–).

Pastora, Edén (1937–) Moderate, non-Marxist Sandinista, leader of the Southern Front faction of the FSLN.

Primo de Rivera, Miguel (1870–1930) Spanish prime minister and dictator, 1923–30.

Ramírez, Sergio (1942–) Member of *Los Doce* and the Sandinistas who served in the Junta for National Reconstruction, and later as the Vice President of Nicaragua.

Reagan, Ronald (1911–2004) President of the USA, 1981–9.

Robelo Callejas, Alfonso (1939–) Inaugural member of the Nicaraguan Junta of National Reconstruction formed in June 1979, which took power after Somoza's resignation. Robelo resigned in April 1980 when it became apparent that power effectively lay solely with the Sandinistas.

Roosevelt, Franklin D. (1882–1945) President of the USA, 1933–45.

Schick, René (1909–66) President of Nicaragua, 1963–6.

Somoza Debayle, Anastasio (1925–80) President and dictator of Nicaragua, 1967–72 and 1974–9.

Somoza Debayle, Luis (1922–67) President and dictator of Nicaragua, 1956–63.

Somoza García, Anastasio (1896–1956) Nicaraguan president and dictator, 1937–56.

Sun Yat-sen (1866–1925) A pro-democracy revolutionary in China who helped overthrow the Qing Dynasty, serving as the Provisional President of the Republic of China and founder of the Kuomintang or Nationalist Party of China.

Truman, Harry (1884–1972) President of the USA, 1945–53.

Urcuyo Maliaño, Francisco (1915–2001) President of Nicaragua for less than two days in 1979 following Somoza's resignation, before the Junta for National Reconstruction assumed power.

Wilhelm II (1859–1941) German Kaiser, 1888–1918.

Wilson, Thomas Woodrow (1856–1924) President of the USA, 1913–21.

Answers

1 First World War 1914–8

Page 19, Western Front battle match-up

Battle	Definition
Second Battle of Ypres	Took place in 1915. Was the battle where Germany introduced poison gas. Finished in a stalemate
Battle of Verdun	Took place in 1916. Lasted for 10 months, killing 1 million. The Germans gained 8 km of territory
Battle of the Somme	Took place in 1916. Was an attack launched by the British; 20,000 British soldiers died on the first day
Battle of Passchendaele	Took place in 1917. Was an attack launched by the Allies in which they gained 8 km of territory
Battle of Cambrai	Took place in 1917. An example of a battle where the Allies used tanks effectively, gaining 9.5 km of land in a few hours

3 Second World War in Europe and north Africa 1939–45

Page 83, Women's role in war

Country	Combatant roles	Military support roles	War production
Britain		✓	✓
Germany			✓
USSR	✓	✓	✓

Page 87, Resistance groups match-up

Country	Information
Poland	Various groups formed, some of which were Jewish resistance groups. The largest resistance group had a spy network which provided information to the Allies
Yugoslavia	Various nationalist groups were formed which engaged in civil war. The biggest resistance group was formed of communists
France	Carried out acts of sabotage and sought information to send to the Allied forces
USSR	Formed of people who had remained in German-occupied territory. Assassinated German soldiers and disrupted transportation routes

4 Second World War in Asia and the Pacific 1941–5

Page 97, The chronology of long-term Japanese imperialism

Correct order:

- Japan was forced to accept the 'unequal treaties' by the Western powers.
- Iwakura Mission.
- Japan industrialized rapidly.
- Japan defeated China in the First Sino-Japanese War and annexed Formosa.
- Japan defeated Russia in the Russo-Japanese War and gained Port Arthur and the South Manchurian Railway.
- Korea was annexed by Japan.
- As one of the Allies in the First World War, Japan took the German naval base in China at Kiaochow.
- As a result of the post-First World War peace treaties, Japan was rewarded with the South Sea Mandate.

Page 103, Japan in the ascendancy 1941 – why were its victories significant?

Territory conquered by Japan	Why was this victory significant?
Philippines	This was the largest US-held colony in Asia, and its defeat was one of the largest in the country's history
Guam	Its capture by Japan disrupted US communications as it was a junction for undersea cables
Wake Island	Gave Japanese aircraft control over a large area of the Pacific Ocean
Malaya	It gave Japan access to Singapore
Singapore	Resulted in Japanese control of the Indian Ocean, and the capturing of 80,000 British troops
Burma	Gave Japan access to oilfields and large areas of rice paddies to help feed its armies
Dutch East Indies	Japan gained access to huge oil fields, which it needed to fuel transport, industry and the military
Rabaul	Japan built a massive naval and air base on this territory for over 100,000 troops

Page 107, Why did the USA's strategy of island hopping develop as it did?

Territory conquered by the USA	Why was this territory needed by the USA?
Tarawa	This atoll was home to an important airfield
Marshall Islands	This territory was part of the Japanese home islands' outer defences, and the USA needed to take them to get to Saipan
Truk	The USA wanted to neutralize the Japanese military presence on this island, but they did not need to conquer it as part of their island-hopping strategy
Saipan	This island was within bombing range of the Japanese home islands
Philippines	These islands gave Japan access to raw materials, such as rubber, and they were on a key shipping route for oil tankers
Okinawa	This territory was within bombing range of most Japanese cities

Page 107, Why was island hopping an effective strategy for the USA to adopt?

Statement	True or false
Allowed the US army to minimize its casualties	T
Helped US bombers to get in range of the Japanese home islands as quickly as possible	T
Led to increased US casualties	F
Avoided direct US attacks on major Japanese fortified islands	T
Did not contribute to the USA's ultimate victory in the war	F
Was decided on due to the Japanese army's tenacity in defending its empire	T
The eventual plan was to bomb the Japanese home islands into surrender	T

6 Nicaraguan Revolution 1976–9

Page 155, How did the revolution escalate?

The *Terceristas*	FSLN's largest faction
Los Doce	Twelve members of the anti-Somoza coalition
COSIP	An organization consisting of most of Managua's business owners
The Coalition of National Dialogue	Organized in response to growing concerns about the unpopularity of Somoza with the aim of smoothly removing him from power
Miguel Obando y Bravo	The Archbishop who founded the Coalition of National Dialogue
Alfonso Robelo Callejas	President of COSIP and leader of the Coalition of National Dialogue

Page 159, Chronology activity

Event	Order
The Committee of National Dialogue was formed	1
Chamorro was assassinated	2
The US president and Venezuelan president met to discuss how to ensure Somoza's removal	3
Somoza announced reforms to the Nicaraguan electoral system	4
The Frente Amplio de Oposición (FAO) was created and announced a sixteen-point plan for Somoza's removal	5
25 Sandinistas stormed the National Palace	6
Sandinistas launched attacks on the National Guard, leading to the death of 63 rebels	7
The OAS met to discuss the growing crisis in Nicaragua	8